THE
SECRET WAR

THE
SECRET WAR
SPIES, LIES AND THE ART OF DECEPTION IN WORLD WAR II

ANTHONY TUCKER-JONES

This edition published in 2025 by Arcturus Publishing Limited
26/27 Bickels Yard, 151–153 Bermondsey Street,
London SE1 3HA

Copyright © Arcturus Holdings Limited

All rights reserved. No part of this publication may be reproduced, stored in a retrieval system, or transmitted, in any form or by any means, electronic, mechanical, photocopying, recording or otherwise, without prior written permission in accordance with the provisions of the Copyright Act 1956 (as amended). Any person or persons who do any unauthorised act in relation to this publication may be liable to criminal prosecution and civil claims for damages.

AD011237UK

Printed in the UK

Contents

Introduction 9

Part 1 Spymasters and Spies **13**
Chapter 1 Spider's Web 15
Chapter 2 Spymasters 29
Chapter 3 Agents and Double Agents 45

Part 2 Eavesdropping War **61**
Chapter 4 Allied Code Breakers 63
Chapter 5 The Impact of Bletchley Park 77
Chapter 6 Axis Code Breakers 87

Part 3 The Art of Misdirection **93**
Chapter 7 Allied Deception Operations 95
Chapter 8 Deception on the Eastern Front 107
Chapter 9 Japan's Great Con 115

Part 4 Camouflage War **121**
Chapter 10 Hiding in Plain Sight 123
Chapter 11 Dummy Armies 131

Part 5	**Partisans and Guerrillas**	**139**
Chapter 12	European Resistance	141
Chapter 13	Resisting on the Flanks	153
Chapter 14	Guerrillas in the Far East and Pacific	163
Part 6	**Opposition Within the Axis**	**173**
Chapter 15	Defying Militarism	175
Chapter 16	The Jews Fight Back	185
Part 7	**Scientific War**	**191**
Chapter 17	Radar Wars	193
Chapter 18	Wonder Weapons	203
Chapter 12	Conclusion	211

Glossary of Deception and Intelligence Code Names	215
Endnotes	219
Bibliography	227
Index	233

Introduction

In his hugely influential *The Art of War,* Sun Tzu counselled, 'If you know the enemy and know yourself, you need not fear the result of a hundred battles. If you know yourself but not the enemy, for every victory gained you will also suffer a defeat. If you know neither the enemy nor yourself, you will succumb in every battle.' In other words, you need to know your enemy's capabilities and intentions as well as your own to achieve victory. Nothing can replace good intelligence.

While the fighting on land, air and sea during the Second World War is very well-known, the scale of what went on behind the scenes is much less understood or appreciated. Throughout, both sides sought to gather intelligence and deceive each other as much as possible using every means at their disposal. This led to a highly secret war involving spies, lies and the art of deception.

'O divine art of subtlety and secrecy!' wrote Sun Tzu. 'Through you we learn to be invisible, through you inaudible; and hence we can hold the enemy's fate in our hands.' Both the Allies and the Axis resorted to spying, eavesdropping and deceiving in order to gain an advantage. Nothing was off the table. Even Winston Churchill admitted, 'I must say, quite frankly, that I hold it perfectly justifiable to deceive the enemy even if at the same time your own people are for a while misled.'

The use of spies and deception in war is as old as time. Sun Tzu included a section on spies and their employment. He listed five types: local spies; inward spies; converted spies; doomed spies; and surviving spies. Throughout the Second World War the motivation and indeed the success of spies varied enormously. Some spied purely for the sheer excitement of it all; others did it out of patriotism or for ideological reasons. Communism certainly proved a great motivator for many – such as the infamous Cambridge Five. Others simply did it for money. Whatever their motivations, most were viewed as traitors if captured and could expect torture and death. The clandestine nature of their work meant even the successful ones could hardly expect a hero's welcome.

Introduction

Sun Tzu also taught the value of counter-intelligence, saying, 'The enemy's spies who have come to spy on us must be sought out, tempted with bribes, led away and comfortably housed. Thus they will become converted spies and available for our service.' Churchill gained a quite remarkable intelligence advantage when German attempts to penetrate Britain with a spy network were thwarted by the Double-Cross System. These 'converted' or turned agents would feed German intelligence a pack of lies designed to seriously dupe the German war effort. This would greatly aid the opening of the Second Front. In contrast, Joseph Stalin had a very poor opinion of spies and questioned their underlying motives, assuming that they were doing it for their own personal gain, rather than for patriotism or ideology.

Fatefully, Stalin did not warn his generals about Hitler's preparations to attack the Soviet Union in the summer of 1941. Although he had extremely well-placed spies, he refused to believe them, assessing that Hitler was trying to lull Churchill into a false sense of security prior to invading England. Stalin also suspected that intelligence warnings from Churchill were part of a deliberate ploy to get him to side with Britain. Churchill's highly accurate intelligence on Hitler's intentions came via the cracked German Enigma codes. In order to protect this source, he pretended it had come from spies when presenting it to Stalin.

Churchill had three very notable strategic advantages over Hitler. These were: the code breakers of Bletchley Park; the early warning radar network belonging to RAF Fighter Command; and the Royal Navy's sonar, capable of detecting enemy submarines. The vital signals intelligence gathered by Bletchley became known as Ultra, in that it was considered Ultra Secret. This along with sonar would help give the Allies victory in the Atlantic and in numerous other campaigns. It is very important to note, though, that Bletchley did not have a monopoly on such eavesdropping operations. The possession of radar meant that the RAF was in a much better position to fight the Battle of Britain after the fall of France in 1940. Victory in this would help stave off the threat of invasion by Nazi Germany.

Although Stalin's commanders were well aware of Hitler's build-up in eastern Europe in 1941, they were not permitted to mobilize. To get round this they decided to conduct large-scale exercises in western Russia. However, their mobilization was too slow and Hitler's Operation *Barbarossa* crushed the ill-prepared Red Army in a matter of weeks. It would take years for the

Soviet Union to recover from this catastrophic defeat and turn the tide on Nazi Germany.

Misleading an enemy in war is also paramount. Sun Tzu taught the art of deception: 'In making tactical dispositions, the highest pitch you can attain is to conceal them; conceal your dispositions, and you will be safe from the prying of the subtlest spies, from the machinations of the wisest brains.' He also wrote: 'By holding out baits, he keeps him on the march; then with a body of picked men he lies in wait for him.' The Allies would become masters of tactical and strategic deception. This culminated in Operation *Bodyguard*, which was designed to protect D-Day strategies and mislead Hitler about where Britain and America intended to open the Second Front.

Stalin in the summer of 1943 very successfully deceived Hitler over his intentions at Kursk. German intelligence detected massive Russian defensive preparations in the Kursk salient backed by a powerful strategic tank reserve. What they did not fully appreciate was that Stalin had also massed his forces to the north and the south, ready to launch two counter-offensives once the Germans had exhausted themselves on his defences. Hitler's troops stormed into a well-laid trap and paid the price. His defeat cost him the strategic initiative on the Eastern Front and firmly heralded the turn of the tide against Germany. Stalin would pull off a similar trick in the summer of 1944 with Operation *Bagration*.

The Allies also sought to support resistance and partisan movements wherever they sprang up behind enemy lines. They would tie down Axis divisions in ever bloodier security operations that would have been better employed on the front lines. In the case of the Balkans, China and the Soviet Union, determined resistance would spark large-scale partisan wars. The Allies likewise fought a scientific intelligence war as Hitler looked to gain a technological advantage with his so-called 'wonder weapons'. What follows lifts the lid on this secret war, examining how it was fought, by whom and its impact.

Part 1

Spymasters and Spies

Chapter 1

Spider's Web

A variety of organizations were involved in intelligence-gathering, counter-intelligence and other clandestine activities during the Second World War. They moved in the shadows of the conventional war being waged between democracy and totalitarianism. Inevitably, there were turf wars as they jostled for dominance. In Germany, Japan and the Soviet Union, many agencies spied on their own citizens, to prevent espionage and subversion.

BRITAIN

BRITISH SECURITY COORDINATION The British Security Coordination organization conducted black ops or propaganda operations and espionage on American soil, including spying on Indian nationalists in the USA. Such activities convinced the Americans and the Chinese that Churchill's priority was maintaining control of the British Empire rather than defeating Japan.

DELHI INTELLIGENCE BUREAU This collected intelligence on the activities of Indian nationalists campaigning for independence, who were seen as a threat to the authority of the Raj.

FAR EAST COMBINED BUREAU This British organization in Singapore was responsible for co-ordinating intelligence gathering in the Far East. Controlled by the navy, this led to service and departmental friction, which did not help with the assessment of the Japanese threat.

GOVERNMENT CODE AND CYPHER SCHOOL This included the code breakers at Bletchley Park and was responsible for the collection of signals intelligence globally (see Part 2: Eavesdropping War).

Chapter 1

INDIAN POLITICAL INTELLIGENCE OFFICE This was set up before the First World War to closely monitor the activities of Indian nationalists. During the Second World War one of its major concerns was the activities of the Quit India movement, which instigated a revolt against British rule in 1942.

JOINT INTELLIGENCE COMMITTEE The Joint Intelligence Committee (JIC) was only established in 1936 to bring together the fruits of military and naval intelligence; however, its remit expanded to encompass MI5, MI6 and the Government Code and Cypher School. Although the JIC technically came under the chiefs of staff, Churchill gave it direct access to 10 Downing Street.

KENYAN DIRECTORATE OF INTELLIGENCE AND SECURITY During the war Mombasa acted as a centre for British intelligence-gathering in East Africa. Bletchley Park's code breakers operated an outstation eavesdropping on the Japanese fleet. MI5, MI6 and Special Branch also had offices there.

MI5 The British Secret Service Bureau was divided into two in 1910, becoming: MI5 or the Security Service, responsible for counter-intelligence at home; and MI6, responsible for intelligence-gathering abroad. MI5 came under the Home Office and was headquartered in London. By the outbreak of war MI5's activities had expanded overseas with defence security officers permanently stationed abroad; locations included Hong Kong and Singapore. Their task was to help monitor internal unrest and foreign subversion.

MI6 MI6 or the Secret Intelligence Service (SIS) was responsible for overseas intelligence-gathering and came under the control of the Foreign Office. Its headquarters were in No. 54 Broadway in London. Both MI5 and MI6 representatives sat on the intelligence co-ordinating body known as the XX Committee, which created the Double-Cross System.

POLITICAL INTELLIGENCE DEPARTMENT The Political Intelligence Department under this designation became responsible for the BBC's European language services, the Ministry of Information's Foreign Publicity Department and SO1.

POLITICAL WARFARE EXECUTIVE The Political Warfare Executive (PWE) was Britain's main psychological warfare organization, which targeted the Axis nations. It was established in September 1941. However, it often found itself competing with the Special Operations Executive (SOE), the BBC, the Foreign Office, the Ministry of Economic Warfare, the Ministry of Information, MI6 and the armed forces.

PSYCHOLOGICAL WARFARE DIVISION This was an Anglo-American organization at supreme Allied headquarters tasked with conducting tactical psychological warfare against German troops in north-west Europe following the D-Day landings in Normandy in the summer of 1944. Its weapons of choice were leaflet and radio propaganda.

SPECIAL BRANCH This was the security wing of the British police. It operated offices throughout the British Empire and conducted counter-intelligence against enemy agents and nationalists.

SPECIAL OPERATIONS EXECUTIVE The British Special Operations Executive (SOE) came into being in 1940. First led by Hugh Dalton and later Lord Wolmer, it had two priorities: the first was to oblige the German armed forces to maintain large occupation forces in western Europe; the second was to hamper Hitler's ability to utilize Europe's economy in support of the Nazi war effort. SOE initially consisted of two branches: SO1 was tasked with subversion, while SO2 oversaw sabotage. It included both British and foreign personnel. From 1943 it co-operated with the American Office of Strategic Services.

After extensive training, SOE agents were sent to the occupied territories clandestinely by boat, aircraft, parachute and submarine. They operated in groups of between two and 30. They always co-operated closely with local resistance groups. Together they would gather intelligence and carry out sabotage. The SOE developed a large range of equipment and explosives to support these missions.

V FORCE This was an intelligence organization set by up the British Army in Burma to replace the earlier Yomas Intelligence Service. It consisted of British officers with local knowledge who recruited Burmese agents to operate behind Japanese lines. This included fostering double agents who preferred the British to the Japanese. As well as intelligence-gathering, its members conducted small guerrilla operations against Japanese patrols. V Force was considered to be much better than its Japanese counterpart and became ever more important once the Japanese had occupied Burma.

XX COMMITTEE This British co-ordinating body brought together representatives of MI5 and MI6 as well as air, military and naval intelligence with the aim of overseeing counter-espionage and intelligence-gathering. From January 1941 through to the end of the war its members got together every week. The Double-Cross System employing double agents was one of its major triumphs.

Y SERVICE Named after the phonetic abbreviation for wireless, this Bletchley Park organization was responsible for intercepting German and Japanese coded signals overseas. It had outstations on the Cocos Islands in the Indian Ocean; in Colombo, Ceylon (Sri Lanka); in Heliopolis, outside Cairo, Egypt; in Kilindini, Mombasa in Kenya; in Valletta, Malta; and in Kranji, Singapore. It also operated numerous facilities across Britain. As the war progressed the Y Service developed mobile units with the wireless listeners using specially adapted vans. These were deployed in North Africa, Greece and Crete.

YOMAS INTELLIGENCE SERVICE This was established by Bill Gunn, a British intelligence officer in Burma. Before the war he worked for a local trading firm and after the Japanese invasion he recruited Burmese loggers to spy on them, in 1942. They were handled by forestry officials, rangers and British employees from Gunn's company. Time did not permit training the new officers or their agents. Colonial rivalries among the expats also hampered the efficient running of this group. The Yomas Intelligence Service was soon replaced by V Force, which put things on a more professional footing.

CHINA

CENTRAL SOCIAL AFFAIRS DEPARTMENT This was established as the Chinese Communist Party's intelligence organization just before the Second World War broke out. Its task was to spy on the Nationalist authorities and the Japanese as well as to root out their spies. The organization became notorious for the use of torture, which often led to wholesale purges. The Nationalists and Japanese, however, did not have clean hands when it came to such practices.

NATIONAL BUREAU OF INVESTIGATIONS AND STATISTICS Known as 'Juntong', this was the intelligence agency of Nationalist leader Chiang Kai-shek's Kuomintang government (KMT, or Chinese Nationalist Party). Controlled by Dai Li, reporting directly to Chiang, it allegedly controlled 100,000 agents and informants, who operated against Japan's Chinese puppet states and the Japanese armed forces. The Juntong were viewed by many as secret police whose operatives were involved in assassination, espionage and kidnapping. Its main focus was on Chinese collaborators rather than the Japanese, as they were easier to target. Chiang also used it to get rid of political opponents. Dai, despite setting up the Sino-American Cooperative Organization, did not get on with the US Office of Strategic Services (OSS).

NATIONAL REVOLUTIONARY ARMY INTELLIGENCE SERVICE Chiang Kai-shek's armed forces operated their own intelligence units. Among them were the intelligence service of the National Revolutionary Army, which was the military arm of the Kuomintang. This conducted intelligence-gathering and counter-intelligence against the Communist forces, the private armies of various Chinese regional warlords, and the Japanese.

FRANCE

SECOND BUREAU OF THE GENERAL STAFF This was France's external military intelligence agency until 1940, when it was disbanded by the Germans. In the late 1930s it was supplemented by the Central Intelligence Bureau. Following the Armistice with Germany, Vichy replaced both organizations with the Bureau of Anti-national Activities, which was designed to combat the Resistance and Communism.

FREE FRENCH INTELLIGENCE SERVICE General Charles de Gaulle's Free French intelligence service, officially known as the Central Bureau of Intelligence and Operations, was set up in 1940. It included espionage and counter-intelligence sections, which worked closely with the SOE, MI5 and the French Resistance. In 1943 it became the General Directorate for Special Services. This established a network of spies watching developments along Hitler's so-called Atlantic Wall prior to D-Day. In February 1944 de Gaulle created the French Forces of the Interior (FFI) under General Koenig, to unite all the various resistance groups under one command.

GERMANY

ABWEHR The Abwehr, which is German for 'defence' or 'resistance', was Germany's key military intelligence service, formed after the First World War. Although the Abwehr's espionage activities against Britain were not successful, its counter-espionage operations were. They were especially effective in the Netherlands. This was the responsibility of Subdivision III, which was tasked with the penetration of foreign intelligence services. It was abolished in February 1944 and its role was taken over by the Sicherheitsdienst.

GEHEIME STAATSPOLIZEI Nazi Germany had an array of internal security and police organizations.

Key among them was Hitler's plain clothes Geheime Staatspolizei or Secret State Police, better known as the infamous Gestapo. Its job was to root out any opposition and this included counter-espionage. It answered to the Reichssicherheitshauptamt (RSHA) or Reich Security Main office, controlled by Reichsführer-SS Heinrich Himmler. Department E was responsible for security and counter-intelligence, while Department D oversaw activities in the occupied territories. The Gestapo controlled a network of plain clothes agents and informants across Europe. Undercover agents were known as V-men and were understandably greatly feared.

LENA NETWORK Operation *Lena* was an attempt by the Abwehr to set up an intelligence network in Britain prior to Hitler's invasion of England with Operation *Sealion*. The so-called 'Lena' spy ring was a team of 13 inept agents who were dropped into Britain in September 1940. Six were immediately arrested, with five executed and one imprisoned. The seventh agent was caught in London; the eighth was arrested trying to buy a train ticket; the ninth committed suicide; the tenth, the only woman, handed herself in. The 11th accidentally parachuted into the Manchester ship canal and drowned. The last two became double agents.

SICHERHEITSDIENST Germany's Security Service was known as the SD and was created in the early 1930s. Like the Gestapo, it came under Himmler's Reich Security Main Office and was controlled by the Schutzstaffel (SS).

It was Hitler's answer to MI5 and MI6 and was organized into the Interior Security Service and the Foreign Security Service. The interior part of the organization spied on Nazi Party officials.

This is what awaited foreign agents – a prison cell in the Gestapo headquarters in Berlin.

SICHERHEITSPOLIZEI The German Security Police, known as SiPo, like the Gestapo and SD formed part of the Reich Security Main Office apparatus. It was also responsible for internal security. The security police operated alongside the Gestapo and the Kriminalpolizei or Criminal Police, known as KRIPO. All these organizations struck terror into the average German citizen. A knock at the door by any of them meant trouble.

ITALY

MILITARY INFORMATION SERVICE During the war the main Italian intelligence agency was the Military Information Service (MIS), which was the equivalent to the Abwehr. It answered to the Italian Chief of the General Staff and controlled 9,000 agents. It scored a major success in securing the US Black Code employed by Colonel Bonner Fellers in Cairo to communicate British military plans to Washington. SIM achieved this by breaking into the US Embassy in Rome. This breach ended when the Americans changed their codes. The MIS was disbanded in 1943 after the fall of Mussolini.

JAPAN

HAYABUCHI DETACHMENT The Japanese army operated plain clothes units, such as the Hayabuchi Detachment, on special intelligence operations against the Chinese. This often relied on collaboration from members of the local population. They were also used in combat. Hayabuchi were tasked with infiltrating the city of Changsha in September 1941. Although they achieved their objectives they were annihilated before help could reach them.

KEMPEITAI Japan's armed forces operated a number of intelligence organizations, with its embassies overseeing intelligence-gathering overseas. The army had dedicated intelligence departments with the Kempeitai, or military and security police, responsible for counter-intelligence operations in the territories occupied by Japan.

The Kempeitai were also known as Japan's Secret Service. Their task was to crush all resistance to Japanese rule. They gained a reputation for extreme brutality that included torture and murder. Kempeitai field units accompanied the army and were responsible for the discipline of troops and for dealing with anti-Japanese groups among the civilian population. In the occupied territories, the Kempeitai recruited local militias to help maintain law and order and guard prisoners of war. They were also responsible for forced prostitution of females, known as 'Comfort Women', who were provided to the Japanese army wherever it was deployed.

Domestically, the Kempeitai were only responsible for the armed forces. However, they were also involved with intimidating and arresting political opposition. In this they were backed by Prime Minister Hideki Tojo, who was a former Kempeitai officer. In 1939 Japan passed an anti-espionage act that greatly increased the Kempeitai's power. Two years later it thwarted the 'Sorge' spy ring.

Japanese intelligence officers proved to be some of the most diehard and fanatical soldiers even after Japan's surrender. In the case of Lieutenant Hiroo Onoda, who was trained as a guerrilla warfare specialist, he did not give up on Lubang Island in the Philippines until March 1974. During his time in the jungle he had conducted attacks on the police with a few comrades who had either since died or surrendered much earlier.

The Kempeitai headquarters in Tokyo.

KODO-HA Within the Japanese army the Kodo-ha or Imperial Way faction saw the creation of Manchukuo as a stepping stone for much greater things. This included a one-party state under the army's control, run on a war economy. To achieve this aim they conducted clandestine operations employing the various secret societies and brotherhoods that flourished in Japan at the time. They conducted assassinations of senior politicians who opposed the Kodo-ha's policies. This course of action was dubbed 'Government by Assassination'.

KOKURYŪKAI The nationalist Black Dragon Society was founded in 1901 to help keep the Russians north of the Amur River. It established an espionage school and sent agents into China, Korea, Manchuria and Russia to spy on Russian activity. In the 1930s it expanded its spying globally. The Japanese army was known to make use of its agents to conduct assassinations, espionage and sabotage. It was finally disbanded by the Americans in 1946.

ORGANISATION F Japanese army intelligence just before Japan entered the Second World War recruited agents throughout South-east Asia. This network was known as Organisation F, which collected military intelligence ready for the Japanese invasion of the region.

TOSEI-HA The Tosei-ha or Control Group were rivals to the Kodo-ha. This faction was mainly made up of senior officers and the General Staff. They wanted to preserve the status quo but without fractious party politics and the corruption that came with it. The two factions could not agree on the pace of change or tactics and inevitably fell out. The Tosei-ha triumphed by having Kodo-ha officers deployed to remote outposts sparking a short-lived revolt in Tokyo in 1936. The ringleaders were executed. This incident enabled the military to take control of the government, firmly setting Japan on the road to war.

TOKKŌ In Japan, a special bureau of the Tokyo police, known as the Tokkō, was responsible for domestic counter-intelligence. This had been created in 1911 to combat political subversion. By 1932 it had become the country's main counter-intelligence organization. It consisted of four sections: the first spied on left-wing political groups; the second on right-wing groups; the third monitored foreign embassies and foreign residents; and the fourth spied on friendly embassies.

TOKUBETSU KEISATSUTAI The Japanese naval secret police, known as the Tokkeitai for short, were similar to the army's Kempeitai. They served as colonial police in the occupied areas of the Pacific with the role of rooting out enemies of the state. Like their army counterparts, they were responsible for numerous war crimes. The Tokkeitai were also the operational branch of the navy's Jōhō-kyoku or Information Office, with responsibility for conducting undercover operations.

TOKUMU KIKAN The Japanese Military Intelligence Agency reported to the Imperial General Headquarters and along with the Kempeitai carried out espionage, counter-intelligence and fifth column operations.

TO NETWORK The equivalent to Organisation F in Europe was known as the TO network. This was run from neutral Spain and collected information on Allied shipping from agents in America. This was shared with the Germans.

SOVIET UNION

MAIN INTELLIGENCE DIRECTORATE Better known as the GRU, this organization was responsible for gathering foreign military intelligence. During the war its key focus was collecting intelligence on the armed forces of the Axis countries and disrupting their lines of communication. This paid dividends first at Stalingrad and later at Kursk.

It was created by Stalin in its modern form in 1942 and the following year exclusively handled agents outside the Soviet Union. Notably, the 4th Bureau within the GRU controlled overseas agents, such as Richard Sorge. Its rival in this task was the NKVD (see below). The GRU likewise co-ordinated spies and partisans operating behind Axis lines on the Eastern Front. It was fiercely independent of the other Soviet internal security organizations.

PEOPLE'S COMMISSARIAT FOR INTERNAL AFFAIRS The abbreviation for the People's Commissariat for Internal Affairs in Russian is NKVD, which succeeded the OGPU in 1934. Despite its name, it also had an international role, which brought it into conflict with the GRU. It conducted counter-intelligence, intelligence and security operations both domestically and overseas. The NKVD's fundamental role was to ensure the continuance of Soviet rule and was the forerunner of the KGB formed in the 1950s. During the war the NKVD, as well as rooting out enemies of the state, conducted mass deportations of Soviet citizens who had collaborated with the Nazi occupation. The latter was done at gunpoint, with tens of thousands of people sent to miserable fates in Siberia.

'RED ORCHESTRA' This was the name given to the successful Soviet spy network in western Europe by German counter-intelligence. Led by Leopold Trepper, it operated under the cover of the Foreign Excellent Raincoat Company. The network had agents in Belgium, England, France, Germany, the Netherlands and Switzerland. They answered to Moscow and not all of them were in contact with each other. The poor quality of their radios often meant that the agents had to rely on vulnerable couriers. German counter-intelligence captured the cypher employed for messages sent from Brussels. The Germans also managed to identify the network's key members. The most effective group was 'Red Three' operating in Switzerland, run by Alexander Radó. The composition of the network was forever changing as agents moved about Europe or were arrested.

'SILVERMASTER' GROUP This was a network of American Communists who spied for the Soviets during the Second World War. It was one of the most significant Soviet espionage operations in America. The Soviets, who had been struggling on the Eastern Front, were particularly interested in American weapons production, estimates of German strength and when the Allies were planning to open the Second Front in Europe.

SMERSH The abbreviation of *smert shpionam*, meaning 'death to spies' in Russian, was a name personally chosen by Stalin. This was a Soviet umbrella organization for three counter-intelligence agencies formed in 1942 with the task of countering anti-Soviet activity.

UNITED STATES
FEDERAL BUREAU OF INVESTIGATION The Federal Bureau of Investigation (FBI) was first set up as the Bureau of Investigation under the Justice Department in 1908 but did not become a national organization until 1934. By the outbreak of war it was the primary agency responsible for domestic counter-intelligence. This included stopping foreign espionage and sabotage on

American soil. Eight Nazi agents were arrested, six of whom were executed. Following Pearl Harbor, the FBI arrested 5,500 Japanese Americans.

OFFICE OF STRATEGIC SERVICES The American Office of Strategic Services (OSS) set up in the summer of 1942 by President Roosevelt was the predecessor of the Central Intelligence Agency (CIA). It had three branches: Special Operations (SO), Secret Intelligence (SI) and X-2 Counter-intelligence. The SO was modelled on the British SOE and provided aid to resistance movements in Europe and Asia. Its units operated behind enemy lines. The SI was grouped into four geographical desks that dealt with Africa, Asia, Europe and the Middle East. They were supported by other specialist sections. For example, the Technical Section collected intelligence on Hitler's V-weapons. The Ship Observers Unit gathered intelligence on shipping operators and seamen's organizations.

The X-2 counter-intelligence branch ran what it dubbed Controlled Enemy Agents and Wireless Telegraphy or radio agents. It also ran double agents. X-2 had an office in London, which acted as the centre for US counter-intelligence operations in Europe. Special counter-intelligence units were set up to accompany US troops after D-Day. By the spring of 1944 the OSS had around 11,000 service personnel and agents deployed around the world. The organization was closely involved with the Allied landings in Normandy and on the Riviera.

OFFICE OF NAVAL INTELLIGENCE During the inter-war period, the ONI was mainly focused on Japan and liaised closely with the US Army's Military Intelligence Division and the FBI. A key area of interest was he development of Japanese weapons, and it also assumed a counter-intelligence role. When the war broke out its tasks became much broader.

Chapter 2

Spymasters

Handling agents and gathering intelligence was no easy task. It required individuals of exceptional ability who could rise above the detail and grasp the bigger picture. It also required people who could cope with very difficult personalities among both agents and staff.

BRITAIN

HUGH ASTOR He worked for the MI5 section B1a, which detected enemy spies then turned them into double agents. This process was completed by 1943 through the Double-Cross System set up by the XX Committee.

WILLIAM CAVENDISH-BENTINCK Cavendish-Bentinck served as the chairman of the Joint Intelligence Committee during the Second World War. Churchill instructed him that his staff must be ready to produce reports 24/7 for the prime minister, members of the War Cabinet and the chiefs of staff. Fortunately for him, Cavendish-Bentinck rose to the challenge of dealing with all the intelligence chiefs, not all of whom were easy to work with.

RICHARD CROSSMAN Crossman was an Oxford academic employed by the Directorate of Political Warfare. He was responsible for producing anti-Nazi propaganda broadcasts for the BBC German Service and Radio of the European Revolution, set up by the SOE. In late 1943 he was appointed assistant chief of the Psychological Warfare Division at supreme Allied headquarters serving under US Brigadier General Robert McClure.

SEFTON DELMER Delmer was a British journalist born in Berlin and a fluent German speaker; he interviewed Hitler in the early 1930s. Delmer was recruited by the Political Warfare Executive to oversee propaganda broadcasts to Nazi Germany. While serving in the Special Operations Directorate, at Woburn Abbey in Bedfordshire in December 1943, he was given responsibility for covert psychological warfare operations. This included setting up bogus German radio stations.

ALASTAIR DENNISTON Denniston helped set up naval signals interception and decryption known as 'Room 40' in the First World War. Afterwards it was merged with MI1b, its army counterpart. This new organization became the Government Code and Cypher School (GC&CS). Denniston was in operational control of this until 1942. Many of the academics recruited by him were highly strung individuals and this led him to running a very relaxed organization at Bletchley Park. This and a shortage of staff resulted in clashes with Sir Stewart Menzies, who was the director of the GC&CS. Some senior cryptanalysts complained to Churchill and Denniston was replaced by his deputy, Edward Travis.

DR REGINALD VICTOR JONES Jones was a leading member of the British scientific intelligence community. In the mid-1930s he had gone to work for the Royal Aircraft Establishment at Farnborough. In 1939 he was assigned to the intelligence section of the Air Ministry. There he became assistant director of intelligence (science). He and his team were responsible for assessing enemy technology and how to counter it. He worked briefly at Bletchley Park in Hut 3, where he helped set up a team who specialized in scientific decrypts, before returning to London. He was involved in the Battle of the Beams, the development of 'Window' to create false bomber trails, and the war against the V-1 flying-bombs and V-2 rockets.

GUY LIDDELL Liddell served as the highly successful director of counter-espionage at MI5's B Division, which supported Double Cross. In 1943 he was able to inform Churchill that 126 spies had been caught, of which 24 became Double Cross agents. It was a quite remarkable achievement.

ROBERT BRUCE LOCKHART Lockhart was not a spymaster, but he was involved in the dark arts in other ways. As a young man Lockhart first worked in Malaya managing a rubber plantation, until he contracted malaria. Returning home, he joined the Foreign Office and before the First World War served in Moscow and afterwards in Prague. This was followed by a stint as a newspaper editor for Lord Beaverbrook. During the Second World War he was Director General of the Political Warfare Executive. This co-ordinated British propaganda directed against the Axis, which included a number of clandestine radio stations. Previously it had been the propaganda arm of the SOE.

JOHN MASTERMAN Masterman was chairman of the intelligence co-ordination body known as the XX Committee. During the First World War he had been a civilian internee in Germany and was fluent in German.

SIR STEWART MENZIES Menzies served as head of MI6 and director of the Government Code and Cypher School from 1939. He succeeded Admiral Hugh Sinclair as director-general of MI6 following the latter's death on 4 November that year. Menzies was told to feed reports directly to the prime minister. Although he personally delivered Ultra intelligence produced by Bletchley Park's decoders to Churchill, he pointedly made sure that Churchill's liaison officer, Desmond Morton, was not on the distribution list.

MAJOR DESMOND MORTON Morton worked for MI6 and then headed the Industrial Intelligence Centre during the 1930s. He kept Churchill briefed during his wilderness years. At the outbreak of war, he was director of intelligence at the Ministry of Economic Warfare. When Churchill became prime minister he appointed Morton his liaison officer with MI6. Morton made himself unpopular by criticizing both MI5 and MI6. While Morton saw himself as Churchill's intelligence supremo, those around him thought otherwise. The Americans were to dub him 'Desperate Desmond'.

SIR DAVID PETRIE Petrie served as the head of MI5 during the Second World War. One of his many preoccupations was to make sure that the dozen Vichy consuls dotted around Britain and refugee Vichy sympathizers were not conducting espionage on British soil. One of Vichy's targets was Free French activities.

MAJOR THOMAS 'TAR' ROBERTSON Robertson was Hugh Astor's boss and ran MI5's B1a section, which was responsible for running double agents against the Germans.

Chapter 2

COLONEL ROBIN 'TIN EYE' STEPHENS Stephens was in charge of assessing whether captured Abwehr agents could be turned. He ran the Camp 020 interrogation centre in West London, as well as operations at the London Cage, Kensington Palace Gardens.

SIR WILLIAM STEPHENSON Churchill and Menzies appointed Sir William Stephenson to represent MI6 in New York. This was far from just an intelligence liaison post: Stephenson headed British Security Coordination, which was an umbrella organization for MI5, MI6 and the SOE, with almost a thousand staff.

EDWARD TRAVIS During the First World War Travis worked on naval cyphers. He then moved to the Government Code and Cypher School, where he became operational head in February 1942. He helped to streamline operations at Bletchley Park. After the war he took charge of the GC&CS's successor, Government Communications Headquarters (GCHQ).

DICK WHITE White was Guy Liddle's deputy and headed up MI5's B1 Division, a subsection of B Division. He was recruited in the mid-1930s and spent a year in Munich working to recruit German agents. Once back in London, White helped to create the Double-Cross System. In 1943 he was seconded to Allied supreme headquarters as an advisor on counter-intelligence. In the 1950s he headed MI5 and then MI6.

GERALD WILKINSON Wilkinson was an MI6 officer appointed by Churchill as his secret liaison with General Douglas MacArthur, the US commander in the South West Pacific. He and Churchill were old friends. Wilkinson was already in the Philippines before the Japanese invasion, working as a broker for a Hawaiian sugar company. He also worked for MI6, providing intelligence on the Japanese. Wilkinson reported to the MI6 station in Hawaii, where Harry Dawson was the British vice-consul.

Major General Charles A. Willoughby, General MacArthur's intelligence chief, was displeased when he discovered Wilkinson had not registered as a foreign agent. Wilkinson, although he reported to Menzies, briefed Churchill personally. When the Japanese landed, Wilkinson was given the rank of major, in case of capture. He was evacuated from Corregidor by US submarine to Java in early February 1942. Wilkinson was later sent to Washington to monitor both American and Chinese economic threats to British commercial interests in the Far East.

CHINA

KANG SHENG During the 1920s the Chinese Communist Party set up its own secret police, tasked with intelligence-gathering and counter-intelligence. This eventually became known as the Central Social Affairs Department in 1939 and was headed by Kang Sheng. He also controlled the Military Intelligence Department. Despite the atrocities perpetrated by all sides in China, some senior Communists, including Zhou Enlai, were alarmed by Kang's brutal methods. Communist leader Mao Zedong, concerned by Sheng's considerable power, had him removed from both jobs in April 1945.

FRANCE

MAJOR ANDRÉ DEWAVRIN Major André Dewavrin (code-named 'Colonel Passy') headed de Gaulle's Free French intelligence service. He was an army engineer and former Assistant Professor of Fortifications at Saint-Cyr military academy. He set up a transmitter network throughout Normandy, particularly the Caen area, Bayeux, Grandcamp and Sainte-Mère-Église in order to relay intelligence back to the Allies regarding German defences and troop movements. His agents also stole plans for the Atlantic Wall and for the V-1 and V-2 launch sites.

GERMANY

COLONEL FRANZ EGBERT VON BENTIVEGNI He was in charge of Abwehr III, the military intelligence division responsible for German counter-intelligence.

ADMIRAL WILHELM CANARIS Canaris was chief of Amtsgruppe Ausland/ Abwehr intelligence in Oberkommando der Wehrmacht, or Armed Forces High Command, from 1935 to 1944. He was regularly at loggerheads with SS leader Heinrich Himmler, who wanted to take over the Abwehr. As the war progressed Canaris became increasingly anti-Nazi and worked secretly to undermine Hitler's regime. He sent intelligence, via his mistress, to Allen Dulles, head of the OSS Mission in Bern, Switzerland.

Chapter 2

Admiral Canaris, head of the Abwehr.

The German General Staff and the Abwehr eventually came to the conclusion that people high up was aiding Stalin. Colonel Reinhard Gehlen, who was in charge of intelligence-gathering on the Eastern Front, noted, 'Admiral Canaris [head of the Abwehr] came to my headquarters at Anderburg one day and told me in the course of a lengthy conversation whom he suspected to be the traitor, though I believe that he knew more than he was prepared to tell me.' Both were looking in completely the wrong direction. They convinced themselves wrongly that the traitor was Hitler's private secretary, Martin Bormann. Canaris was sacked in early 1944 and subsequently suspected of being involved in the bomb plot to kill Hitler that July. After a lengthy investigation he was executed on 9 April 1945.

GENERAL ERICH FELLGIEBEL Fellgiebel was head of communications for both OKW and OKH (Oberkommando des Heeres, the army's high command) from 1940 to 1944 and 1942 to 1944 respectively. As General of the Communication Troops he had encouraged the introduction of Enigma encryption. Along with his deputy, Lieutenant General Fritz Thiele, he was an ardent anti-Nazi. To some they were patriots trying to undermine Hitler; to others they were traitors intent on Germany's defeat. Every step Hitler took to formulate Operation *Citadel* in mid-1943 was relayed by Fellgiebel to the 'Lucy' spy ring in Lucerne and on to Moscow. He was executed as one of the 20 July 1944 bomb plotters.

COLONEL REINHARD GEHLEN Head of intelligence on the Eastern Front from 1942, Colonel Reinhard Gehlen tried to warn Hitler of the danger gathering on the Volga and the threat this posed to the German army and its Axis allies at Stalingrad in the winter of 1942. Hitler refused to listen and would not authorize a tactical withdrawal. 'By 9 November 1942, ten days before the beginning of the Soviet counter-attack, which was to lead eventually to the Stalingrad disaster,' recalled Gehlen, 'my branch had clearly predicted precisely where the blow would fall and which of our armies would be affected.' From the north massed Soviet forces cut across the Don and surrounded Stalingrad with ease.

Gehlen then tried to call off Hitler's Kursk offensive, warning that it was another trap, but left it too late. The following year he again tried to warn that Army Group Centre was at risk from a third Soviet Reserve Front but once again failed to get Hitler to withdraw. As a consequence, Army Group Centre was annihilated before Minsk and the remnants driven all the way back to Warsaw.

HANS BERND GISEVIUS Before the war Gisevius was recruited by the Gestapo but subsequently joined the Abwehr. Like his boss, Admiral Canaris, he was opposed to Hitler. He was posted to Zurich, where he met with Allen Dulles from the OSS. Upon his return to Germany he went into hiding following the failed July 1944 assassination attempt on Hitler. He fled back to Switzerland the following year.

COLONEL EBERHARD KINZEL At the start of the war Kinzel was responsible for German intelligence-gathering in eastern Europe in his role as head of the General Staff's Branch 12 'Foreign Armies East'. Kinzel failed to impress upon Hitler the danger posed by Stalin's Reserve Front and the Reserve Armies gathering beyond the Volga. The Reserve Front coalesced around Moscow to hold off Operation *Typhoon* in 1942 while the Reserve Armies were mobilizing. This meant Hitler had one chance and one chance only to capture Moscow before losing momentum.

Following General Zhukov's winter counter-offensive around Moscow, by March 1942 Kinzel was optimistically reporting, 'Only a meagre reserve is available over and above the armed forces already existing, and in my view of the prevailing conditions in Russia one must be sceptical as to whether this reserve can be built up to the theoretical estimate. The Russians will never again be able to throw reserves into the scales as they did in the winter of 1941/1942.' He was subsequently sacked for being the bearer of bad tidings. Kinzel was to end the war as chief of staff of Army Group Vistula, tasked with defending Berlin.

Chapter 2

MAJOR KARL-ERICH KÜHLENTHAL Kühlenthal headed German intelligence operations in Madrid. Although Spain was neutral, it remained pro-Nazi thanks to Hitler's support for General Franco during the civil war. Although Kühlenthal was partly Jewish, he had been granted full Aryan status. He was completely duped by Operation *Mincemeat*, which suggested the Allies would attack Greece or Sardinia and not Sicily.

Heinrich Müller, who controlled the infamous Gestapo.

HEINRICH MÜLLER Müller was in charge of the Gestapo throughout the war. His secret police oversaw espionage and counter-intelligence operations in direct competition with the Abwehr. His greatest success was in 1942 when he infiltrated the Soviet 'Red Orchestra' network. This enabled him to feed false intelligence to the Soviets. Müller was one of the architects of the Final Solution and helped with its implementation. He also oversaw the investigation into the assassination attempt on Hitler in July 1944.

CAPTAIN NIKOLAUS RITTER Ritter was chief of air intelligence in the Abwehr's espionage department. He was British double agent Arthur George Owens' handler.

ITALY

COLONEL CESARE AMÈ Amè headed the Italian Military Information Service (MIS) from 1940 to 1943. He tried to persuade Benito Mussolini not to enter the war because of the country's lack of preparedness. He was removed from office after the fall of Mussolini.

GENERAL VITTORIO GAMBA Gamba was in charge of Section 5 within the MIS, which listened in on Allied communications.

GENERAL GIACOMO CARBONI Carboni led the MIS from September 1939 to June 1940. His reports to Mussolini about Italy's inadequate preparations for war got him sacked and he was sent to command the Modena Military Academy. In 1943 he failed to defend Rome against the German takeover.

JAPAN

HIROSHI ŌSHIMA He served as the Japanese ambassador to Germany and had a close relationship with Admiral Canaris. Intelligence gathered was relayed to Tokyo via the TO network (see page 25 and below).

YAKICHIRO SUMA Suma was a minister in the Japanese Embassy in Madrid. He cultivated Ramón Serrano Suñer, the Spanish foreign minister who was General Franco's brother-in-law. From Madrid, he co-ordinated Japan's European intelligence operation, known as the TO network. It shared its intelligence with Germany.

SOVIET UNION

ELIZABETH BENTLEY Bentley was an American who worked as a Soviet spymaster handling agents within the FBI and OSS known as the 'Silvermaster' group. She became active in the late 1930s with Communism after being recruited by Jacob Golos, who she had a romantic relationship with. He suffered a fatal heart attack in 1943, so Bentley took his place. Becoming disenchanted with the Soviets in 1945, she handed herself in to the FBI and defected. She implicated almost 150 people as Soviet spies, 37 of whom were federal employees. Kim Philby alerted Soviet intelligence, and they broke off all contact with Bentley. This prevented the FBI from using her as a double agent.

LAVRENTIY BERIA Beria headed the NKVD from 1938 to 1946 and as such wielded enormous power within the Soviet Union and abroad. His organization conducted espionage and counter-espionage. He provided Stalin with a list of 457 'enemies of the people' in mid-January 1940, of whom 346 were executed. This, though, was just the start. Beria was a sadist who throughout the war not only sanctioned torture, but also carried it out personally.

ALEXANDER DEMYANOV Demyanov was an NKVD double agent who penetrated the Abwehr. He ran the fake 'Monastery' spy network in the Soviet Union, which recruited agents from the equally fictitious resistance movement code-named 'Throne'. The Germans were led to believe that the latter consisted of pro-tsarists working in the Soviet high command, who were prepared to enlist Germany's help to bring down Stalin. Demyanov was never unmasked.

ARNOLD DEUTSCH Deutsch was a Communist European émigré who lived in London before the war. Under the guise of an academic, he worked for Soviet intelligence recruiting agents who included Anthony Blunt, Guy Burgess and Kim Philby. In the late 1930s he went to Moscow and during the war he disappeared.

GENERAL FILIPP GOLIKOV From his office in the central Arbat District of Moscow, General Filipp Golikov, head of the GRU, knew exactly what was going on in the first half of 1941. He watched as Adolf Hitler massed three powerful army groups in Prussia, Nazi-occupied western Poland and then Romania. His credible and well-placed sources all indicated that Hitler was poised to strike between mid-May and mid-June 1941. Golikov had direct access to 'The Boss' in the Kremlin and was regularly at his side. When it came to briefing Joseph Stalin, he did not even have to bother going through the General Staff.

Golikov was relatively new in post, and he understood that it was best not to disagree with 'The Boss'. He had replaced Ivan Proskurov, who had been sacked for not sugar-coating intelligence on Hitler's intentions. Proskurov had gone the way of his six predecessors. Golikov appreciated that being head of military intelligence for someone like Stalin was a poisoned chalice. 'The Boss', naturally supported by Golikov, had very set views on what was going on. In his mind, Hitler's build-up was all part of an elaborate plan to force Britain to the negotiating table. Therefore, it was very clear to Stalin and Golikov that war with Germany was not imminent.

According to Zhukov it was Golikov who persuaded Stalin in late March 1941 that Hitler would not attack in the summer. Ironically, he produced an accurate report that warned that three German army groups were indeed massing on the Soviet Union's western frontier, which could strike for Leningrad, Moscow and Kiev between 15 May and 15 June 1941. Golikov concluded his report by saying Hitler would not attack until after a victory over England and that rumours of war were a result of misinformation coming from the English or German intelligence services. Admiral Kuznetsov also had credible intelligence from Berlin about an imminent attack, but he considered it false.

Stalin had little time for Golikov's abilities, branding him 'inexperienced and naïve'. He also observed that human intelligence should not be relied on: 'A spy should be like the devil; no one should trust him, not even himself.' Stalin chose to believe none of it. 'This information,' he wrote, 'is an English provocation. Find out who the author is and punish him.' Golikov knew better than to antagonize Stalin. By April he was flagging up the significant German troop movements towards the border and stopped reassuring his boss about Hitler's intentions. However, he avoided making any assessments that might deviate from Stalin's already set views. Stalin's mantra was: Don't tell me what you think. Give me the facts and the source!

Golikov, who had helped contribute to Stalin's delusion that Hitler was not going to invade, was summoned to see the Soviet leader on 21 October 1941. By then the enemy were approaching the capital he must have feared that he was facing a firing squad; instead, remarkably, he was given command of the 10th Reserve Army gathering south-east of Moscow. He was replaced by Alexei Panfilov as head of the GRU, who in turn was replaced by Ivan Ilyichev.

ANATOLI GORSKY Gorsky was recruited by the Soviet secret police in the late 1920s, then in 1936 he joined intelligence and was sent to London as a cypher clerk to assist the resident spy handler. There, during the war he was put in charge and was responsible for 18 British spies, including the Cambridge Five. His team at the embassy grew to a dozen and they collected intelligence on the Allied war effort, including the Anglo-American atomic bomb programme. In 1944 Gorsky was sent to America, but his cover was compromised by the defection of Soviet spy Elizabeth Bentley, and he was recalled to Moscow.

NATHAN GREGORY SILVERMASTER Silvermaster headed a large Communist spy ring inside the US government during the war. He worked for the US Treasury and the US Production Board, which gave him and his fellow conspirators access to highly sensitive information regarding America's war effort. Elizabeth Bentley acted as a courier, transferring documents from Washington to her Soviet handler in New York.

Chapter 2

RICHARD SORGE 'The story of Richard Sorge, Soviet master spy, falls into this category of security surveillance,' wrote General Douglas MacArthur. 'It represents a devastating example of a brilliant success of espionage.' Sorge was born in the Soviet Union with a German father and Russian mother. Afterwards they moved to Berlin, where Sorge became a Communist. During the early 1930s, working as a journalist, he established a Soviet network in Shanghai with the aid of Agnes Smedley, to spy on foreign garrison forces.

Sorge recalled, 'Unlike Japan, Shanghai at that time was comparatively safe for persons engaged in activities such as ours.' One of his other tasks was to gather intelligence on Anglo-American and Japanese dealings with anti-Nationalist factions. He was also interested in the activities of Germany in China, which was supporting the Nationalists with training and weapons. Sorge cultivated Chinese contacts who were Communist sympathizers but not members of the party. He code-named them 'Wang', 'Chiang' and 'Chui' to conceal their identities. While there he also met Japanese journalist Hotsumi Ozaki.

Sorge was then sent to Tokyo in 1933 to spy on the Japanese. Posing as a German journalist, he was accredited to the German Embassy staff. He befriended the German military attaché Eugene Ott and renewed his relationship with Ozaki. 'The espionage group which I operated in Japan was a special arm of the USSR Communist Party,' said Sorge, 'and all of its members have frankly confessed that they were working to advance the cause of Communism and not for money or personal gain.'

Sorge also wrote: 'I stood firm on the view that Japan had no intention of waging war against the Soviet Union.' The two countries had fought a brief border war in 1939, which the Soviets won. Stalin was concerned that the Japanese build-up in Manchukuo indicated that Japan was planning to attack the Soviet Union again. The last thing he wanted was a two-front war. Sorge was able to report just three days after Hitler's invasion of the Soviet Union that the Japanese preferred the pickings of French Indochina and the Dutch East Indies to renewed aggression against the Soviet Union.

Once Sorge's spy network had let Japanese intentions towards American interests in the Pacific be known, Red Army divisions began to head west to help defend Moscow. Japanese intelligence, though, was increasingly suspicious of Sorge's activities. He was arrested in October 1941 by the Kempeitai and hanged on 7 November 1944.

Richard Sorge worked as a Soviet spymaster in Shanghai and Tokyo.

Chapter 2

LEOPOLD TREPPER Known as 'Big Chief', Trepper went to Brussels in 1938 to lead the Soviet 'Red Orchestra' spy network. Trepper's work was hampered by Stalin not trusting spies. After the German invasion of France in 1940 Trepper moved to Paris and became a contractor for the German army. Trepper warned Stalin of the impending German invasion of the Soviet Union, but Stalin ignored him. He was arrested in 1942 but convinced the Germans he was a double agent and managed to escape. He spent the rest of the war in hiding.

UNITED STATES

GENERAL WILLIAM J. DONOVAN Donovan was a highly decorated First World War veteran. In the inter-war years, he worked as a US attorney and travelled extensively. Having developed a relationship with President Roosevelt, he acted as an informal emissary to Britain in 1940 and 1941. This brought him into contact with Winston Churchill and King George VI. Donovan, like Roosevelt, was supportive of the British war effort. Shortly after, he was put in charge of the Office of Strategic Services (OSS) to oversee America's espionage activities. Returning to active duty, he was first promoted from colonel to brigadier general and then major general. He made the OSS a global organization despite rivalry from other organizations, such as the FBI, MI6, SOE, and some force commanders.

ALLEN DULLES Dulles, like Donovan, was a lawyer and worked in the diplomatic service. In the 1930s he was involved in arms control negotiations at the League of Nations. In 1933, while in Berlin, he met Adolf Hitler and Joseph Goebbels. During the war he served as the OSS station chief in Bern, Switzerland. There he liaised with German émigrés and anti-Nazis gathering technical intelligence on German weapons programmes. Dulles was also made aware of the plot to kill Hitler. He went on to become the director of the CIA.

CAPTAIN CARL EIFLER Eifler commanded OSS secret operations conducted by Detachment 101 from April 1942 to December 1943. This unit was trained by the SOE in Canada. It was sent to conduct guerrilla warfare behind Japanese lines in Burma. There Eifler enlisted the help of the local Kachin people. Detachment 101 reached a strength of 500 supported by 10,000 Kachins. Combined, they inflicted over 15,000 casualties on the Japanese.

J. EDGAR HOOVER Hoover was the director of the FBI during the war and was responsible for counter-intelligence in America, including dealing with Communist activists and German agents. His previous preoccupation had been the Mafia and organized crime. He tried unsuccessfully to bring foreign intelligence-gathering under his control. Hoover was regularly at loggerheads with America's other security organizations.

BRIGADIER GENERAL ROBERT MCCLURE In 1942 McClure was appointed Eisenhower's chief of intelligence for the European theatre of operations. He was then asked to head the newly formed Allied Forces Information and Censorship Section, which was a cover for American psychological warfare. This brought together civilian staff from the US Office of War Information, the OSS and the British Political Warfare Executive. He then became the head of the Psychological Warfare Division at Supreme Headquarters Allied Expeditionary Force.

WILLIAM PHILLIPS Phillips, head of the OSS in London, was made Roosevelt's personal representative in India in 1943. This gave the clear impression that the OSS was not only supporting anti-Japanese nationalist movements in South-east Asia, but also nationalists in India. Churchill's fears were confirmed when it became apparent that Phillips was very pro-Indian independence and did not support the British administration. Phillips further incurred Churchill's displeasure when he suggested a meeting of imprisoned Indian leaders adjudicated by an American.

To keep Roosevelt happy, Churchill agreed to the establishment of a 'special OSS mission' in New Delhi, but he was not pleased about it. He responded by permitting the interception of mail to the American consulates in India and the tapping of their telephones. This included bugging General Albert Wedemeyer, the most senior American officer in India. Indian Political Intelligence also kept a close eye on Phillips's efforts to encourage mediation, even after he had returned to America.

Chapter 3

Agents and Double Agents

Agents fall under the category of human intelligence or HUMINT and were very active during the Second World War on both sides. Space understandably does not permit the listing of every single spy involved in the conflict. Therefore, the following only briefly covers some of the major characters and the part they played. In the case of the Axis spies, most were turned and became double agents for the Allies, so are listed as Allied assets.

ALLIED SPIES

EDWARD 'EDDIE' CHAPMAN Chapman was released from prison in Nazi-occupied Jersey and sent to Britain by German intelligence in December 1942. He was a career criminal who specialized in safecracking and had been awaiting trial in Scotland before escaping to the Channel Islands. In Britain, his mission was to blow up the De Havilland Mosquito aircraft factory at Hatfield. Instead, he handed himself in. Thanks to Bletchley Park's intercepts, MI5 was already expecting him. Given the code name 'Zigzag', it was made to look as if his operation had been a success, and he was sent back to Germany. There he was awarded the Iron Cross, becoming the only British citizen to ever receive it. He returned to Britain in June 1944 and fed false information to the Germans about the effectiveness of the V-2 rockets hitting London.

WILLIAM EGAN COLBY Colby served with the OSS in France and Norway during the war, where he carried out sabotage alongside local resistance groups. After the war he joined the OSS's successor, the Central Intelligence Agency, and became its director during the 1970s.

SIDNEY COTTON Cotton was sent by MI6 to Ireland to search for U-boats along the creeks and inlets of western Eire. Through the summer of 1940 and into the following year, intelligence confirmed that the Germans continued to land agents in Eire, though with very mixed results.

PIETER DIEPENBROEK Diepenbroek, along with Johan Ubbink, was a Dutch SOE agent dropped by the British into the Netherlands. After being captured by the Germans in August 1943, they escaped. This threatened to wreck the successful German double agent network in the Netherlands. However, the Germans claimed the pair were working for the Gestapo. When they reached England they were arrested. Shortly after, the Germans admitted they had comprehensively compromised the SOE Dutch operations.

KARL EITEL Eitel was an Abwehr handler in Portugal. He recruited Juan Frutos to spy on France. In November 1943 Eitel defected and gave up Frutos to the Americans.

JUAN FRUTOS Frutos, a Spaniard living in the port of Cherbourg in France, was recruited as a double agent by the US Office of Strategic Service's X-2 counter-intelligence unit. He had been an Abwehr agent since the mid-1930s and reported on French naval activity. In May 1944 he was put on alert to monitor any Allied invasion of the continent. He transmitted intelligence following the D-Day landings and was arrested by the Americans on 8 July 1944. Agreeing to work as a double agent, he was code-named 'Dragoman'. He then proceeded to feed the Germans fake naval intelligence.

JUAN PUJOL GARCÍA García was a Spanish national recruited by German intelligence. When he was sent to Britain in 1942 he offered his services to the British and became Agent Garbo. Through Double Cross he was able to help undermine the Abwehr. It was Garbo who suggested where the Germans should send their agents to in Britain. He was a key player in the implementation of Operation *Quicksilver*, which was intended to fool the Germans into believing D-Day would take place in the Pas-de-Calais. Garbo told his German handler he was operating a network of 27 agents across Britain. None of them existed; he simply made up their fictitious reports. Garbo was awarded the Iron Cross First Class for his services to Nazi Germany.

TOR GLAD Tor Glad, along with John Moe, was a Norwegian who served the Abwehr. On 7 April 1941 the pair were flown across the North Sea by the Luftwaffe in a flying boat. When they came ashore by dingy at Covie on the Moray Firth in northern Scotland, they handed themselves in. Glad had spied for the Germans before the invasion in April 1940 and was treated with some caution. Although he became a double agent, code-named 'Jeff', he was kept under close surveillance. Glad did not perform well and was eventually confined to an internment camp on Dartmoor.

ANDRÉ JARROT Jarrot was a hero of the French Resistance. A motorcycle racing champion before the war and a garage mechanic and local politician after it, he rose to become France's first minister of quality of life. Born in Lux, he left school in his early teens and devoted his time to motorcycle racing, becoming a French national champion in 1937. Jarrot was mobilized in 1939 and captured by the Germans in June 1940. After escaping, he became involved in some of the very first clandestine arms drops to the Resistance by the British. Then, following training in England, he parachuted into occupied France on several occasions to conduct sabotage missions.

Awarding him the Cross of Liberation, General Charles de Gaulle wrote that Jarrot had 'seriously harmed German industries on French soil'. The Basset–Jarrot team in August 1943 had blown up the power station at Chalôn-sur-Saône, which was supplying electricity to the industries at Le Creusot serving the Nazi war machine. The power station was put out of action for six months. He also helped organize the escape routes that enabled shot-down Allied airmen to get out of occupied France. Jarrot was also honoured with American, British and Belgian decorations for his resistance work.

PAUL JEANNIN Jeannin was an Abwehr agent in Marseille, southern France, who was turned by the Americans. In early 1945 he was involved in a deception operation designed to make it look like more American troops were arriving at the port than was really the case. This was intended to convince the Germans that an attack across the Italian border was imminent. Two German divisions were prevented from redeploying north from the Franco-Italian frontier as a result.

JOHANN JEBSEN Jebsen was a German playboy who studied at Freiburg university, where he met Serb Dušan Popov. Both were to become Double

Chapter 3

SOE agent Noor Inayat Khan was captured and executed by the Nazis.

Cross agents. Jebsen was code-named 'Artist' and stationed in Lisbon. There he enjoyed a nice lifestyle in part financed by stolen Abwehr funding. His controller directed him to contact the British with a view to spying on them. Instead, he became agent 'Artist' in 1943, betraying the Abwehr and feeding it false intelligence. The following year he was charged with currency violations and taken to Germany to face interrogation. This threatened the security of Operation *Fortitude*. Despite being tortured, Jebsen revealed nothing and was shot in Oranienburg concentration camp.

FRITZ KOLBE Kolbe was an anti-Nazi German diplomat employed by the German foreign ministry. In 1943 he became a diplomatic courier travelling to Bern in Switzerland. There he approached the British Embassy but was rebuffed, so he approached the Americans. They gave him the code name 'George Wood' and put him to work. Kolbe provided intelligence regarding German assessments of D-Day landing points, Hitler's V-weapons, German jet fighters and much more. His OSS handler, Allen Dulles, viewed him as one of the best agents of the war. However, although he provided over 1,600 documents, much of his information was superseded by Ultra intelligence gathered by Bletchley Park.

NOOR INAYAT KHAN Noor Inayat Khan was an Indian Muslim who also served the SOE. She had an Indian father and American mother and grew up in Paris. After the German invasion of France her family fled to England. Joining the Women's Auxiliary Air Force, she was later recruited by the SOE. During her training she adopted the name 'Nora Baker'.

On 16/17 June 1943, with the cover name 'Jeanne-Marie Regnier', she landed in northern France, where she travelled to Paris to work as a wireless operator. She was betrayed to the Germans, but on 25 November 1943 escaped with John Renshaw Starr and Leon Faye, only to be recaptured. Noor Khan and three other women were moved to Dachau concentration camp and on 13 September 1944 all four were executed. For her sacrifice, she was awarded the George Cross and Croix de Guerre.

HUBERT LAUWERS Lauwers was an SOE agent dropped into the Netherlands. Captured in March 1942, he was recruited as an Abwehr double agent. Although he tried to warn the SOE, his warnings were missed. As a result, the SOE continued to send agents, who were all captured. By October 1943, of the 56 agents sent to the Netherlands only eight survived; 36 were executed.

HANS FERDINAND MAYER Mayer was more of a dissident than a spy. He was a German mathematician and physicist who worked in telecommunications before the war. After the German invasion of Poland he decided to share Nazi military secrets with Britain. In late October 1939 he travelled to Oslo, Norway, where he typed a seven-page report. This outlined, among other things, German aircraft carrier, bomber, glider and radar programmes. Mayer mailed it to the British Embassy.

The British intelligence community largely dismissed what became known as the Oslo Report as a plant. Dr R.V. Jones, who was in charge of British

Chapter 3

scientific intelligence, assessed the information to be accurate and found it an invaluable insight into German developments. In 1943 Mayer was arrested for political reasons; the Gestapo had no idea about the Oslo Report, and he survived incarceration.

JOHN MOE Moe was a Norwegian working for the Germans. When he and Tor Glad arrived in Britain he became a double agent known as 'Mutt'. He took part in Operation *Solo I*, which was designed to fool the Germans into believing the Allies were going to attack Norway in late 1942. He then played a part in Operation *Oatmeal* in February 1943, in which he convinced the Germans he had been involved in sabotage operations in Aberdeen. The results were faked by MI5 and reported in the newspapers. He joined the Norwegian army in exile in 1944 after it was feared news of Glad's internment might compromise his cover.

JACQUELINE NEARNE Nearne was recruited from the First Aid Nursing Yeomanry (FANY) by the SOE. They trained her in Morse code signals using a suitcase radio. She was sent to France in 1943 as a courier and acted as liaison for a number of SOE groups in the Paris area. Nearne was later awarded the MBE for her brave service.

ARTHUR GEORGE OWENS Owens, code-named 'Agent Snow', was by the mid-1930s working for the Abwehr and MI6. He had patented an electric storage cell, which he had sold to both the Royal Navy and the Germany navy. MI6 soon dispensed with his services when he proved to be a poor source of intelligence. The Germans offered him money to spy on the RAF, so he reported this to MI5. He ended up taking money from both sides. However, Owens did provide MI5 with the names of three agents operating in England as well as German codes. The latter were supplied to Bletchley Park. This facilitated the recruitment of more double agents. MI5 stopped using him in 1941, following a largely fruitless trip to Lisbon.

Jacqueline Nearne served as an SOE courier in occupied France.

Agents and Double Agents

DUŠAN POPOV Serbian Popov was the heir to a shipping magnate. While studying in Germany he was arrested for expressing opposition to Hitler. Popov was subsequently recruited by the Abwehr. By 1940 he was managing a law firm in Belgrade, where he made it known to the British he had been approached by the Germans. Popov travelled to Britain and became Double Cross agent 'Tricycle'.

The Abwehr sent him to Pearl Harbor, Hawaii to gather intelligence on US naval facilities for the Japanese. Popov informed the FBI of the threat four months before the Japanese attack on Pearl Harbor. J. Edgar Hoover, the FBI chief, did not believe him. Popov subsequently played a leading role in Operation *Fortitude*.

HANS-THILO SCHMIDT Schmidt was a German former soldier and spy who sold details of the Enigma cypher machine to French intelligence in the early 1930s. He was able to do this because he worked at the German Amed Forces Cypher Office. Schmidt sold details over a number of years, meeting French agents across Europe. The French were unable to penetrate the encryption but shared the information with the Poles. This helped Polish mathematician Marian Rejewski, who was trying to crack Enigma. His work enabled the Poles to read Enigma until the outbreak of the Second World War in 1939.

WULF SCHMIDT Code-named 'Tate' by the British, Schmidt was a Dane working for the Abwehr. After landing in Britain by parachute in September 1940 he got as far as Willingham in Cambridgeshire before being arrested. He was betrayed by a fellow agent who had already been captured. He was recruited as a double agent as part of the Double-Cross System and made radio transmissions to Germany. He also took part in Operation *Bodyguard* by spying on the fake First United States Army Group. For this he was awarded the Iron Cross First and Second Class.

ODETTE SANSOM Odette Sansom was born in France, the daughter of First World War hero Gaston Brailly, who was killed at Verdun in 1918. She married Englishman Roy Sansom in 1931 and moved to England. She was recruited into the SOE and in 1942 landed near Cannes to act as a courier with the code name 'Lise'. Tragically, she and her supervisor, Captain Peter Churchill, were betrayed and arrested on 16 April 1943. After being tortured by the Gestapo she was condemned to death and sent to Ravensbrück concentration camp. By good fortune she survived, and testified against the prison guards after the war. She also remarried.

Odette Sansom is the only woman to have received the George Cross while still alive; all other female George Cross recipients were posthumous. She was also appointed a Chevalier de la Légion d'honneur by the French for her brave work with the Resistance. Of the 55 female SOE agents, 13 were killed in action or in the Nazi concentration camps.

LILY SERGEYEV Sergeyev was a French journalist of Russian extraction who was recruited in occupied Paris by the Abwehr. She was ordered to infiltrate Britain via Madrid. There she approached the British and was flown to London. She served as a double agent with the code name 'Treasure'. By early 1944 the XX Committee had her sending numerous bogus messages to the Abwehr. There were concerns, unfounded as it transpired, that she might be a triple agent, and she was dismissed after the D-Day landings.

VIOLETTE SZABO Violette Szabo, code-named 'Louise', was another heroine of the SOE and French Resistance. She first parachuted into occupied France near the port of Cherbourg in April 1944 to help the Resistance and gather intelligence. On her second visit on 7 June 1944, immediately after D-Day, she flew to Limoges. Three days later she was captured after the car she was travelling in ran into an SS roadblock. She was eventually sent to Ravensbrück concentration camp and at the age of just 23 was executed on 26 February 1945. Szabo was the second woman to be awarded the George Cross and also received the French Croix de Guerre.

HALINA SZYMAŃSKA Szymańska was a Pole recruited by the British who had an affair with Admiral Canaris, the head of the Abwehr, in Switzerland and Italy. He helped her escape from occupied Poland to Switzerland with her three daughters, where she became a conduit to the anti-Nazi group Schwarze Kapelle (Black Orchestra). There she met with Hans Bernd Gisevius. Halina obtained intelligence on the German attacks on France and the Soviet Union. During the war she became a highly effective MI6 agent, regularly travelling into occupied France.

CHARLES TEGART Tegart, a veteran Anglo-Irish intelligence officer, was sent by MI6 to Dublin in May 1940 to ascertain if Hitler had gained a foothold. A major concern was whether the German Legation in Dublin was being used as a hub for espionage and subversion. Tegart was soon sending back highly alarming and exaggerated reports that German U-boats had delivered 2,000 agents to join the IRA, who were planning for a German invasion of western Britain. None of this was true.

AMY ELIZABETH THORPE Born in Minneapolis, Thorpe had a series of affairs with foreign diplomats in Washington. Known during the war as 'Cynthia', she worked for US intelligence. One of those who was seduced by her was Italian naval attaché, Admiral Alberto Lais. It has been alleged that information supplied by him helped with the British naval victory at Matapan in 1941.

NANCY WAKE Nancy Grace Augusta Wake served as a British agent and became one of the Allies' most decorated women. She was the Gestapo's most wanted person, and they dubbed her the 'White Mouse'. Born in New Zealand, Wake's family moved to Sydney, Australia when she was just two. Abandoned by her father, her mother was left to raise six children on her own. After running away from home at 16, Wake, inheriting some money, travelled to New York to become a journalist. During the 1930s she worked in Paris and witnessed the rise of the Nazis under Adolf Hitler.

In 1939 she married French industrialist Henri Edmond Fiocca. Living in Marseille when the Germans invaded France, she became a courier for the Resistance and joined Captain Ian Garrow's escape network. By 1943 the Gestapo had put a 5 million franc bounty on her head. Wake was forced to flee Marseille, but her husband was captured, tortured and executed by the Germans. He died refusing to give away her whereabouts. Eventually making her way to England, she joined the SOE and on the night of 29/30 April 1944 parachuted into France to become the liaison officer with a local Resistance group.

It was at this stage that the Resistance began to seriously escalate its activities in preparation for the Normandy landings. In particular, it fought running battles with the Waffen-SS as it sought to impede German troop movements. On one occasion, during a sabotage raid, Wake killed an SS sentry with her bare hands to prevent him from raising the alarm.

On another occasion she cycled over 800 km (500 miles) in order to replace some radio codes.

After the war she received the George Medal, the American Presidential Medal of Freedom and the French Médaille de la Résistance and Croix de Guerre with two palms and a star for her brave work. In 1970 she was appointed a Chevalier de la Légion d'honneur and in 1988 the French promoted her to Officer of the Legion of Honour.

FOREST FREDERICK EDWARD YEO-THOMAS Wing commander Forest Frederick Edward Yeo-Thomas was a secret agent code-named 'The White Rabbit' serving with the SOE. Although he was born in London, early in his childhood his parents had moved to Dieppe, France, so he spoke both English and French fluently. He gained a taste for adventure early on; during the Polish–Soviet War of 1919–20 he had fought for the Poles. After being captured by Soviet troops he strangled his Russian guard and made good his escape.

Between the wars, Yeo-Thomas worked for a successful fashion house in Paris. After the Fall of France he fled the Nazis and returned to England, where he worked as a volunteer for Charles de Gaulle's Free French forces. He was soon lured away by the promise of excitement with the newly created British intelligence and subversion organization – the SOE.

Initially, Yeo-Thomas found himself in an administrative role, but he was soon liaising with the Free French intelligence agency. On 25 February 1943 he was parachuted into occupied France for the very first time. In Paris, he helped a French officer evade a Gestapo agent and also escorted a shot-down American pilot safely back to England. He returned to France a second time on 17 September 1943 and narrowly escaped arrest on six different occasions. Back in England, Yeo-Thomas, dismayed at the lack of help the Resistance was receiving, managed to get a meeting with Prime Minister Winston Churchill.

Unfortunately, Yeo-Thomas's luck ran out when he parachuted into France again in February 1944. He was betrayed and arrested at the Passy metro station in Paris on 21 March. The Gestapo proceeded to torture him, employing cold-water immersion, beatings and electric shocks. Held in shackles, he contracted blood poisoning through the cuts on his wrists and almost lost his left arm. Throughout his ordeal never once did he tell the Germans anything.

He made two failed attempts to escape from Fresnes prison and was sent to Compiègne prison and then to Buchenwald concentration camp. Sixteen of his travelling companions were executed and cremated shortly after arrival. Escaping from Buchenwald, he ended up in a camp near Marienburg. On 16 April 1945 he and 20 others made a break for it; half of them were gunned down. Yeo-Thomas was recaptured just half a mile from American lines; a few days later he tried yet again and finally reached Allied lines.

After the war he served as a witness at the Nuremberg trials, helping to identify Buchenwald officials. He also served as a defence witness for Otto Skorzeny, whose commandos had worn American uniforms during the opening stages of the Battle of the Bulge. Yeo-Thomas testified that he had masqueraded in German uniforms behind enemy lines while on SOE missions.

In recognition of his unflinching bravery, on 15 February 1946 he was awarded the George Cross. His citation recorded: 'Wing Commander Yeo-Thomas thus turned his final mission into a success by his determined opposition to the enemy, his strenuous efforts to maintain the morale of his fellow prisoners and his brilliant escape activities. He endured brutal treatment and torture without flinching and showed the most amazing fortitude and devotion to duty throughout his service abroad, during which he was under the constant threat of death.'

HE YIZHI Japan made extensive use of spies in China. The Japanese army recruited Chinese student He Yizhi, who studied at the Imperial University in Tokyo, in the late 1930s because he could speak fluent Japanese. He was sent to southern China to work for the Japanese military as an interpreter. When He Yizhi met Chinese general Li Zongren he offered to spy on the Japanese. He was working for Colonel Wachi Takaji, who felt Japan should be fighting the Soviet Union rather than China, which would make a valuable ally against the Soviets. This view was shared by General Li. Wachi began passing military secrets to Chinese intelligence via He Yizhi.

He Yizhi proved an extraordinary success thanks to Wachi and his supporters. He built a secret radio transmitter in a Japanese friend's house in the French Concession in Shanghai. From there he provided Chinese intelligence with advanced warning of Japanese deployments for a series of battles from Xuzhou to Wuhan. In 1941 he was forced to flee Shanghai suspected of spying after the Japanese occupied the International Settlement. He Yizhi escaped back to Chinese lines just in time.

AXIS SPIES

ELYESA BAZNA Bazna was the Albanian valet of the British ambassador to Turkey, Sir Hughe Knatchbull-Hugessen. He was also an agent for the Nazi intelligence service Sicherheitsdienst during 1943 and 1944. Bazna stole the keys to the ambassador's safe and photographed the contents, which related to the Moscow, Cairo and Tehran conferences and the opening of the Second Front. He was rewarded for his service with £300,000. Bazna did not discover the money was counterfeit until after the war.

ALFRED GABAS Frenchman Gabas worked as an Abwehr agent in the Cherbourg area. He was given up to the Americans by Juan Frutos in late August 1944.

HERMANN GÖRTZ Just five days before Churchill took up residence in Downing Street on 10 May 1940, German agent Hermann Görtz parachuted into County Meath to the west of Dublin. He was already well-known to MI5. He had been arrested in Britain in the 1930s for spying on the RAF and jailed for four years. During his time in Maidstone prison he became acquainted with members of the Irish Republican Army (IRA). He had been deported in February 1939, but was now back with a new mission to help the IRA plan attacks in Northern Ireland. He was also to discuss Operation *Kathleen*, an IRA-supported German invasion of Ireland.

Görtz's presence was compromised on 7 May 1940 when the IRA tried to capture the courier bearing correspondence to Britain's representative, Sir John Maffey. A gun battle followed with the police and Irish Prime Minister Éamon de Valera ordered another clampdown. Several weeks later Irish police raided a known safe house. They seized documents relating to Kathleen, £20,000, Görtz's uniform and his parachute. Görtz, though, managed to remain on the run for 18 months before he was captured.

KAREL RICHARD RICHTER Czechoslovak citizen Karel Richter was recruited by the Abwehr and parachuted into Britain in May 1941. He job was to check whether fellow agent Wulf Schmidt had been turned by

British intelligence. Richter was caught, tried for espionage and hanged on 10 December 1941.

GENERAL YOSHIOKA YASUNORI From 1935 to 1945 Yoshioka served as the Japanese military attaché to Emperor Pu Yi in Changchun (Xinjing), Manchukuo. His real task was to spy on Pu Yi and control him on Japan's behalf. Everything the emperor did was reported back to Tokyo. Manchukuo was an unwilling Japanese ally in its war against China, Britain and America. As the state was a Japanese creation, no one recognized it.

SOVIET SPIES

ANTHONY BLUNT Soviet intelligence proved highly adept at recruiting British Communists during the 1930s. Most notable were the Cambridge Five, who were all Cambridge University graduates. They consisted of Anthony Blunt, Guy Burgess, John Cairncross, Donald Maclean and Kim Philby. Blunt, while working for MI5, was also a Soviet mole who leaked Ultra intelligence from Bletchley Park. After the war he became a respected art historian and was knighted in 1956. His treachery went undetected until 1964 and was not made public until 1979.

GUY BURGESS Burgess joined the British Communist Party and was recruited by Soviet intelligence in 1935. He worked for MI6 for a time before joining the BBC in 1941 and then the Foreign Office three years later. This gave him access to British policy documents, which he passed on to the Soviets. After the war he defected to the Soviet Union.

JOHN CAIRNCROSS Cairncross spied for Soviet military intelligence while working at Bletchley Park during 1942 and 1943. He was recruited as a spy by James Klugmann of the British Communist Party. He did not confess until 1964.

DONALD MACLEAN Maclean became a Soviet agent during his last year at Cambridge University and joined the diplomatic service as a mole. He then went to work for the Foreign Office and was posted to the British Embassy in Paris. Following the German invasion of France in 1940 he was evacuated to London. Back at the Foreign Office he became an expert on economic warfare.

In 1944 he was sent to the British Embassy in Washington, where he worked for four years. He defected to Moscow in 1951.

ALLAN FOOTE Foote was born in Liverpool and briefly served in the RAF before deserting in 1936. He fled to Spain, where he fought for the Communist international brigades against General Franco's Nationalists. He then joined the Soviet 'Red Orchestra' network and became a radio operator working for Soviet military intelligence in Lucerne, Switzerland. He was eventually arrested by the Swiss police in 1943. It has been alleged that he was a double agent.

LEO LONG Long was an intelligence officer working for Soviet military intelligence at the War Office. While at Cambridge University he became a member of the Communist Party and was recruited by Anthony Blunt. From 1940 to 1944 he served in MI14, the section at the War Office responsible for assessing German military intentions. He had access to Ultra-based intelligence, which he passed on to Blunt. After the war he served as an intelligence officer with the Control Commission in Germany. He claimed he did not spy for the Soviets while there. He confessed in 1964 but was not prosecuted.

YOTOKU MIYAGI Miyagi was born in Okinawa and moved to California as a teenager, where he ran a restaurant and became a Communist. In 1933 he moved to Japan and was recruited by Soviet spy Richard Sorge. He gathered economic and military intelligence and translated Japanese documents. Miyagi's contacts included a Japanese general's secretary. He was arrested in 1941 along with other members of Sorge's network and died two years later in prison.

HOTSUMI OZAKI Japanese Communist and journalist Ozaki was also recruited by Sorge after they met in China in the early 1930s. Returning to Japan, he gathered intelligence on Japanese economic and political affairs for Sorge. He was arrested along with Miyagi and was hanged for treason on 7 November 1944.

SÁNDOR RADÓ (ALEXANDER RADÓ) Operating from Geneva, Sándor Radó, code-named 'Dora', and Englishman Allan Foote developed a contact in

Lucerne known as 'Lucy' via German émigré Christian Schneider. 'Lucy' was a German exile by the name of Rudolf Roessler, who was a committed anti-Nazi with extremely well-placed sympathizers within the German high command and military intelligence.

By June 1943 Foote was aware that he was being watched by the Swiss police. Three months earlier the Abwehr had also placed Radó and most of his co-conspirators under surveillance. He had not helped matters by having an affair with one of his female wireless operators, who was half his age. The girl concerned was also seeing an Abwehr agent. Foote had wanted to reduce the rate of his transmissions but Moscow refused. Germany put diplomatic pressure on the Swiss to arrest them and it became increasingly difficult for the authorities to turn a blind eye. Radó fled to France and was later flown to the Soviet Union and imprisoned.

RUDOLF ROESSLER By profession, Roessler was a journalist and publisher who in the early 1930s had incurred the displeasure of the Nazis. Exiled in Switzerland, he lived in fear of being handed over to Hitler's henchmen. By way of insurance he worked for both Soviet and Swiss intelligence. He ran the 'Lucy' spy ring and was arrested in May 1944, but later escaped.

CHRISTIAN SCHNEIDER Schneider was a German émigré working for Soviet intelligence in Switzerland. For security purposes, code-named 'Taylor', he was Roessler's only point of contact. He was arrested in April 1944.

AGNES SMEDLEY Smedley was an American journalist who came to the notice of US and British intelligence during the First World War due to her dealings with Indian nationalists with ties to Germany. She was arrested by the Office of US Naval Intelligence for espionage in 1918 but was released and the charges were dropped. She worked in China during the 1930s and supported the Chinese Communists, though she also visited Nationalist-held areas. While in China she had a relationship with Richard Sorge and introduced him to Hotsumi Ozaki.

Smedley was clearly anti-Japanese and tried unsuccessfully to join the Chinese Communist Party in 1937. Four years later she returned to America to champion China's Communists. At her funeral in Beijing a decade later

Arthur Clegg, a member of the British Communist Party said, 'She fought for the cause of the Indian people struggling against British oppression, for the cause of the Chinese people struggling against Japanese oppression and against the terror of Chiang Kai-shek.'

BRANKO VUKELIĆ Vukelić was a Yugoslav journalist who was also part of the 'Sorge' spy ring. He studied in Paris and was a firm supporter of the Communist cause. In Japan, Vukelić provided Sorge with information mainly from foreign correspondents and French contacts. After being arrested, he died in a Japanese prison in January 1945.

Part 2

Eavesdropping War

Chapter 4

Allied Code Breakers

Signals intelligence, or SIGINT, played an equally vital role during the war and helped shape Allied strategy and bring them ultimate victory. Afterwards its contribution in Britain remained Ultra Top Secret until Group Captain Frederick Winterbotham published his book *The Ultra Secret* in 1974. This lifted the lid on the work carried out by the men and women of Station X.

BRITISH SIGINT

GOVERNMENT CODE AND CYPHER SCHOOL The British Government Code and Cypher School (GC&CS) developed a good track record intercepting German signals during the First World War. Throughout the inter-war period it turned its attentions to French, Italian, Russian and US codes and cyphers. When the storm-clouds of war began to gather over Europe once more it was clear to Alastair Denniston, the GC&CS's head, and his boss Admiral Hugh Sinclair, the then head of MI6, that it would need to expand its operations in order to keep the British government as well-informed as possible.

BLETCHLEY PARK Showing great foresight, Sinclair purchased Bletchley Park Mansion in 1938 as a base of operations for both MI6 and GC&CS outside London. The house was designated 'Station X', as it was the tenth property that MI6 numbered with Roman numerals. Located in Buckinghamshire, near the town of Bletchley, it was mainly chosen because it was a safe distance from the threat posed by the Luftwaffe but was still reasonably close to London for meetings. MI6 planned to evacuate to Bletchley Park in the event of a threat to London. In the meantime it moved all its pre-war files there for safekeeping.

When the cypher staff began to arrive, improvised wooden huts were built to accommodate the various intelligence sections. Denniston had hoped the huts would be built in a star shape around the house, but instead they ended up dotted around the grounds in a random fashion. The working conditions at Station X were very basic and the crude heating stoves in the huts often filled them with acrid smoke. In light of the sensitive nature of the work being conducted, security was paramount, so the sections operated on a need-to-know basis and were strictly compartmentalized. The work was divided up as follows:

The Cottage This housed the Enigma Research Section.

Hut 1 The very first hut was built as a radio transmission and reception station, thereby connecting Bletchley Park to the outside world.

Hut 2 This was built as a mess to provide refreshments for the staff and included a NAAFI kiosk. It soon became known as 'the beer hut' and was a popular place to congregate and socialize.

Hut 3 This functioned as home to the intelligence reporting section, which turned the deciphered messages into the all-important intelligence reports for customers spread across Whitehall.

Hut 4 This housed the Naval Section that worked on German and Italian naval communication codes. It proved vital during the dark days of the Battle of the Atlantic.

Hut 5 Initially assigned to the Naval Section, this dealt with general military intelligence from across Europe. The hut also included a sunray parlour, which was intended to help keep up the night shift's vitamin D levels.

Hut 6 The staff of Hut 6 focused on the German army and Luftwaffe Enigma systems. They were brought great bundles of messages collected by the outstations across the country. Huts 6 and 3 operated 24 hours a day with three eight-hour shifts.

Hut 7 This was built some distance from the other huts because it housed noisy tabulating machinery.

Hut 8 This housed the Naval Enigma Section and became the most famous hut thanks to the presence of Alan Turing.

Hut 9 Huts 9 and 18 were used by Oliver Strachey for what became known as Intelligence Service Oliver Strachey.

Hut 10 The occupants of this hut dealt with low-grade coded messages that were not encrypted by Enigma.

Hut 11 The mechanical bombes that helped speed up breaking Enigma were located in Hut 11 and at Bletchley's outstations.

Elmers School Situated on an adjacent site to Bletchley Park, code breakers here dealt with Japanese diplomatic codes.

The new blocks As the war progressed the rudimentary accommodation was improved with the construction of new, purpose-built concrete blocks. These were extremely utilitarian but were better-heated than the spartan wooden huts. Blocks A and B were the first to go up. Block D housed the Enigma processing sections from Huts 3, 6 and 8 from November 1943 until the end of the war. In total, around 9,000 men and women worked at Bletchley in continuous shifts. Others were deployed in Bletchley's numerous outstations.

UK OUTSTATIONS Listening stations were dotted all along the British coastline, from Dover to Wick. From these, the operators were able to eavesdrop on the rest of Europe. There were at least eight key facilities:

Beaumanor Hall Located in Leicestershire, Beaumanor Hall intercepted German Enigma signals for Bletchley. The Y Service staff, like their colleagues at Bletchley, operated from wooden huts.

Eastcote At this outstation, Alan Turing's revolutionary bombe machines were allocated to separate territories. The bombes were large cabinets full of rotating drums. These worked through thousands of code combinations with the drums rotating endlessly. They made their debut at Bletchley in the summer of 1940.

Chapter 4

Station X, better known as Bletchley Park, was home to Britain's war-winning code breakers.

HMS Flowerdown Masked as a naval base, this wireless-intercept facility was a shore base in Hampshire outside the city of Winchester.

Isle of Man Interception training was conducted in seclusion on the Isle of Man in the midst of the Irish Sea between Britain and Ireland. Recruits enjoyed being there because there seemed to be no shortage of foodstuffs.

Letchworth Here, Harold Keene and Oliver Lawn with the British Tabulating Company oversaw the construction of the first bombe machines in 1940.

Skegness The Butlin's holiday camp at Skegness was also used as a location to train wireless operators.

Southwold The Y Service stationed in the seaside town of Southwold in Suffolk found themselves at risk of being shelled by German ships or by bombers jettisoning their remaining bombs on the way home.

Wavendon Manor Royal Navy Wrens working at Bletchley were billeted at the nearby Wavendon Manor.

OVERSEAS OUTSTATIONS

Algeria Following the Allied landings in French North Africa in late 1942 a Bletchley team was sent to Fort Sidi M'Cid, overlooking Constantine in Algeria, to break low-level German cyphers.

Ceylon (Sri Lanka) HMS Anderson was a shore base in Colombo that acted as home to the Far East Combined Bureau after it relocated from Hong Kong and Singapore. It eavesdropped on the Japanese and tracked their shipping and submarines using direction finding. The island was bombed by the Japanese in April 1942 and came under threat of invasion.

Cocos Islands Situated in the middle of the Indian Ocean, these isolated islands provided a location from which to secretly monitor Japanese naval movements. This was one of the most isolated and secretive Y Service stations.

Egypt A disused museum in Heliopolis, just outside Cairo, was the location for the Combined Middle East cypher operation. Once the war progressed its operators became mobile out in the desert, using vans to eavesdrop on the Axis communications.

Bombing of Bletchley

Despite its location, Bletchley Park briefly found itself on the front lines when the Luftwaffe accidentally bombed it on 21 November 1940. A lost lone bomber sought to jettison its bombs on the neighbouring railway station and missed. Instead, a bomb struck Elmers School. A direct hit destroyed its telephone exchange and the typists' room. The vicarage next door was also damaged by a bomb exploding in the garden. Two more landed in the grounds of Bletchley Park, one of which narrowly missed Hut 4. The blast was such that the hut was shifted a few inches off its foundations and some of its windows were blown in. Fortunately, no one was harmed. The other fell to the ground metres from the Cottage, but luckily it failed to go off. Inside, Dilly Knox and Mavis Lever were hard at work on the Italian Naval Enigma.

Hong Kong This was the initial home of the Far East Combined Bureau, established in 1935 to monitor Chinese, Japanese and Soviet radio traffic. Four years later it moved to Singapore. After the Japanese invasion of the island in February 1942 it relocated to Colombo, Ceylon (Sri Lanka).

India Bletchley ran a little-known operation in India called the Wireless Experimental Centre outside Delhi at Ramjas College. Section C ran the wireless intercept station, which monitored Japanese traffic. There were also facilities in Abbottabad, Bangalore and Barrackpore. The former eavesdropped on the Soviets during the inter-war years. Code breakers Maurice Allen and Wilfrid Noyce broke the Japanese water transport code at Ramjas in 1943.

Kenya The Far East Combined Bureau relocated to Kilindini, Mombasa in April 1942 because of the Japanese threat to Ceylon. The cryptologists and Wrens monitored Japanese codes from a requisitioned 19th-century school building. The bureau moved back to Colombo the following year.

Malta The Y Service operated on Malta as well as in Egypt. There it helped track Axis aircraft and shipping movements, especially those keeping General Rommel's Afrika Korps resupplied in Libya.

The Y Service

The global scale and complexity of Bletchley's operations was to be one of the best-kept secrets of the war. It is not widely known that Station X and the GC&CS staff operated facilities not only across Britain but also overseas, collecting communications intelligence. These were manned by what was known as the Y Service. This name helped conceal the exact nature of what its operators were up to.

Deployment overseas for many must have felt like being sent on holiday to a tropical sun-kissed paradise, where there was little or no rationing. However, those sent to the Far East had to relocate a number of times because of the constant Japanese threat.

Allied Code Breakers

Singapore The Y Service had an interception station at Kranji, on the northern coast of Singapore, monitoring Japanese naval communications. It also monitored the diplomatic traffic to the Japanese consular-general in Singapore. The Far East Combined Bureau was located at Seletar Naval Base. Both organizations had to be evacuated when the Japanese invaded.

BREAKING THE CODES

Enigma British code-breaking operations in the First World War led to the development of cypher machines (a cypher represents a letter or figure with another letter or figure, whereas a military code uses a group of randomly selected letter or figures to represent a word or phrase). In the late 1920s the German armed forces began employing the Enigma machine. This looked like a small typewriter housed in a wooden box. At the top was a lampboard with a light for each letter of the alphabet. When the keys were depressed an electrical current lit up the enciphered letter on the lampboard. This was used to create the enciphered message.

The British found the three rotor version relatively easy to solve, but the Germans added a plugboard that increased settings to a staggering 159 million, million, million. Alfred Dillwyn ('Dilly') Knox worked on the Enigma machine and cracked the less complicated versions, which had been supplied by the Germans to their Spanish and Italian allies during the Spanish Civil War. Afterwards Knox struggled until the British began to co-operate with the

Special Liaison Units

Group Captain Winterbotham, serving with MI6 at the outbreak of war, was well aware of the work being carried out by Bletchley. This led him to consider how its intelligence could best be disseminated to commanders without revealing the source. To this end he created Special Liaison Units (SLUs), which were attached to field headquarters. These consisted of RAF officers and a few enlisted men. Decrypted messages were re-encrypted in a British cypher and sent to the Allied commands, where the SLUs would decode them and share them only with the cleared senior commander. Secrecy surrounding the origin of the Ultra intelligence remained paramount throughout the war.

Poles. Marian Rejewski, a Polish mathematician and code breaker, managed to reconstruct Enigma mathematically. The Poles then built an electromechanical key to Enigma known as the *bomba kryptologiczna* (Bletchley would later build a version known as 'bombe'). However, it did not work very well.

Despite this, the initial Polish success convinced Denniston to recruit mathematicians to help Knox. The first to arrive was Peter Twinn in February 1939, followed by Alan Turing. The GC&CS's code breakers were instructed to move to Station X on 15 August 1939, just before the German invasion of Poland. Bletchley became home to 110 code breakers, though just 13 were working on German codes and cyphers, and just four – Knox, Twinn, Turing and Tony Kendrick – were tackling Enigma. Denniston then embarked on a major recruitment drive.

The first wartime Enigma message was cracked in January 1940, when Knox broke the 'Green' system that was used by Germany's regional military headquarters. This was followed by the 'Red' system used by the Luftwaffe to liaise with the German army. The German Naval Enigma proved much more complex but Alan Turing was determined to crack it. He and Peter Twinn set up the Naval Enigma Section in June 1940. Their goal was to crack 'Dolphin', the Enigma cypher employed by the U-boats' wolf packs in the Atlantic. They did this in July 1941, which enabled Allied aircraft to hunt the U-boats and the Admiralty to re-route vulnerable Allied convoys. The German Railway Enigma was broken by John Tiltman.

Lorenz The Lorenz SZ40 enciphered teleprinter system was introduced in 1940. This was used by the German high command to keep its communications secure. This was code-named 'Tunny' by Bletchley. There were, however, a number of different German teleprinter cypher machines, which the code breakers gave the collective code name 'Fish'. Lorenz was cracked by John Tiltman and Bill Tutte in late 1941, enabling the Allies to read Hitler's orders to his generals. This proved to be yet another major intelligence windfall.

Jellyfish In March 1944, aided by the first Colossus computer, Bletchley broke the 'Jellyfish' enciphered teleprinter connecting Berlin with Field Marshal Gerd von Rundstedt, the German commander in Paris. In the run-up to D-Day, this was a major coup. Bletchley was able to confirm that Hitler anticipated that the Allies' main force would land at Calais rather than in Normandy. It also proved that Operation *Bodyguard*, designed to deceive the Germans about the exact location of Operation *Overlord*, had worked.

Ultra and 'Boniface' The signals intelligence derived both from Enigma and Lorenz were designated Ultra because it was considered Ultra Secret and was only released on a strictly need-to-know basis. To hide its origin, Ultra intelligence was attributed to the fictitious 'Boniface' spy network operating in Germany. Initially, Bletchley intelligence was distributed under the code word 'Boniface', until it was replaced by Ultra in June 1941.

ALLIED SIGINT

While Bletchley received all the credit for breaking Enigma, Lorenz and many of the Japanese army and navy codes, American and Australian code breakers also played a vital role, especially in South-east Asia and the Pacific.

US SIGNAL INTELLIGENCE SERVICE The US Army's Signal Intelligence Service (SIS) code-breaking division founded in 1930 under William F. Friedman was renamed the Signal Security Agency in 1943. Its headquarters were in Arlington, across the Potomac River from Washington, and it formed part of the US Army Signal Corps. Friedman gathered a team that included Frank Rowlett, Abraham Sinkov, Solomon Kullback, Ann Z. Caracristi and Leo Rosen. During the war the SIS had six fixed stations that concentrated on Axis diplomatic traffic. Four of these were on American soil in Alaska, California, Hawaii and Virginia; the other two were in New Delhi, India and Asmara, Ethiopia. By the end of the war the SIS had some 10,500 staff, the majority of whom were female. Eventually the organization became part of the newly formed National Security Agency.

In 1940 Frank Rowlett's team of cryptanalysts broke Japan's diplomatic 'Purple' cypher, by replicating it without ever seeing one, thereby revealing Japan's diplomatic secrets before the USA entered the war. During the six months preceding Japan's attack on Peal Harbor over 7,000 Japanese messages were intercepted, decrypted and translated. This averaged nearly 300 per week. Perhaps not surprisingly, in 1941 Friedman was hospitalized suffering from nervous exhaustion. A four-man team including Sinkov and Rosen was sent to Bletchley to hand over a 'Purple' machine in exchange for very limited details on Enigma. Friedman later travelled to Bletchley in April 1943.

Chapter 4

In the Philippines, the US Army's 2nd Signal Service Company conducted radio intelligence-gathering in the Pacific. Initially, its task was to intercept Japanese diplomatic traffic to Washington, but they also shared local radio intelligence with the US Navy code breakers on Corregidor. From the summer of 1941 General MacArthur's chief of staff, General Sutherland, regularly received copies of these intercepts. After the Japanese attack on the Philippines the focus became the Japanese air force. This enabled them to pinpoint Japanese radio stations in Formosa and the southern Philippines and give advance warning of air attacks. The 2nd Signal Service Company was eventually evacuated to Australia.

The Japanese General Army Administration Code, known as '7890', was cracked in April 1943 thanks to Japanese sloppiness. Failing to change position in the addend book, Japanese operators sent similar messages, allowing sufficient depth for cryptanalysts to break the code.

The SIS also ran the Venona project, which was a counter-intelligence operation that started in February 1943 to decrypt messages sent by the Soviet intelligence agencies. This was instigated by Colonel Carter W. Clarke, Chief of Special Branch of the Military Intelligence Service, who did not trust Stalin. Clarke feared that the Soviet Union might seek a separate peace deal with Hitler, leaving the USA and Britain to fight on alone. Therefore, he felt it was vital to have an inside track on Soviet intentions.

CENTRAL BUREAU The Central Bureau was a joint Australian and US Army signals intelligence facility initially located in Melbourne and then Brisbane. It was designed to support the Supreme Commander, Allied Forces, South West Pacific Area, General Douglas MacArthur, whose headquarters moved to Australia after the fall of the Philippines. In July 1942 Abraham Sinkov was sent to take charge of the American contingent at the Central Bureau. MacArthur's chief signal officer, General Spencer Akin, was appointed director but he rarely visited the organization and was content to let Sinkov get on with it. Under him the Central Bureau became a very trusted source of intelligence for MacArthur and his commanders. It regularly decoded intercepts regarding the Japanese order of battle, as well as their defensive and offensive plans. MacArthur rather foolishly excluded naval intelligence from the bureau, which resulted in a poor working relationship with the US Navy. The Central Bureau grew to employ 4,000 men and women by the end of the war.

Allied Code Breakers

US OFFICE OF CHIEF OF NAVAL OPERATIONS The US Navy's cryptanalysis organization was aptly known as OP-20-G (Office of Chief of Naval Operations, 20th Division of the Office of Naval Communications, G Section/Communications Security), or the Communications Security Unit, under Commander Laurance F. Safford. By 1941 its two key branches were located in the Philippines and Pearl Harbor, which were supported by a chain of outlying intercept stations. Understandably, their efforts were concentrated on Japanese naval codes.

The most important code breaking in the Pacific was 'JN-25', the standard Japanese naval operational code. It was introduced in the summer of 1939 and proved far more secure than earlier Japanese navy codes. The US Naval Intelligence unit at Pearl Harbor, Station Hypo, under the leadership of cryptanalyst Commander Joseph Rochefort, and Station CAST in the Philippines had figured out much of 'JN-25' by the time war broke out. However, just before the attack on Pearl Harbor it was changed. It then took time to reconstruct the code books and useful intelligence did not become available until March 1942. They also managed to crack the Japanese weather forecasting cypher.

Rochefort and his code breakers were able to identify Port Moresby as a Japanese objective that would involve two of their carriers. Admiral Nimitz was able to intercept them and this resulted in the Battle of the Coral Sea in early May 1942. The far-flung nature of the Japanese conquests also helped the American code breakers because it became a logistical headache for the Japanese to keep updating and reissuing their code books. After Midway, the Office of Naval Intelligence sought to take OP-20-G away from the Office of Naval Communications' control but failed. By the end of the war it had over 5,000 staff.

FLEET RADIO UNIT, MELBOURNE Fleet Radio Unit, Melbourne (FRUMEL) was an American, Australian and British facility in Melbourne, with stations also in Canberra and Darwin. It came under the command of the chief of naval operations in Washington and not MacArthur. FRUMEL was tasked with monitoring Japanese naval signals. Commanded by Lieutenant Rudolph Fabia, US Navy, he was not prepared to co-operate with the Central Bureau and insisted when briefing MacArthur that Major General Charles Willoughby,

Chapter 4

his chief of intelligence, be excluded. Willoughby complained that FRUMEL failed to provide his boss with timely intelligence, which was not entirely true.

FLEET RADIO UNIT PACIFIC Fleet Radio Unit Pacific (FRUPAC) was a sister signals unit, to FRUMEL based in Hawaii (it replaced Hypo) answering to the US commander-in-chief, Pacific, Admiral Nimitz and the chief of naval operations in Washington DC, Admiral King.

IMPACT ON PEARL HARBOR Extremely poor co-ordination meant that the fruits of being able to read the 'Purple' code were not shared with the US Fleet at Pearl Harbor. Nagao Kita, the Japanese consul in Honolulu, Hawaii received a message on 24 September 1941 from Japanese Naval Intelligence. This requested that Pearl Harbor be divided into five distinct geographic areas and the warships in them listed. The SIS team at Fort Shafter, Honolulu intercepted this message. Unfortunately, they had no decrypting facilities so instead they had to send the messages to Washington by air.

Bad weather meant that this particular message was sent by ship and did not arrive until 6 October. It was another three days before the SIS decrypted the contents. This was then sent to the US Navy. Both the army and the navy rightly deduced that the Japanese were putting together a grid system to support an air attack. Disastrously, the information was not forwarded to Admiral Husband Kimmel, commander of the Pacific Fleet.

This was not the only warning that was missed. Three other messages to Kita from Tokyo were intercepted that showed the Japanese navy was taking a deep interest in Pearl Harbor. The first instructed consular official Ensign Takeo Yoshikawa to report twice a week on US warship movements. Yoshikawa was a member of Naval Intelligence and had been sent to Hawaii with the task of spying on the Americans. The second message ordered him to scout out Oahu's airbases. This clearly suggested an interest in American air defences. On 8 November 1941 a third message requested data on points around Honolulu. None of these were sent to Kimmel either. He was denied the opportunity to put his forces on alert and disperse his ships.

IMPACT ON MIDWAY In contrast, the cracking of 'JN-25' meant that Admiral Nimitz was informed of Japan's entire operational plans before their naval task force ever reached American-controlled Midway in June 1942. Ignoring the diversionary activities of the Japanese Northern Force heading for the western end of the Aleutian Islands, and the Second Carrier Striking Group making for the middle of the chain, the US fleet sailed on Midway. Code breaking could not guarantee an American victory but it greatly helped to make it possible.

Thanks to superior intelligence and improved tactics the Americans thwarted a Japanese force five times the size of their own. What followed was a deadly game of cat and mouse involving carrier-based dive-bombers and culminated in a significant American victory. In the space of just five minutes Admiral Nagumo's flagship, the *Akagi*, as well as two other Japanese carriers, the *Kaga* and *Soryu*, were hit by aircraft from the US carriers *Yorktown* and *Enterprise*. Midway proved to be decisive. The defeat was a serious blow to Japan's carrier force and Japan could simply not match America's major carrier-building programme. From that point on the Japanese were mainly on the defensive in the Pacific, permitting the American and Allied fleets to take the initiative.

The Japanese defeat at Midway had immediate repercussions for their plans in China. Their main objective was the Nationalists' last stronghold in Sichuan province. However, the necessary resources could not be brought to bear for such an enormous undertaking after Midway and the American landings on Guadalcanal in early August 1942. The gathering of 16 divisions in south-central China redeployed from Japan, Manchuria and the South Seas to reinforce the Japanese Expeditionary Force had to be abandoned. It also impacted on the Japanese forces operating in Burma, who were at the very limit of their supply lines. Japanese plans in China were similarly hampered by the massive influx of American weapons supplied to the Nationalists. Their last grand offensive in China was not conducted until May 1944.

After Midway the Japanese changed their codes in June and again in August 1942, fearing their security had been breached. However, American code breakers were helped when Japanese code books were captured in the Solomons. When the Americans cracked the Japanese convoy code this aided their submarine operations, though it did not necessarily guarantee more vessels were sunk. In April 1943 the interception of Japanese radio communications at Rabaul enabled American fighter aircraft to shoot down Admiral Yamamoto's plane. His death was a great blow to Japanese morale.

Chapter 5

The Impact of Bletchley Park

BATTLE OF BRITAIN

Bletchley Park, even before the evacuation of the British Expeditionary Force at Dunkirk, had broken the Luftwaffe's codes. This meant that it was reading up to a thousand messages a day, though little of it was of much value. 'Enigma gave a general warning of the approach of the Battle of Britain,' recalled code breaker Harry Hinsley. 'The fact that Enigma had now been producing intelligence for some months on the German Air Force's organization [...] was also of great strategic value.' This, though, had weakened the efforts to break the Naval Enigma.

In mid-July 1940 Hitler issued instructions for the preparation of an invasion of England. Churchill was informed that an initial air offensive was expected to start in early August. The Luftwaffe would first have to clear the skies of the RAF before a seaborne assault could be contemplated. Bletchley's intelligence was so sensitive that Churchill did not clear Air Chief Marshal Sir Hugh Dowding, who was in charge of RAF Fighter Command, to see it. He was only granted access to Ultra in mid-October 1940 and even then Dowding was not permitted to share it with his commanders.

Churchill visited Fighter Command's 11 Group Operations Room at RAF Uxbridge on 15 September 1940. Although it was quiet, Churchill knew very well that trouble was brewing. Bletchley's decoders had already warned him that the Luftwaffe was planning to throw everything it had at London that day, prior to invasion. Churchill watched as the RAF fighter squadrons were stretched to breaking point. It was subsequently hushed up just how close Fighter Command had come to being overwhelmed. Nonetheless, the RAF successfully turned the tide in the air war and forced Hitler to postpone his invasion until the following year.

THE BLITZ

The 'Red' cypher used by the Luftwaffe provided Bletchley with indications of potential German targets and the numbers of bombers and fighters involved in the raids. Bletchley was also helped by the Germans using code names that included the same letters as their intended targets, such as 'Bild' for Birmingham and 'Liebe' for Liverpool. Unfortunately, the code breakers would miss 'Korn'. Bletchley during the Battle of Britain and the Blitz also broke the 'Brown' cypher used by the Luftwaffe stations in France. This would help thwart the Luftwaffe's night raids on Britain's cities.

In mid-November 1940 Churchill faced a dilemma when Ultra indicated a major British city was to be bombed. It has since been claimed that Churchill deliberately sacrificed Coventry to the Blitz rather than reveal that Bletchley Park was decoding Enigma and intercepting the bombers. However, Ultra did not identify which city was to be attacked and Churchill thought that London was to be the target. 'Ultra never mentioned Coventry,' confirmed head of Air Section Peter Calvocoressi. 'Churchill – so far from pondering whether to save Coventry or safeguard Ultra – was under the impression that the raid was to be on London.'

Coventry was actually a victim of poor intelligence co-ordination within Whitehall. A captured Luftwaffe pilot had warned of a full-moon raid against Coventry and Birmingham. The Air Ministry dismissed this and stuck with its own analysis of German messages regarding their 'Moonlight Sonata' using radio navigation. They deduced the target was once again London. As for the navigational beams being aimed at the West Midlands, air intelligence assumed it was just another trial. It was only later that it was realized that the code word 'Korn' had been missed – this was the German name for 'Corn' and the cover name for Coventry. Nonetheless, the point about source protection remains valid – the secrecy surrounding the vital work at Bletchley Park was paramount. This was exemplified by the hunt for the *Bismarck* and the Battle of Matapan.

BATTLE OF THE ATLANTIC

Harry Hinsley, who worked in Bletchley's Naval Section, warned for weeks that two German battleships were heading for the North Sea to attack British

The Impact of Bletchley Park

shipping. The Admiralty ignored him and the aircraft carrier HMS *Glorious* and two destroyers were lost. When the German battleship *Bismarck* sailed from the Baltic in early 1941 Hinsley reported she was heading for a French port. Again the Admiralty dismissed this intelligence, only to have it confirmed by a deciphered message stating her destination was Brest. The *Bismarck* was caught, damaged and forced to scuttle on 27 May 1941. However, the RAF flew reconnaissance flights over the *Bismarck* before the attack to hide the use of signals intelligence.

In early February 1942 the German U-boats started using an Enigma machine with a fourth rotor. Bletchley code-named this 'Shark'. For ten months vital intelligence on U-boat movements was lost in what became known as 'the Shark Blackout'. For the first half of the year the Germans concentrated on the US coast, but in August attacks were resumed on Atlantic convoys. Hugh Alexander, who had taken over Hut 8 from Alan Turing, and his team struggled to break 'Shark'. During August and September the U-boats caught 21 of the 63 convoys and sank 43 ships. During November almost a hundred ships were lost. Finally Bletchley broke 'Shark' in December 1942, helping to slow the losses.

BATTLE OF MATAPAN

Bletchley also helped the Royal Navy track the Italian fleet and then maul it at the Battle of Matapan off southern Greece. In the early hours of 27

Ultra was highly instrumental in winning the Battle of the Atlantic.

79

Chapter 5

March 1941 the Italian fleet sailed from Naples, and Admiral Cunningham at Alexandria was notified. The British did not want it interfering with British troop movements to Greece. Cunningham's challenge was to intercept the Italians without making it apparent their naval codes had been compromised. This was achieved by sending a flying boat from Crete on a 'routine' patrol. Not only did it have to find the Italians, but it was vital the Italians saw the aircraft. Cunningham was 'officially' made aware of the Italian warships' location by the flying boat at 12:20 hours. It reported seeing three Italian cruisers and a destroyer some 130 km (80 miles) east off south-eastern Sicily.

Cunningham at his headquarters stuck to his routine and went to his country club to play golf. There he ran into the Japanese consul and ensured he was overheard saying that he was going to a dinner party that night. All this was intended to give the impression that it was business as usual. Although Cunningham planned to deploy his fleet to the west of Crete, he felt, 'it was important to maintain an appearance of normality [...] lest the enemy should "smell a rat".' The Italians, still keen to confirm the British fleet was not at sea, sent a reconnaissance plane from Rhodes to see what was going on at Alexandria. It flew over the port at 14:00 hours and reported all was as anticipated.

Cunningham did not go to the party; instead, he went to the docks. By 19:00 hours on 27 March he was aboard HMS *Warspite*, supported by the *Barham* and *Valiant*, the *Formidable* and two flotillas of destroyers, and they departed Alexandria. At the same time Admiral Sir Henry Pridham-Wippell, with a second force consisting of four light cruisers and three destroyers, set sail from Piraeus. Vessels escorting the convoys from Alexandria and in the waters off northern Crete were alerted. Battle soon commenced.

The Italian navy lost five ships along with 2,400 men by 29 March. Only three British lives were lost when a torpedo-bomber was shot down. Cunningham's ships were largely unscathed and the Royal Navy was ecstatic. Admiral John Godfrey, director of Naval Intelligence, rang Bletchley and left a congratulatory message: 'Tell Dilly [Knox] that we have won a great victory in the Mediterranean and it is entirely due to him and his girls.' Not long after, Cunningham travelled to Bletchley to personally thank the code breakers for their exceptional work.

THE INVASION OF YUGOSLAVIA

Bletchley predicted Hitler's invasions of Yugoslavia and Greece, which took place in April 1941. Unfortunately, this did little to save the Greeks and Yugoslavs or the British Expeditionary Force sent to Greece from North Africa.

NORTH AFRICA

Up until 1940 Bletchley's main customers had been the Royal Navy and the RAF. Then in early 1941 intercepts of Luftwaffe messages showed that Hitler was about to intervene in Libya to prop up Mussolini. The War Office dismissed this intelligence and the British military authorities in Cairo were not warned. As a result, General Rommel's arrival came as a nasty shock to the British Army and it suffered a series of embarrassing defeats. The code breakers then broke a Luftwaffe Enigma cypher and the Italian navy's 'Hagelin C38m' cypher, which revealed the routes and timings of Rommel's supply convoys from Italy. This enabled the Royal Navy and the RAF to throttle his lines of communication.

'By the summer of 1942,' said Aileen Clayton, who was working for the Y Service in Malta, 'there can have been little Enigma traffic between the German forces in Africa and their masters back in Berlin and Italy that we did not intercept […] it was almost like being a member of Rommel's staff.' When General Montgomery took command of the British 8th Army in August 1942 Bletchley warned him that Rommel was planning to attack the British positions at Alam el Halfa. It also ensured Montgomery was fully appraised of Rommel's numbers and dispositions.

While Bletchley helped Montgomery achieve victory at El Alamein in November 1942, it appears he did not altogether trust Ultra. He was subsequently criticized for the slowness of his pursuit of Rommel. 'We told Monty over and over again how few tanks Rommel had got,' said code breaker Ralph Bennet. 'So Monty could have wiped Rommel off the face of the earth. Why he didn't, I simply do not know.' In consequence, the Axis forces in North Africa would hold out in Tunisia until May 1943.

THE INVASION OF RUSSIA

From mid-March 1941 Bletchley Park began picking up indications that Hitler was poised to attack Stalin. Although Soviet military intelligence was aware of Bletchley Park, which they called 'Krurort', they were unaware of the exact nature or indeed the scale of the work being conducted there. Churchill waited a few weeks before he felt moved to warn the Soviet leader. He drafted his warning in early April, but did not want to reveal that Bletchley had broken Hitler's Enigma codes. His message, as a result, was vague and not delivered until 27 April. It mattered little, as Stalin saw this as British subterfuge in order to get him to enter the war against Hitler.

While Bletchley's code breakers and Churchill were firmly of the view that Hitler intended to invade the Soviet Union, the British Joint Intelligence Committee remained unconvinced by Ultra. 'They appeared only on 12th June to have come to the conclusion that Hitler would attack Russia,' recalled Churchill's scientific advisor Dr R.V. Jones, 'earning the comment from Churchill, "I had not been content with this form of collective wisdom and preferred to see the originals [messages] myself [...] thus forming my own opinion sometimes at much earlier dates."'

This change of heart was due to an intercepted telegram from the Japanese ambassador in Berlin. On 10 June 1941 Bletchley's Japanese Diplomatic Section translated a message from the ambassador to Tokyo. This confirmed that the German invasion of the Soviet Union was about to take place. JIC chairman William Cavendish-Bentinck was instructed to immediately brief the Soviet ambassador. 'I remember saying that the attack would take place on 22 or 29 June,' recalled Bentinck, 'and that I would put money on the 22nd.' The ambassador relayed the warning to the Kremlin. His predicted date for Hitler's Operation *Barbarossa* proved spot on.

Bletchley then started intercepting messages confirming the Germans were committing large-scale atrocities on the Eastern Front. Stalin was convinced that Churchill's help came with an agenda. In 1941 he had largely ignored Churchill's warnings about Hitler's impending invasion. His main concern was that if the Germans had broken the Soviet cypher system then the British had as well.

PEARL HARBOR

Bletchley prior to the Japanese attack on the US fleet at Pearl Harbor had shared Japanese codes with the US Navy and the US Army. In late 1938 British code breaker John Tiltman cracked the Japanese army's main enciphered code. The following June he broke 'JN-25', the Japanese navy's key code. These results were shared informally with the Americans. In December 1940 a more

Thanks to Ultra, Stalin knew all about Hitler's Kursk offensive in 1943.

formal arrangement led to Bletchley revealing how to break Enigma while the Americans provided the solution to cracking the Japanese diplomatic cypher machine, the Alphabetic Typewriter 97, which was code-named 'Purple'. In early 1941 the first US liaison officers arrived at Bletchley.

KURSK

By 1943 the prognosis for the rejuvenated Red Army was good, despite friction between Churchill and Roosevelt on the one hand and Stalin on the other, over intelligence sharing and the delivery of weapons supplies. The British Joint Intelligence Committee now doubted Hitler's chances of victory, assessing 'the prospect of a German defeat of Russia has receded to vanishing point'. It was also of the view that Hitler had passed the point where he could hope to reach a peace settlement with Stalin. Churchill was in agreement and wrote: 'The Russians, both on land and in the air, had now the upper hand, and the Germans can have had few hopes of ultimate victory.'

Thanks to Bletchley's decoders, Churchill was forewarned that a battle was looming at Kursk that summer. Not only had Bletchley cracked Enigma used by the German armed forces, but also the Lorenz system used by their high command. He resolved to inform Stalin but was at pains to conceal the true source of this information. Captain Jerry Roberts, working at Bletchley, explained: 'We were able to warn them what army groups were going to be used. And most important, what tank units were going to be used. [...] We

Chapter 5

had to wrap it all up and say it was from spies, that we had wonderful teams of spies, and other sources of information.'

It has been speculated that Bletchley intelligence was also deliberately passed through Rudolf Roessler and his 'Lucy' spy network in Switzerland, but there is no evidence to support this. Churchill's warning was simply sent via diplomatic channels on 30 April 1943 to Moscow. Stalin did not altogether trust Churchill and it is doubtful he took much heed of Britain's help. After all, this intelligence simply confirmed what he already knew.

Again Stalin had a spy right in the heart of Bletchley: Captain John Cairncross, known as 'Liszt', who was passing large quantities of decrypts to the Soviet Embassy in London. He worked at Bletchley from 1942 until the summer of 1943, when he transferred to MI6. Cairncross could not believe just how lax security was at Bletchley. The code breakers were daily intercepting and decrypting German, Italian and Japanese coded signals, yet the place leaked like a sieve.

Stalin did not really need Churchill's official or Cairncross's unofficial help, as his own military intelligence was already well aware of Hitler's build-up around the Kursk salient. Ironically, the intelligence provided by Cairncross helped convince Stalin that the 'Lucy' spy ring was part of a deliberate German deception operation, because some of the information matched. It seems Stalin could not accept or appreciate that Bletchley Park and his Swiss spies were drawing on the very same sources within the German high command.

Cairncross worked in Hut 3 and regularly scooped the processed decrypts from the floor, adding them to his own translations, which he then hid in his trousers. Curiously, Cairncross was never patted down by Bletchley's guards, nor did he seem particularly surprised that he always managed to find useful stuff on the floor, which would be of help to his foreign friends. Once at the local railway station he put the decrypts in a bag and travelled to London to meet 'Henry', his Soviet handler – Anatoli Gorsky.

In particular, he gained valuable information that showed Hitler was planning to pinch off the Kursk salient. What he did not know was that Leo Long, a military intelligence officer working in the War Office, was also leaking Bletchley intelligence on Kursk. He was doing so via Soviet mole Anthony Blunt, who worked for MI5. Despite initial fears that it might be part of a deliberate British deception plan, Soviet military intelligence deemed it to be 'very valuable'.

It is notable that Soviet generals Khrushchev and Zhukov said that they were tipped off that Operation *Citadel* was about to commence against both the Central and Voronezh Fronts by prisoners captured just hours before. It is highly improbable that lowly privates from the German army and the Waffen-SS would be privy to such information. Even if they were, it seems a convenient coincidence that the two fronts received the same warning at about the same time from the same type of source.

It may be that Khrushchev and Zhukov wanted a plausible reason for opening fire before Hitler attacked. Could it be that Stalin and his high command already knew the exact day and hour that Operation *Citadel* was due to commence? This is more than likely. Was this knowledge derived from Bletchley's intelligence? It is impossible to tell.

D-DAY

Regarding the Second Front, the Allies knew that their deception plans were working thanks to Bletchley Park's code breakers. Captain Jerry Roberts and his colleagues were able to confirm 'that Hitler and his commanders expected an Allied invasion along the French coast at Calais, preceded by a feint at Normandy'. They could do this because they had cracked the Lorenz cypher. 'It was crucial,' said Roberts, 'for us to know whether the main bulk of the German army was held in the Calais region (as Hitler wanted) or in the Normandy area (as his generals wanted).'

On D-Day, code breaker Harry Hinsley had the job of alerting the Allied command the moment that the German navy detected the presence of the Allied invasion fleet. Understandably, there was considerable concern about the damage German E-boats and U-boats could cause if they intercepted the invasion forces. This was well-founded after the losses incurred during Exercise *Tiger* off Slapton Sands. Just before 03:00 hours on 6 June 1944 the first German naval signal was decrypted by Bletchley and the contents transmitted to the Admiralty. Shortly after, Hinsley received two personal calls from Churchill demanding updates on the German response.

After D-Day, Bletchley's Special Liaison Units kept the Allied commanders well-informed of German intentions. Although US General Patton had a reputation for being an impetuous, if not reckless, commander, he always ensured that his decisions were backed by the latest intelligence. Initially, Patton was not a fan of Ultra-derived intelligence, but that soon changed.

Chapter 5

Group Captain Frederick Winterbotham was largely responsible for this. 'Patton studied every Ultra signal and, knowing where every enemy soldier was in his path, would tread his way round or through them and find an undefended spot,' recalled Winterbotham. Patton 'never failed to use every opportunity that Ultra gave him to bust open the enemy', concluded the group captain.

At Bletchley, the code breakers watched in amazement in late July 1944 as Patton swiftly cut through the German defences. Selmer Norland, from Minnesota, one of the Americans working there, recalled: 'I remember a particular night when I was working on a message and some German unit reported that the American tank spearheads were in the outskirts of Rennes.' She immediately informed the duty officer and they consulted a map. 'We were astonished to find that it was almost all the way across to the Brittany peninsula.'

Bletchley's code breakers ensured that Generals Eisenhower and Bradley were well aware of Hitler's plans to counter-attack in Normandy at Mortain. This was designed to cut off Patton's breakout westwards into Brittany and eastwards towards Le Mans. The Ultra intercepts revealed on 3 August 1944 what Hitler was intending to do. It also monitored Field Marshal von Kluge's grumbling that it would be difficult to disengage his forces from elsewhere, particularly in the Caen sector facing the British and Canadians, in order to conduct the operation.

Code breaker John Prestwich was astounded that Hitler was intent on trapping his army: 'Then there came through this detailed order that four or five German armoured divisions were to go hell for leather for Avranches and this opened up the whole possibility of wiping out the cream of the German armed forces.' Prestwich could not believe that Hitler would be so foolish. 'It cannot be true,' he said in surprise to his colleagues.

Four days later, when Hitler launched Operation *Lüttich*, the Americans were waiting for him. Prestwich concluded the German generals must have thought that Hitler's order was 'lunatic'. Bletchley also knew when Hitler gave up on 16 August 1944. Code breaker Susan Wenham recalled: 'The message was to say how the Germans were planning to get out of this impasse.' Shortly after, the entire German army collapsed and was trapped in the Falaise pocket.

Chapter 6

Axis Code Breakers

The Allies did not have a monopoly on signals intelligence. Germany, Italy and Japan conducted varying levels of signals interception and decryption work. They also regularly monitored domestic communications in order to stamp out political opposition.

GERMANY

There was no German equivalent to the British Government Code and Cypher School. During the war there were at least eight organizations conducting decryption work in Germany but they lacked central focus and co-ordination. These were split across the army, navy, Luftwaffe, Abwehr, SS and Foreign Ministry. Each concentrated on their own specific areas of interest.

ARMY AND LUFTWAFFE SIGNALS SCHOOL The old Reichswehr cypher training academy, which was located in Jüterbog, moved to the General Maercker Barracks in Halle in 1935 to help create a radio intelligence training facility. The following year the German army and Luftwaffe Signals School separated into two parts on the same site under the command of General Ernst Sachs. The Luftwaffe conducted its air intelligence training there as well.

CYPHER DEPARTMENT OF THE HIGH COMMAND OF THE WEHRMACHT This was the signals agency of the German armed forces high command based in Berlin. It was tasked with keeping Germany's military communications secure and monitoring enemy signals traffic. However, it had no authority to set policy when it came to signals intelligence and signals security. Furthermore, liaisons with Italy and Japan in this field proved very poor; the Germans did not altogether trust the Italians.

Chapter 6

The German Cypher Bureau had first been set up in the 1930s with a focus on foreign diplomatic and military traffic. When Hitler came to power the bureau was greatly expanded to become the Cypher Department, though at its height it only had 800 staff compared to the 9,000 employed by Bletchley. It was given oversight of the cyphers used by the army, navy and Luftwaffe, such as Enigma.

The Cypher Department had a number of outstations, with one in Madrid, Barcelona, Las Palmas and Seville, and others in the cities of Bordeaux, Belgrade, Budapest, Rome, Sofia and Vienna. The Barcelona outstation was designed to monitor naval radio traffic in the Atlantic and the Mediterranean.

In the first half of 1944 the Cypher Department was producing about 2,000 reports a month, which were circulated to the three services and the Abwehr. Following the Normandy landings in the summer of 1944 the Barcelona and Seville outstations were closed, leaving just Madrid operating until May 1945.

By the end of 1944 the Cypher Department was struggling to function due to the effects of the Allied bombing campaign. This forced it to relocate to the Army Signals School at Halle in mid-February 1945. Work continued on an extremely limited basis until mid-April, when the staff were evacuated by train to Werfen in Austria, where they were disbanded.

AIR INTELLIGENCE DEPARTMENT This was the signals agency of the Luftwaffe and dated back to the mid-1930s. It was supported by eight regiments that were responsible for intercepting signals, jamming and tracking enemy aircraft. It was largely concerned with tactical intelligence, which was shared with the Luftwaffe's various commands. Monitoring stations were located in Belgium, Denmark, northern and western France, the Netherlands and the German Bight. These were steadily lost following D-Day. There were also three outstations in Spain.

OBSERVATION SERVICE Formed in the early 1930s, the Beobachtungsdienst – B-Dienst for short, or Observation Service – was a department of the German Naval Intelligence Service that dealt with intercepting and decoding enemy signals. By 1935 it had broken the most widely used British naval code as well as a number of American ones.

Most notably, B-Dienst broke British Combined 'Naval Cypher No. 3' in October 1941, which was used to encrypt all communications for Allied North

Atlantic convoys. This enabled B-Dienst to provide valuable intelligence for the German navy in the Battle of the Atlantic. This security breach ended when the Admiralty introduced 'Naval Cypher No. 5' on 10 June 1943. Likewise, the U-boats were able to run amok off the east coast of America until the US Navy changed its code system in April 1942.

PERS Z S The German Foreign Office had its own signals intelligence agency, known as Special Service of Z Branch. Its task was to crack foreign diplomatic cyphers and codes. The sister Personal Z Cipher Service was responsible for the security of the Foreign Office codes and cyphers. Both were collectively known as Pers Z S. Its work covered 25 countries, which proved difficult, as it was constantly short of staff. In late 1943 it was evacuated from Berlin due to the bombing.

REICH MAIL SERVICE The Reichspost was able to descramble transatlantic radiotelephone conversations. A facility was built at Noordwijk near the Hague, which meant descrambling specialists were able to hack the telephone conversations between Churchill and Roosevelt. Sir Edward Bridges, the cabinet secretary, warned on 16 March 1942 that the Americans in telephone conversations between Washington and London 'still reveal a gross lack of discretion'. The worry was that they might give away Ultra.

In 1943 the facility was relocated to a bunker in Valkenswaard, south of Eindhoven, for fear it might be bombed. It remained operational until August 1944 when the Allies' advance forced it to move to Germany. A major telephone coup was prior notification that the Italians planned to surrender, which gave Hitler the opportunity to occupy northern Italy and seize Rome.

RESEARCH OFFICE OF THE REICH AIR MINISTRY Run by Luftwaffe chief Hermann Göring, this functioned as the Nazi Party's signals intelligence and cryptanalytic agency between 1933 and 1945. It was also known as Göring's Research Bureau or Göring's Cypher Bureau. This was a purely Nazi Party institution rather than an armed forces military signals intelligence and cryptographic agency. Although its headquarters was located in Berlin and despite its name, it was not connected to the Luftwaffe.

Its role was to spy on the German people, including officers and members of the clergy, and their dealings with foreign countries. This included the interception of mail, telegrams, telephone calls and wireless broadcasts. Such activities led to the growth of an enormous internal spy network that served the Nazi police state. The Research Office produced daily brown sheets that were distributed to government ministries and the security services, most notably the Gestapo.

SECURITY POLICE One of the departments of the Sicherheitspolizei conducted radio surveillance. Like the Research Office, this was against German citizens.

ITALY

Other Axis countries, most notably Italy and Japan, conducted signals interception and code breaking. Like Germany, though, this was never on the same scale as Britain and America. In the early part of the war the Italians were quite successful, but they never gained any significant strategic advantage from their code breaking.

SECTION 5 Within the Italian Military Information Service (MIS), Section 5 was responsible for penetrating foreign military and diplomatic codes. This included Britain, France, Romania, Turkey, the USA, Yugoslavia and even the Vatican. At its height, Section 5 was intercepting 8,000 signals a month, of which 6,000 were examined and 3,500 were translated. A digest of the reporting was shared with Mussolini, his Chief of the General Staff and the Italian foreign minister, Count Galeazzo Ciano. Mussolini's real concern was Greece, which by late 1940 was distracting him from his ill-judged campaign against Britain in Egypt.

In 1941 the MIS broke the Yugoslav military codes and pre-empted an

Target Intelligence Committee

The Target Intelligence Committee (TICOM) was a secret Allied project conducted at the end of the Second World War to locate and seize German intelligence assets, particularly in the field of cryptology and signals intelligence. The Allies were particularly keen to get their hands on the German wide-band receivers, known as 'Russian Fish', used to intercept Soviet high-level radio teletype signals.

attack on Italian forces in Albania by sending a fake message to the Yugoslavs ordering them to postpone their offensive. Hitler's intervention in Yugoslavia and Greece in April 1941 subsequently secured Italy's eastern flank. Following the Axis invasion of Yugoslavia MIS broke three codes used by the Chetnik and Communist partisans, enabling them to tip off Italian forces on garrison duty. Section 5's work ceased after the fall of Mussolini from power in 1943.

JAPAN

The Japanese army mainly concentrated on breaking Chinese and Russian codes in the 1930s. This was because Japan ended up at war with both nations at one point. Japan conquered Manchuria in 1931, but it was another six years before there was all-out war with the rest of China, which was to last until 1945. Then in 1939 Japan fought a brief border war with the Soviet Union over Outer Mongolia, which it lost. This was followed by an uneasy peace, as Japan had no desire to fight a two-front war with China and the Soviet Union.

JAPANESE ARMY INTELLIGENCE In July 1937 the Ōwada Receiving Station, which monitored Chinese and American signals traffic, successfully intercepted and decoded Nationalist Chinese defensive plans for its 27th Army. By the spring of 1940 the Japanese had cracked the Chinese 'Mi-ma' code, which permitted them to track Nationalist military movements.

Despite this success, Japanese operations in 1941 did not significantly advance Japan's strategic position in China, which it had found easy to invade but fiendishly difficult to conquer. In contrast to the Nationalists, the Chinese Communists were more security-conscious and the Japanese were only able to periodically break their codes. This presented a problem when tackling the Communist forces occupying a large area of Anhui and Jiangsu in central China.

At the end of 1941 Japan diverted its attentions to attack Western interests in the Far East and Pacific, thereby taking the pressure off China. Nonetheless, the Japanese only belatedly shifted their main intelligence-gathering efforts on to the Americans in the summer of 1943, by which time it was largely too late.

JAPANESE CYPHER BUREAU The Japanese Cypher Bureau operated within Japan's Foreign Office and was responsible for the security of the country's diplomatic traffic. It oversaw the introduction of the Type A and Type B cypher machines. The Japanese penetrated the US State Department's 'Brown' and 'Gray' diplomatic codes by breaking into the US consulate in Kobe and photographing the code books. They shared their findings with the Germans in 1941, but Germany did not reciprocate. The Americans had first successfully broken Japanese diplomatic codes in the 1920s.

JAPANESE NAVAL INTELLIGENCE The Japanese Naval Intelligence Division came under the control of the Ministry of the Navy run by Admiral Shigetarō Shimada. This included a radio and radar division. Its main concern was the US fleet and subsequently the US Marine Corps. Japanese navy cryptography only achieved limited success. Crucially, there were no major Japanese breakthroughs comparable to those made by Allied cryptographers in cracking 'JN-25'.

INSIDE THE EMPIRE OF JAPAN Japan's other security organizations conducted eavesdropping operations to track down enemies of the state. The Tokkō, the Special Higher Police, monitored external telephone and radio communications inside and outside Japan. This undoubtedly involved foreign embassies. Across the occupied territories, the Kempeitai and the Tokumu Kikan conducted surveillance activities that included monitoring radio transmissions and telephone lines. This encompassed traffic from both the Chinese military and Chinese civilians. Anyone accused of sedition was usually tortured and executed.

In Manchukuo, the Japanese needed to ensure that Emperor Pu Yi remained compliant with their wishes and was not seeking to treat with the Nationalists or Communists. This meant keeping him a virtual prisoner and closely monitoring his communications. They likewise kept a close eye on the communications of Prince Teh Wang, the ruler of Inner Mongolia, who was another Japanese ally not altogether trusted.

Part 3

The Art of Misdirection

Chapter 7

Allied Deception Operations

While spying and eavesdropping played a part in the secret war, so did deception. This was regularly used as a way of hiding military intent. It was also employed as a deterrent to bluff an enemy into not taking an undesired course of action.

THE MEDITERRANEAN

EL ALAMEIN In Cairo, the nondescript 'Advanced Headquarters, A Force' was set up under Lieutenant Colonel Dudley Clarke in March 1941. General Wavell instructed that this would be a 'special section of Intelligence for Deception'. Its job was to deceive the Germans and the Italians. After the German invasion of Crete in May 1941 the British began to worry that Cyprus would be next. This could then provide a staging post from which to threaten the Levant and the Suez Canal. Clarke's 'A Force' were instructed to do all they could to deter a German invasion of British-controlled Cyprus. They did this by reinforcing the garrison with the fictitious 7th Division. This was achieved through the creation of dummy camps, equipment and radio traffic between fake divisional units. They also arranged for fake defence plans for the island to go astray in Cairo in the hope they fell into Abwehr hands. The Germans refrained from attacking Cyprus.

The summer of 1942 was a decisive time for Rommel in North Africa. His troops captured the strategically important port of Tobruk, which meant it was much easier to supply his drive on the Nile. In Cairo, an Axis team of agents known as the Kondor mission had been rounded up and their cypher system broken. Fake intelligence was then passed on to Rommel suggesting that General Montgomery (also known as 'Monty') was planning to try and hold him south of Alamein along a ridge called Alam el Halfa. These reports also claimed that Montgomery was far from ready and was awaiting reinforcements.

The British baited the trap with further deception. During one night in August 1942 a British vehicle ran into a minefield. A German patrol was sent forward to investigate the commotion and discovered a wrecked British scout car. Among the debris they found a case. Inside was a map that showed all the safe 'hard going' for vehicles in the Alam el Halfa area. It also helpfully pointed out where the going was much more treacherous thanks to shifting sands and rocky outcrops. When Rommel's intelligence officer examined it they could see that it was worn and covered in tea stains. They assessed it was real. The map, though, was a fake prepared by 'A Force'. What they had done was deliberately reverse the good and bad routes on the map.

Rommel launched his attack on the night of 30 August. Montgomery was waiting for him, in part thanks to Bletchley Park's Ultra reports. The British guns were dug in and well-camouflaged. Rommel's infantry and panzers were met by much stronger resistance than anticipated and failed to gain any of

Axis forces at El Alamein were deceived about safe routes for vehicles.

their objectives. Come daylight, his panzers and other vehicles soon began to run into soft sand and became bogged down. At that point the British Desert Air Force began to pound them.

'The enemy certainly got badly "bogged down" in this area,' noted Major General de Guingand, Montgomery's chief of staff, 'but how much the map was to blame I don't quite know.' Nonetheless, he added, 'From the interrogation of prisoners, however, we did obtain confirmation that a falsified map led the enemy to send their tanks into this sandy terrain, which trebled their fuel consumption.' This proved a major problem for Rommel.

By 4 September 1942 Rommel was forced to retreat having lost 4,800 men, 50 panzers and 70 heavy guns. It would then be Montgomery's turn to go on to the attack. He planned to strike in the northern sector of El Alamein, but first he conducted a massive fake build-up to the south near the Qattara Depression, to dupe Rommel again. At the same time he had to hide his real northern build-up. This deception would work wonderfully and contributed to Rommel's defeat.

SICILY After the Allies had cleared the Axis from North Africa their next operation was to be the invasion of Sicily in July 1943, code-named 'Husky'. This was to deliver another blow to the already very weakened Italian armed forces. Field Marshal Albert Kesselring, the German commander in the Mediterranean, observed, 'Sicily lay within striking distance; the capture of the island would be an important step on the road to Italy.' Kesselring, in light of Allied forces being concentrated in Tunisia, thought the Allies were most likely to act in the western Mediterranean.

The presence of the Luftwaffe on the Greek islands in the eastern Mediterranean presented a good deterrent to Allied operations there. However, Kesselring also noted, 'But if the Allies were to land in the Balkans and launch an offensive against the rear of the German eastern front with the objective of joining up with the Russians their success would not only affect the military situation; it would have political repercussions of at least equal importance.' Kesselring knew Mussolini would need the backing of German divisions to hold Sicily.

To confuse the Axis about their true intentions, the Allies conducted a highly elaborate deception operation known as *Mincemeat*. This involved a drowned Royal Marine from the staff of Vice Admiral Lord Louis Mountbatten,

Chief of Combined Operations. The Marine would be carrying fake letters from Mountbatten and Lieutenant General Sir Archibald Nye, Vice Chief of the Imperial General Staff. When authorization was sought from Churchill he quipped that if the plan did not succeed, 'we shall have to get the body back and give it another swim'.

The body of Captain William Martin was stumbled upon along the shore at Huelva on the Spanish coast by a fisherman on 30 April 1943. He had documents identifying him as a courier from the War Office to Generals Alexander and Eisenhower and Admiral Cunningham. The corpse was actually that of Glyndwr Michael, a drifter who had died after deliberately ingesting rat poison, which had been jettisoned from a British submarine. It has since been argued the dead man was Seaman John Melville, who was killed with the loss of the carrier HMS *Dasher*. However, the consensus remains that it was Michael.

'Captain Martin' was carrying fake letters in a brief-case chained to his wrist showing that operations were being planned against Sardinia and Greece, with Sicily being just a feint. The photo on his fake identification card was really of an MI5 officer who looked just like Michael. In his pockets was a photo of his girlfriend 'Pam' in a swimming costume, who in reality was an MI5 secretary, love letters and some London theatre ticket stubs dated 22 April. In light of Spain being a neutral country, the Spanish authorities should have notified the British Embassy and returned the body and the brief-case. While the former was quickly handed over, the brief-case went missing.

Pro-Nazi Spanish officials obligingly copied the documents and passed them on to the Abwehr. Convinced that they were real, Major Karl-Erich Kühlenthal, the head of German intelligence in Madrid, flew them to Berlin. There, they were judged to be authentic and Hitler ordered, 'Measures regarding Sardinia and the Peloponnese take precedent over everything else.' In response, the Germans sent reinforcements to the region, which would have been more useful on Sicily. A squadron of Kriegsmarine R-boats were redeployed from Sicilian waters to the Aegean. Kesselring, though, was not blind to the threat. 'At the time of the capitulation of Tunis [on 13 May 1943],' he noted, 'the outlook in Sicily, as everywhere, was very black.' On that date the Spanish finally returned the brief-case and its contents.

The following day Churchill, while seeing Roosevelt in Washington, was sent a message stating: 'Mincemeat swallowed rod, line and sinker by right people and they look like acting on it.' Captain Stanley Pack, who served with the Combined Chiefs of Staff in Washington during the planning for Operation *Husky*, concluded: 'The deception bolstered the German High Command's assumption that the Balkans would be the objective for the next attack.' Christopher Andrew in his official history of MI5 writes: 'Soon afterwards ULTRA decrypts revealed that the Germans had been comprehensively deceived.'

Kesselring, though, was not entirely convinced. On Sicily, he ensured German flak guns were concentrated around Messina. This meant that when the time came for the Axis to evacuate the island, the Strait of Messina was well protected from air attack. As a result, the bulk of the Axis garrison would escape. There were also two German armoured divisions on the island at the time of the invasion, which helped slow the Allied advance. Likewise, there were German forces on Sardinia and Corsica that still had to be dealt with.

Mincemeat has since been immortalized by a number of books and movies. The first film, *The Man Who Never Was*, came out in 1956 and *Operation Mincemeat* in 2021. Over the years its contribution to *Husky* has reached almost mythic proportions. In reality, *Mincemeat* was simply part of a much wider deception scheme conducted across the Mediterranean.

THE WESTERN FRONT

D-DAY Before the Allies were ready to open the Second Front in France they conducted a series of elaborate deception operations in the latter half of 1943 to alleviate pressure on Allied operations in Sicily and on the Red Army on the Eastern Front. These came under the overall moniker of *Cockade*, directed by Lieutenant General Sir Frederick Morgan, chief of staff to the Supreme Allied Commander. He was also responsible for planning Operation *Overlord*.

Initially, Operation *Harlequin* was envisaged as an amphibious training exercise in the English Channel, which would include a feint towards the German defences in the Pas-de-Calais. The idea was that five real divisions from the British 12th Corps and the Canadian 2nd Corps would move to Dover, Newhaven, Portsmouth and Southampton. Rather than embarking, they would then quietly disperse. Only anti-aircraft units would be loaded before sailing. The exercise, however, was cancelled due to a lack of landing craft.

Subsequently Operation *Starkey* was intended to deceive the Germans into believing that British and Canadian troops were to seize the French port of

Boulogne during late August and early September 1943. To make it look like this was imminent the RAF and US Army Air Force were to conduct a major air offensive in the area. An assault force of 300 ships was then to appear off Boulogne to suggest to the Germans that the Allies were trying to repeat the Dieppe raid of August 1942.

However, the American air force commanders were not keen on diverting resources from the ongoing strategic bomber campaign against Germany. Nor was the Royal Navy keen to provide two battleships to support the ruse. Nonetheless, German defences in the Boulogne area were extensively bombed from 25 August 1943 onwards. This culminated with attacks on German coastal batteries. On 9 September a bogus invasion fleet comprising barges, steamers and destroyers, carrying no troops, sailed across the English Channel. After thoroughly alarming the Germans they then turned back.

Operation *Wadham*, as part of *Cockade*, was supposed the convince the Germans that the Americans planned to land in Brittany with the aim of capturing Brest after the liberation of Boulogne. This task fell to the US 5th Corps stationed in Britain. The Americans went through the motions of giving the impression that an assault group would sail from the USA to join another one departing from Britain. In total this force would number 13 divisions. The problem with *Wadham* was that it was outside the range of tactical air support, which undermined its credibility.

German occupation forces in Norway were likewise distracted. Operation *Tindall* prepared a fake operation to seize Stavanger and its airfield. As Norway was outside tactical aircraft support, taking the airfield made the attack more plausible. Five real divisions stationed in Scotland were assigned to *Tindall*.

Overall, the Germans took little notice of *Cockade* and it noticeably made little impact. The Germans seriously doubted that the Allies had the ability to open the Second Front in 1943. Apart from the threat to Boulogne, none of the others seemed plausible. However, the Germans did keep a dozen divisions in Norway and grossly overestimated the strength of Allied forces in the British isles. Despite the best efforts of Hitler's generals, these forces would remain there until after the war.

The subsequent Allied strategic deception plan for the opening of the Second Front, designed to shield *Overlord* from German intelligence, was appropriately called Operation *Bodyguard*. This covered a series of operations designated *Copperhead*, *Fortitude*, *Graffham*, *Ironside*, *Quicksilver*, *Royal*

Flush, *Vendetta* and *Zeppelin*. All of these were designed to thoroughly confuse the Germans about where the Allies intended landing.

Just before *Overlord* commenced a ruse was carried out to deceive the Germans regarding Montgomery's whereabouts. An audacious plan called Operation *Copperhead* involved a body double travelling around the Mediterranean to draw Axis attention away from the English Channel. By good fortune, Lieutenant Meyrick Edward Clifton James, who was a professional actor, bore an uncanny resemblance to Montgomery. James found himself duly recruited to be Monty's double. He set about studying Monty's mannerisms, which concluded with meeting him. Reassuringly, Montgomery told James, 'Everything will be all right. Don't worry about it.'

James arrived in Gibraltar on 27 May 1944, just nine days before D-Day was scheduled to start. There he met with the governor, Lieutenant General Sir Ralph 'Rusty' Eastwood. The governor knew Montgomery, having been at the Royal Military Academy at Sandhurst with him. James and Eastwood ensured that they were overheard by known spies discussing 'Plan 303'. James then flew on to Algiers to meet with General Sir Henry Maitland Wilson. The city had long been a hotbed of espionage. A double agent dutifully reported the arrival of Montgomery to his Abwehr handler in Dijon. Two Italian spies likewise picked up on Monty being in the city to prepare for an attack on southern Europe. James, once more donning the uniform of a lieutenant, was flown secretly to Cairo and then back to Britain.

According to Captain Harry C. Butcher, General Eisenhower's naval aide: 'From all I could gather, the plan worked to perfection. It was just another example of detailed planning to throw the Germans off balance.' In contrast, historian Jock Haswell concluded: 'In fact there was nothing in Ultra messages or in German documents examined after the war to indicate that any account had been taken of Montgomery's visit to the Mediterranean.' Part of the reason for this was the success of Operations *Fortitude South* and *Quicksilver* directing German attention to the Pas-de-Calais. Likewise, in the Mediterranean, Operation *Royal Flush* convinced the Germans that the Allies intended to attack Turkey.

Captain Butcher claimed rumours circulated that James had been sent home after Montgomery heard that he had got drunk and had been smoking cigars in Gibraltar. Montgomery was a non-smoking teetotaller. James received no official recognition for his mission. After the war a ghost-writer helped him write a book about his exploits, called *I Was Monty's Double*. This was made into a film in 1958. James was cast both as the double and Montgomery, while part of the plot involving submarine-borne German commandos was fictionalized. Writer Harry Pearson noted James's unusual situation: 'thus playing himself being himself as well as playing the man he had been playing at being. The war had already gone postmodern.'

FAR EAST

BURMA Once the Japanese had overrun Thailand, Malaya and Singapore it only seemed a matter of time before they pushed north through Burma to attack India. British, Indian and Chinese forces were steadily being driven northwards from Rangoon to Mandalay and then onwards towards the Indian frontier. General Wavell, as British commander-in-chief in India, wanted to devise a ruse that might persuade the Japanese that British forces in Burma were stronger than they really were. This task fell to Peter Fleming, who was serving in New Delhi as Wavell's General Staff Intelligence (Deception). 'It is a one-horse show,' noted Fleming, 'and I am the horse.'

Fleming and Wavell cooked up a plan that would be known as Operation *Error*. This was intended to make it look like Wavell had been involved in a car accident while visiting Burma and unintentionally left behind his brief-case. This would contain top-secret documents suggesting the British had two armies in Burma and that their air strength was growing. Fleming and Captain Sandy Reid Scott, Wavell's aide-de-camp, landed in Burma on 29 April 1942. General Alexander's chief of staff recommended a place 97 km (60 miles) south of Shwebo at Sagaing and the Ava Bridge over the Irrawaddy River. This was just down from Mandalay, where the British Burma Corps was withdrawing. The bridge had been allocated to the Chinese 5th Army but was also to be used by the British 7th Division and the 7th Armoured Brigade.

Fleming, accompanied by Mike Calvert, deliberately crashed a staff car off the road south of the river. In the boot they left a brief-case containing the fake documents, along with one of Wavell's jackets. After everyone had crossed over the Irrawaddy the bridge was dropped into the water to impede the Japanese advance. General Slim recalled, 'With a resounding thump it was blown at 2359 hours on 30th April, and its centre spans fell neatly into the river – a sad sight, and a signal that we had lost Burma.' It is unknown what the Japanese made of the crashed car or its contents, though they never successfully invaded India.

By late 1944 General Slim's British 14th Army was poised to cross the mighty Irrawaddy River in Burma with a view to liberating Mandalay on the far bank. His 33rd Corps would strike towards the city in a pincer movement, but he wanted to persuade the Japanese that his 4th Corps was on his left, not on his right. Slim planned for his main assault, led by the latter, to be conducted much further south towards Meiktila, from where it would then swing northwards to Mandalay. The Meiktila-Thazi airfield, communications, hospital and supply hub was the key administrative centre for both the Japanese 15th and 33rd Armies.

'The stage was set for the most dramatic of all military operations,' said Slim, 'the opposed crossing of a great river.' The Japanese knew that his assault to force the Irrawaddy was inevitable but the question was where. The Japanese intelligence system had largely collapsed as they retreated and their commanders in many instances were operating blind.

Slim, in a brilliant piece of deception under Operation *Stencil*, created a fake '4th Corps' at Tamu while the real one moved into position at Pauk on the Myittha River. Wireless operators at Tamu transmitted spurious signals to confuse the Japanese. Operation *Cloak* spread false information that 20,000 troops were moving down the Yaw Chaung way to the north-west of Meiktila. The 28th (East African) Brigade was given the task of generating bogus radio traffic and masquerading as the 11th (East African) Division, which was not at the front. It was hoped that the Japanese would assume this was just a feint. Indeed, the Japanese failed to appreciate the significance of the reports filtering in about this advance. They reasoned that if '4th Corps' was at Tamu then it would surely head east to the Irrawaddy.

The real 4th Corps meantime pushed 483 km (300 miles) south under radio silence along a winding track through tree-covered hills. 'The gradients and the dust were at times such that the tanks had to tow their own transporters,' reported Slim. Overhead, the RAF made sure that no Japanese reconnaissance planes caught sight of the columns. 'The Japanese, as far as we knew, were still unaware of our change in plan and of the stealthy march of 4 Corps,' added Slim. 'Their eyes, we hoped, were still fixed on Mandalay, not Meiktila.'

Lieutenant General Katamura, commander of the Japanese 15th Army facing Slim, had no idea where 4th Corps was. He assessed that only two of its four divisions were combat-worthy after the others had suffered heavy casualties. Katamura assumed that if it came south it would cross just downstream of Mandalay then strike north-east towards the city, not south-east towards Meiktila. He felt that 4th Corps' southern movement was simply a raid and not a main thrust. The Japanese were also distracted by a perceived threat to Indochina. On 13 February, fearing American landings there, the Japanese redeployed their entire air force in Burma, along with an infantry division, to repel any seaborne invasion.

Slim's 4th Corps crossed the Irrawaddy at Nyaungu in mid-February 1945 in the face of varying degrees of resistance. 'The enemy had no suspicion that a major crossing was about to be attempted here,' Slim wrote. 'His troops were strung out along the river.' Nyaungu happened to be the boundary between the Japanese 15th and 28th Armies and was held by the ineffective remains of the Indian National Army. To put more pressure on the Japanese, feints were conducted north and south of Nyaungu at Pakokku and Chauk. The Japanese were unable to prevent Slim from rapidly creating and enlarging his bridgehead. Once his tanks were over there would be no stopping them. The 4th Corps, in the face of determined resistance, liberated Meiktila in early March and 33rd Corps took Mandalay at the end of the month.

To screen the left flank of Slim's advance down the Irrawaddy and Sittang towards the Burmese capital Rangoon, he conducted another deception scheme known as Operation *Conclave*. The city was liberated in early May, with the Japanese retreating into Thailand before surrendering. Slim's dash for Meiktila has gone down in history as a fine example of an all-arms battle; however, the extent of his highly successful deception operation still remains little-known.

PACIFIC

PEARL HARBOR The US Pacific Fleet had been in the Hawaiian islands since May 1940 with the aim of acting as a deterrent to Japanese aggression towards British and Dutch colonial interests in South-east Asia. In some US naval circles it was thought to be the height of folly having the fleet so far forward, especially as the support facilities in the Hawaiian islands were clearly inferior to those on the American West Coast.

Since June 1940 Hawaii had experienced three major security alerts as well as numerous air-raid and anti-submarine drills. Yet despite Japanese–American relations spiralling downwards, no preparation had been made for the possible outbreak of war. Two reports in March and August 1941 had specifically identified the threat of a surprise carrier air attack. Instead, the US armed forces preferred to remain in a state of denial. General George C. Marshall, the US Army chief of staff, described Hawaii as 'the strongest fortress in the world'. Besides, intelligence increasingly indicated the Japanese were mustering their strength to attack British and Dutch possessions in South-east Asia. A simultaneous attack on American interests in the Pacific was dismissed as highly unlikely.

Japan's 1st Air Fleet assembled in Tankan Bay in the Kuril Islands on 22 November 1941 and began to sail four days later. The Imperial Japanese Navy took great pains to hide its tracks and avoided the sea lanes frequented by merchant shipping. They also avoided passing near any American naval air installations from which reconnaissance aircraft operated. MI6 tried to warn the Americans on 3 December. British agent Colonel Gerald Wilkinson, who was at General MacArthur's headquarters in Manila, sent a message to the US Army in Hawaii stating: 'It is our considered opinion that Japan envisages early hostilities against Great Britain and the United States.'

Although heavy seas and foul weather greeted the Japanese task force, it arrived undetected off Oahu on the evening of 6 December 1941. It reached its attack position some 443 km (275 miles) north of Pearl Harbor at 06:00 hours on the following day. An hour later the first wave of fighter-bombers was in flight to their targets. The Japanese managed to hit eight battleships, three light cruisers and three destroyers in the attack. The Americans lost almost 200 aircraft, mostly on the ground. Fortunately for the US fleet, its aircraft carriers were not at Pearl Harbor, otherwise the Japanese assault would have been far more decisive than it was.

Chapter 8

Deception on the Eastern Front

OPERATION *BARBAROSSA*

In the spring of 1941 Hitler very successfully deceived Stalin. He told the Soviet leader he was moving his troops to the border with the Soviet Union to lull Churchill into a false sense of security. He would shortly be conducting Operation *Sealion* – his invasion of England – and needed the British to lower their guard. In 1939 the pair had carved up Poland, so Stalin had no reason to see Hitler as a threat. Even when Soviet intelligence and Churchill warned him that invasion was imminent, he did not heed them.

Both the commissar for defence Marshal Semyon Timoshenko and chief of staff General Georgy Zhukov lobbied Stalin until the very last moment to mobilize but he would not listen. Despite this they attempted to create a reserve under the guise of conducting a large-scale military exercise. The net result, though, was that the Red Army was ill-prepared for the coming conflict.

General Voronov, deputy chief of the Artillery Directorate, felt that the General Staff did not believe there would be war and that this was as a result of Stalin's overbearing influence. He astutely noted the dilemma faced by Timoshenko and Zhukov: 'The troops stationed on our western borders were not moved up to their defence line along the border for fear of provoking war. But at the same time, there were large-scale shifts of troops from the interior of our country to the western borders. Units which were not combat ready, which needed more personnel and armaments, were sent there.'

Barring the road to Minsk and Moscow was General Pavlov's Western Military District (or West Front). Pavlov was in the unenviable position of holding the Białystok salient trapped between German East Prussia and

Chapter 8

German-occupied Poland. There was a suspicion that Stalin and Zhukov considered Pavlov's command a sacrificial lamb and that it was the Reserve Front's job to hold Hitler at the old frontier. Certainly, by June 1941 Pavlov's forces were far from up to strength.

General M.I. Kazakov, chief of staff of the Central Asian Military District, who was conducting officer training in Tashkent, found himself summoned to Moscow to brief Timoshenko on 11 June 1941. Following military district exercises it was routine for senior officers to attend an annual conference at the People's Commissariat of Defence or Soviet Defence Ministry, but these were normally held in November or December.

Kazakov flew to the capital on 12 June and once the transport aircraft was in the air he checked over his report. Afterwards, he settled down for the long flight and, peering out the windows, noticed, 'A railroad stretched beneath us almost the whole time. A great many trains were moving along it, and it soon became clear to me that these were military trains. They were headed in one direction – northwest. I knew very well that no troops had been despatched from our military district, and that there were no plans to do so. So these were troops from Eastern Siberia or the Transbaikal.'

At the General Staff's headquarters in Moscow, Kazakov bumped into commanders from the Transbaikal, Urals and Volga Military Districts. He felt, 'It was clear that they were not travelling to manoeuvres.' It transpired that it was forces from the Transbaikal that he had seen moving by rail. General Pavlov was also in Moscow. Major General M.F. Lukin from the Transbaikal met Kazakov in passing but was not at liberty to discuss the destination of his troops. However, his men had been summoned to help create the new Reserve Front. Lukin's 16th Army, some 6,437 km (4,000 miles) away, was ordered on 25 May to move to Starokonstantinov in Ukraine south-west of Kiev. It was to join General I.S. Konev's 19th Army from the North Caucasus and General A.K. Smirnov's 18th Army in the Kharkov Military District as part of the Reserve Front in the Southern Sector.

Lukin's boss, Lieutenant General P.A. Kurochkin, commander of the Transbaikal Military District, was ordered back to Moscow to take command of a new 20th Army, also destined to form part of the Reserve Front armies in the Western Sector. General F.A. Ershakov, commander of the Urals Military District, was instructed to send his men to the Vitebsk area while the Orel Military District under General F.N. Remizov sent troops to the area of the middle Dnieper River. It was clear to Stalin's generals that war was brewing.

All this, though, was simply too late. The strategic east–west redeployment was only partially completed when Hitler attacked; in the case of Lukin's 16th Army, just the 5th Mechanized Corps had reached Ukraine by this stage. The late arrival of the 16th Army meant it would be committed to the battle piecemeal when trying to defend the city of Smolensk.

When Kazakov asked the deputy chief of operations, General Aleksandr Vasilevsky, when war would break out the response was, 'We'll be lucky if it doesn't begin in the next fifteen to twenty days.' Instead of delivering his report, much to Kazakov's dismay, he was invited to watch a two-hour-long Nazi propaganda film about Hitler's invasion of the Balkans, after which Timoshenko and Zhukov calmly went off for dinner together.

When Pavlov was asked by a colleague why he was in the capital he responded calmly, 'Everything is normal with us. And so I decided to take advantage of the calm situation and come to Moscow for one thing and another.' It all sounded so casual. Nevertheless, this may have been a polite way of saying it's on 'a need-to-know basis'. Putting the Red Army on full alert, Stalin would hear none of it; he did not wish to provoke Hitler into war. This was despite the very evident massing of German troops and constant Luftwaffe reconnaissance flights over eastern Poland, Byelorussia and Ukraine.

Despite his best efforts, Kazakov never got to brief Timoshenko and instead briefly saw Zhukov before returning to Tashkent on 21 June. The following day Hitler invaded the Soviet Union and his forces swept to the very gates of Moscow.

'URANUS'

Stalin's operations during the summer of 1942 misled Hitler into believing that towards the end of the year the full weight of any Soviet offensive would fall on Army Group Centre. Instead, Stalin gathered his forces for a major thrust either side of the beleaguered city of Stalingrad and Army Group B. The Soviet South-western Front and Stalingrad Front forces were to link up between Kalach and Sovietsky behind the Axis armies, thereby encircling the Germans at Stalingrad.

Stalin was able to fool Hitler in part thanks to Operation *Monastery*. Its success was comparable to that of the Allies' Operation *Fortitude*. Originally

Chapter 8

this had been conceived as a counter-intelligence mission to root out Nazi spies; it then developed into something comparable to the Double-Cross System. The GRU and NKVD created a fake pro-Nazi resistance movement within the heart of the Soviet high command. This was headed by Alexander Demyanov, an NKVD counter-intelligence agent working at Moscow's Central Cinema Studio. He was trusted in anti-Soviet and Nationalist circles and, furthermore, he was already on the Abwehr's list as a potential spy.

Demyanov defected in late 1941 and was recruited by the Abwehr, who code-named him 'Max'. He was sent back in February 1942 and dropped by parachute west of Moscow. Demyanov then conveniently got a job as a communications officer at the Soviet high command. Under the guidance of Soviet intelligence he proceeded to create a network of bogus agents in Leningrad, Kuibyshev and Novorossiysk. They sent regular reports to the Abwehr and Reinhard Gehlen, who was in charge of intelligence on the Eastern Front. These really originated from the GRU and NKVD. Dr Wagner Delius, the head of the Abwehr station in Sofia, began to voice his doubts about 'Max'. However, the failure of the Red Army's offensive in the Leningrad area convinced the Abwehr that the 'Max' network was legitimate.

Hugh Trevor-Roper, who was working for MI6, began to see 'Max' decrypts in the autumn of 1942 and warned Moscow they had a mole, but no action was taken. British intelligence, like the Abwehr, was duped. 'MAX must be regarded as a success [for the Abwehr]', reported Guy Liddell at MI5. 'Reports have been singularly accurate in forecasting Russian operations and the theory that it is a Russian double-cross rather goes by the board.' 'Max' fed the Germans intelligence suggesting that there was a planned thrust against Army Group North and Army Group Centre. The Soviets were clever enough to ensure these reports were detailed and in many cases verifiable.

Stalin appreciated that a successful offensive at Stalingrad would have one of two results: force the Germans to withdraw or be trapped in a pocket. Either way, it was a winning scenario. Stalin and Zhukov were concerned not only with local German efforts against Stalingrad, but the wholesale destruction of all weaker Axis forces supporting German operations against Stalingrad. It was an ambitious undertaking, intent on reversing the course of the war, which up to this point had seen Hitler holding the strategic initiative.

Despite repeated intelligence warnings, Hitler refused to believe his forces at Stalingrad were in danger, remarking, 'All there is left to take is a couple of little scraps of land. [...] Time is of no importance.' He was soon distracted by the Allied landings in North Africa, which threatened to trap Rommel, who was being pursued by Montgomery. Hitler ordered the seizure of Tunisia to safeguard Rommel's rear. Stalin's offensive, code-named 'Uranus', commenced on 19 November and overwhelmed everything in its path. By the New Year he had forced the surrender of the German army trapped at Stalingrad. In a stroke, the tide began to turn on the Eastern Front and Hitler was humiliated.

OPERATION *BAGRATION*

While the Allies were trying to deceive Hitler about where the Second Front would open in the summer of 1944, Stalin sought to confuse Hitler as to where his next blow would fall. Little did Hitler know that Stalin was planning to liberate Minsk and Byelorussia with Operation *Bagration*. Hitler and his staff were convinced that Stalin's goal was northern Ukraine; the republic's vast steppes had provided few defensive barriers for the German army groups in the south. If this happened, Hitler reasoned, Army Group Centre in Byelorussia could strike south and cut the Red Army off. Unfortunately for him, Stalin had every intention of striking again in Ukraine, but this was not scheduled to commence until three weeks after the start of *Bagration*. Stalin was planning to destroy two entire German army groups in one go.

Intelligence pointed to Stalin attacking the Kovel-Lvov area with a push on Warsaw or an offensive in the Baltic. Also as part of the Allied D-Day deception plans for the invasion of Normandy, Operation *Bodyguard* resulted in German intelligence picking up rumours of Soviet-American planning in Novorossiysk for a naval attack on the Romanian coast in the Black Sea. Such co-operation was nonsense in light of the difficulties experienced by the American shuttle-bombing campaign, but to Hitler it was another threat that could not be dismissed out of hand.

Hitler knew an assault on the occupied Baltic states could cut off Army Group North and Centre, but the geography in this region favoured the defenders and the area was of little strategic importance. Similarly, Byelorussia favoured the defenders, as it was heavily forested and swampy, plus the roads were poor. Army Group Centre had successfully withstood everything that the Red Army had thrown at it since early 1942.

Nonetheless, during Soviet operations in December–January 1944 the German-held Byelorussian city of Vitebsk had been threatened, with the Red

Chapter 8

Army capturing Gorodok, an advanced strongpoint of Vitebsk. They also cut the Vitebsk–Polotsk railway and approached Vitebsk along the northern bank of the Dvina River. Fortunately, thanks to the bad weather and German counter-attacks the Vitebsk operation was abandoned.

Many of Hitler's commanders were uneasy about maintaining the 'Byelorussian Balcony' as the vast bulge in Army Group Centre's line was nicknamed. To no avail Field Marshal Ernst Busch, commanding Army Group Centre, had been pleading with Hitler to pull out of Byelorussia, or at least to shorten the line. General von Mellenthin, serving with the 48th Panzer Corps, Army Group North Ukraine, supported the view that Busch should pull back: 'Despite persistent attacks Army Group Centre had retained a considerable part of White Russia, including Vitebsk and the important railway junction at Orsha. The Eastern Front was still too long for an effective defence, and we would have gained much by evacuating Estonia and White Russia.'

While German intelligence estimated the Soviet summer offensive would strike south of the Pripyat Marshes through Romania, Hungary and Slovakia, they were alert to troop build-ups in the Kovel–Tarnopol area. In April Hitler designated Bobruisk, Mogilev, Orsha and Vitebsk as fortified places to be held to the last. All were to be defended by a division except for Vitebsk, which was to be held by an entire corps. Tying up a third of 3rd Panzer Army's strength to Vitebsk was a recipe for disaster. It meant that 3rd Panzer Army had no way of stabilizing its front unless these forces were freed up.

Busch saw Hitler on 20 May 1944, just as Stalin was conferring with his generals, and requested a strategic withdrawal. He presented two plans, developed by his staff: the 'Small Solution' advocated a withdrawal to the Dnieper River, while the 'Large Solution' proposed withdrawing to the Berezina River. These were in violation of Führer Order No.11 and Führer Order No.7 instructing Army Group Centre to establish contact with Army Group South via Kovel.

Hitler flatly refused, remarking he had not thought Busch to be one of those generals always looking over his shoulder. This was unfortunate because five days earlier Field Marshal Model had floated the idea of an offensive operation using Army Group North Ukraine and practically all Busch's armoured formations. For Busch, this was a disaster. While his front shrank by 6 per cent, in one fell swoop he lost up to 15 per cent of his divisions, along with 88 per cent of his panzers, 23 per cent of his assault guns and 33 per cent of his heavy artillery.

Army Group Centre's intelligence officers began to assess that a threat was manifesting itself on their front by late May and early June 1944; this assessment was fuelled by the build-up of Soviet artillery and aircraft, though they missed other factors, particularly the tank build-up. The movement of Stalin's artillery, so vital for softening up Busch's defences, was conducted eight to ten days before the start of the operation. This ensured that Busch's intelligence officers failed to spot the main concentrations and, just as importantly, the breakthrough sectors.

By 14 June Busch's staff were expressing their concerns with the army's high command or Oberkommando des Heeres (OKH) representatives. General Reinhardt's 3rd Panzer Army was anxious about a main attack south-east of Vitebsk. The presence of three new divisions, 100 tanks and artillery support also seemed to suggest a supporting attack north-east of the city.

Poor camouflage discipline on the part of General Chernyakhovsky's 5th Artillery Corps from 13 June also meant that General von Tippelskirch's 4th Army was aware of a concentration north of the Smolensk–Minsk highway through Orsha. While Reinhardt was aware of this, his greatest concern was Vitebsk, which it seemed the Red Army were preparing to envelop. From mid-June the 4th Army detected another build-up opposite Mogilev and accurately anticipated an attack on 22 June.

Similarly, Jordan's 9th Army was not totally ignorant of what was going on. From the end of May they had watched preparations for an attack towards Bobruisk. They also suspected an attack west of the Berezina River and south of Bobruisk. By 12 June Jordan's intelligence officers were telling him that both locations would be main attacks, with the one west of the Berezina the most threatening. By 20 June they anticipated an attack within two days, rightly with the intention of seizing Bobruisk, dividing the army and isolating those forces east of the Berezina.

It appeared all three armies had a better appraisal of Stalin's impending offensive than Busch's Army Group headquarters in Minsk. Yet all these little warnings did not come together in time to indicate that something simply enormous was about to be unleashed upon them. In the run-up to *Bagration*, on the night of 14 June, the Red Air Force attacked Luftwaffe airfields at

Chapter 8

Brest-Litovsk, Pinsk, Minsk and Orsha. Despite these attacks, Busch was not unduly alarmed and five days later went home on leave.

Within 24 hours of his departure Soviet partisans blew up numerous railway lines in Byelorussia. Colonel Count Kielmannsegg, 1st General Staff Officer OKH, telephoned Minsk on 20 June and warned them that the main Soviet effort lay near Polotsk. Army Group Centre's HQ did not believe him. Two days later Operation *Bagration* commenced and within a matter of weeks Army Group Centre had completely collapsed. Busch was sacked for incompetence.

Chapter 9

Japan's Great Con

In the run-up to Japan's dramatic entry into the Second World War it pulled off a strategic con of epic proportions. Japan's long-running feud with Russia and its wars with China indicated that Japanese militarism was not a threat to Western interests in the Far East. Japan had struck Imperial Russia in 1904, attacking her fleet at Port Arthur (Lüda), taking over the latter and gaining Russia's rights in the southern part of Manchuria. The total humiliation of Russia's armed forces ensured simmering resentment marred their relations throughout the 1920s and 1930s. After the Japanese occupation of Korea and Manchuria, friction between Japan and the neighbouring Soviet Union became inevitable.

NORTH OR SOUTH?

Notably, Japan coveted the Russian port of Vladivostok, but to keep the Red Army at bay the Japanese first needed to cut the vital Trans-Siberian railway. However, when it came to expanding Japan's empire the Japanese military were always divided over a 'Strike North' against Russia or a 'Strike South' against the Western powers' colonial interests. By the late 1930s the Soviet Union, weakened by decades of infighting and Stalin's purges, seemed easy prey. The Soviets, though, to protect Vladivostok pre-emptively seized the tactically important Changkufeng Hill near the mouth of the Tyumen River south-west of the port.

Throughout the summer of 1938 the Japanese probed Soviet defences with a series of border incidents at Lake Khasan near Vladivostok. Fighting broke out when the Japanese tried to force Soviet troops from Changkufeng on 11 July 1938. The Soviets, though, had fortified it and remained in possession following an armistice in August. The Japanese army now risked losing face

Chapter 9

with the formal ceasefire; however, Emperor Hirohito agreed to the Japanese army's plan to act much further to the north-west against independent Outer Mongolia.

The Japanese were in a position to do this because in 1933 they had invaded Jehol, the eastern province of Chinese-controlled Inner Mongolia. This placed Japanese forces up against Outer Mongolia's border to the north and along the Great Wall to the south, facing China. Outer Mongolia was protected by the Soviet Union thanks to a mutual assistance pact dating back to March 1936, but the Japanese hoped that the Red Army would be too stretched to intervene in its latest land grab.

Soviet intelligence confirmed that a Japanese build-up in Jehol signalled that something more than a border raid was being planned. The activities of the Japanese air force indicated that a major operation was to take place. Indeed, the Japanese were preparing for Operation *Second Period of the Nomonhan Incident*, which was intended to surround and rout the weak Soviet-Mongolian forces east of the Khalkhin-Gol River, then strike across it to destroy their reserves.

Red Army General Georgi Zhukov was ordered to Outer Mongolia in early June 1939 by Stalin. He was told by the Soviet People's Commissar of Defence, Marshal Kliment Voroshilov, 'Japanese troops have made a surprise attack and crossed into friendly Mongolia which the Soviet Government is committed to defend from external aggression.' Afterwards Zhukov saw the acting deputy chief of the General Staff, General Ivan Smorodinov, who instructed him, 'pull no punches'. To the rest of the world it was clear that Japan and the Soviet Union were about to go to war. This would be a major distraction from the growing tensions in Europe.

The Japanese had massed about 38,000 men supported by 135 tanks and 225 aircraft east of the Khalkhin-Gol River by July 1939. The outnumbered Zhukov could muster little more than 12,500 Soviet-Mongolian troops, though they were backed by a powerful force of 186 tanks and 226 armoured cars. Both sides would pour in reinforcements. The Japanese fatally underestimated Zhukov. By the end of August he had comprehensively defeated their invasion.

The Japanese claimed they lost 17,200 killed and wounded, while the Soviets reported 9,284 casualties. However, losses for the Japanese have been put as high as 45,000 dead and Soviet casualties at well over 17,000. Certainly, of the 60,000 Japanese troops eventually trapped by Zhukov some 50,000 were listed as killed, wounded or missing.

MIXED MESSAGES

'I had to keep a constant watch on Japan's troop strength in China,' recalled Soviet spy Richard Sorge, 'because it was possible for Japanese forces to be quickly dispatched from occupied areas there to the Soviet border.' However, rather than renewing hostilities the Japanese turned back to their war with the Chinese. They were greatly helped by ongoing tensions between China's Nationalist and Communist forces who had been fighting each other since the mid-1930s. While some Communist units had escaped north on the Long March to Shaanxi others remained in central China. By the end of 1940 the Communist New Fourth Army was occupying a vast area of Jiangsu and Anhui in central China with some 35,000 men.

Chen Yi, later to succeed Zhou Enlai as Mao Zedong's foreign minister, was one of the divisional commanders who played a deadly game of cat and mouse by harassing the Japanese at every turn. When the New Fourth Army was ordered north of the Yellow River it ended up fighting the Nationalists as well. This broke the uneasy alliance against Japan and weakened the Chinese war effort. At this stage Japan's main priority in China was to crush the Nationalists by invading their last fortress in Sichuan.

Japan in April 1941 signed a neutrality pact with the Soviet Union. This freed considerable numbers of Japanese forces to attack South-east Asia and

Japan's wars against China and Russia convinced the colonial powers that it was not a threat to them.

Pearl Harbor. It did not include the division of China between Japan and the Soviet Union. Mao failed to get a Poland scenario, which could have provided him with a secure base of operations under Soviet protection. He made it clear to colleagues he would not support the Soviet Union if attacked by Japan. In July he warned, 'It is not a good idea [...] to undertake large-scale action [...] our armies are weak.' Mao added that any co-ordination with Stalin was to be 'strategic and long-term – not in battles'. In other words, the Soviet Union was on its own.

Japan also sought to lull the Chinese into a false sense of security. 'I remember in particular [Hotsumi] Ozaki's report on his meeting with [Japanese prime minister] Prince Konoye in 1941,' said Richard Sorge, 'which revealed clearly what great efforts the prince was making to settle the China problem.' Konoye wanted the Chinese Nationalist government to merge with the Japanese-backed government in Nanking and recognition of Manchukuo. None of this was going to happen.

Strategically, Japan still retained the options of striking north into the Soviet Union or south from its territories in China into French Indochina and the Pacific. 'To everyone's surprise, the Japanese armed forces had carried through a very large reinforcement programme and a wide reorganization,' reported Richard Sorge, 'which, it was considered, were aimed not solely at China but at the Soviet Union as well.'

Traditionally, the Japanese army preferred the northern approach, while remaining on the defensive in the south. The rapidly expanding Japanese navy favoured a strike south. 'A correct knowledge of the scope of the [Japanese] mobilization and its direction (north or south),' observed Sorge, 'would give the most accurate answer to the question of whether or not Japan wanted war with the Soviet Union.' His spies kept a close watch on the South Manchurian Railway.

Logically, though, Japan had unfinished business with the Soviet Union. The Japanese army wanted to expand its Chinese empire rather than carve out a new one in South-east Asia. The navy, however, argued that America's mounting hostility to Japan's militarism and its support for China's Nationalists would constitute a threat to Japanese security. The navy won the argument. Sorge concluded that Japan was unlikely to attack the Soviet Union until spring 1942 at the earliest. 'I maintained that the great mobilization of August 1941 was not directed primarily against the Soviet Union,' he said.

TURNING SOUTH

The Battle of Khalkhin-Gol helped to convince the Japanese to strike south into South-east Asia against British, French and Dutch interests and south into the Pacific against the Americans at Pearl Harbor and the Philippines. Japan rightly assessed that with Britain and its allies distracted by the war against Hitler and Mussolini they would not have sufficient resources to counter Japanese ambitions towards their colonial possessions. These contained key natural resources, including oil and rubber, all of which were needed by the Japanese war machine.

Japanese spies in Burma, Malay, Indochina and the Philippines were able to report on the weakness of British, French and American defences and how unpopular their administrations were. In Burma, a small group of nationalists, known as the 'Thirty Comrades', were sent to the Japanese-occupied island of Hainan to undergo guerrilla warfare training. Afterwards they were deployed to Thailand to recruit men for the anti-British Burmese Independence Army.

In the Far East and Pacific, both Britain and America had to decide what Japan's true intentions were. Increasingly, the balance of probability was that rather than pick another fight with the Soviet Union it would now push southwards. This was especially the case after the British were driven from Europe and facing eviction from North Africa. Furthermore, it was hard to imagine the Japanese would ignore the strategically important Burma Road for long. Running from Rangoon to Lashio, this was used to ship vital American military supplies to the Chinese Nationalist armies struggling to keep the Japanese at bay. A push into Indochina would enable the Japanese to cut this route and threaten India.

Britain and America were about to face a series of cataclysmic events that they should have seen coming. Winston Churchill and his commanders were privy to regular intelligence reports that suggested a Japanese attack was imminent. MI6 gained information in early November 1941 that Japanese troops were gathering on Hainan ready to be deployed to Indochina. In mid-November another report stated that the Japanese were poised to attack both Burma and Thailand. Things happened very rapidly.

MI6 in the space of just a week, between 30 November and 7 December 1941, produced numerous reports warning of Japanese 'preparations for Southward Move'. On 5 December MI6 reported the Japanese were landing in Cam Ranh Bay in Indochina and that 48,000 troops had come ashore supported by 250 aircraft. The distraction of Japan's wars with China and the Soviet Union had fatally delayed the Western powers from taking the growing Japanese threat seriously until it was far too late: Japan was able to pull off a massed surprise attack.

Hitler achieved a very similar stunt by persuading Stalin his troops were massing in eastern Poland, in order to lull Churchill into a false sense of security before invading Britain. On 7 December the Japanese navy launched its air attack on Pearl Harbor. Shortly after, Japanese troops successfully stormed into Burma, Malaya, Singapore, the Dutch East Indies and the Philippines. The Japanese proceeded to wage aerial, land and naval war on a truly grand scale that made the fighting in Manchuria and China pale into insignificance.

Britain and America were not the only ones unprepared for what happened. 'The Russians were so prone to suspect that the Japanese and German foreign policies were aimed at the USSR,' noted Richard Sorge, 'that in 1941, when Japan took the last great turning in her career, Moscow was taken completely by surprise.' Stalin was relieved; Churchill and Roosevelt were not, as the Second World War had widened considerably.

Part 4

Camouflage War

Chapter 10

Hiding in Plain Sight

In warfare, military equipment always needs to be concealed in order to dupe an enemy. The most basic forms of camouflage were achieved through the application of disruptive paint patterns to break up the outline of aircraft, vehicles and other military equipment. When stationary, covering them with canvas awnings and netting had the same effect. Netting often proved highly effective from the air. In Europe, units had the added advantage that they could disperse beneath trees, behind ridges and among buildings, making it much easier to hide, especially from aircraft.

LAME-DUCK DECOYS

In the open deserts of North Africa, troops were horribly exposed and they had to do their upmost to minimize the risk of detection from the air, which could result in air attack or artillery fire. On the whole, the digging of trenches and weapons pits in such terrain was impossible. The only real option in the desert was camouflage netting and wide dispersion. The use of desert scrub and the building of low fortifications, known as 'sangers', from stone or sandbags also helped with concealment. On occasions, though, commanders did not want to hide their presence and sought to deceive an enemy about their exact location. Hiding in plain sight became almost an art form.

Both the Allies and the Axis regularly employed decoys to fool each other, using dummy or obsolete equipment to draw fire away from the real target. In North Africa, as the air war turned against them, both the Italians and the Germans left damaged and cannibalized aircraft on their runways to act as decoys in the hope they would divert attention away from operational planes. These were often moved about to give the impression that they were still taking off and landing. The key Axis airbases were at Tripoli, Benghazi and Tobruk.

Chapter 10

The forward airfields in the Tobruk area were at El Adem, Gambut and Sidi Rezegh and as the war progressed they came under increasing air attack.

When Australian troops entered Benghazi on 6 February 1941 they found unserviceable Italian aircraft lining the airfield as if on parade. When the Allies finally captured the main Axis airbase at Tripoli in January 1943 they discovered a huge array of abandoned aircraft out in the open. Aerial reconnaissance had detected at least 40 aircraft there on the ground. When the Allies overran Tunisia that May, El Aouina aerodrome and the airfields at Bizerte were found to be in a similar condition.

Decoy tactics were likewise used by Axis ground forces. In January 1941, when the 6th Australian Division took Bardia from the Italians, they captured 400 guns. Among them were ancient museum-piece fortress muzzle loaders. The Australians naturally assumed they were decoys but the fact that the guns were in carefully constructed stone sangars seemed to suggest otherwise. However, this was no doubt the Italians' intention. Paint schemes also played a part. The Italian technique of using light grey and dirty white colours to camouflage their guns out in the desert made then almost invisible at 450 m (500 yards). After General Rommel's intervention in North Africa he was known for requisitioning abandoned Italian equipment, which he either repurposed or used as decoys. The Italians were understandably never happy about this.

In the Battle for Normandy in 1944 the Germans became masters at camouflaging their vehicles. Allied air superiority meant that it was highly dangerous for German divisions to move during the day unless conducting an attack. When massing for such operations their panzers were transformed into mobile shrubs by being covered in real foliage. This often did not help shield them from the Allies' prowling fighter bombers, though.

'Every vehicle was covered with tree branches and moved along hedges and the edges of woods,' recalled General Fritz Bayerlein, commander of Panzer Lehr Division, when he marched on Normandy following the D-Day landings. Such measures did not prevent his division from suffering a severe mauling from continual air attacks. 'By the end of the day I had lost forty tank trucks carrying fuel, and ninety others. Five of my tanks were knocked out and eighty-four half-tracks, prime-movers and self-propelled guns,' added Bayerlein.

Concealing troops was one tactic; faking their presence was another. During the Second World War the Allies became masters in creating the illusion of armies. In March 1941 'Advanced Headquarters A Force' was established in Cairo under Brigadier Dudley Clarke to conduct deception operations for Middle Eastern Command.

Among his recruits was Major Victor Jones, who had been experimenting with the use of dummy tanks. He was placed in charge of physical strategic deception. Major Mark Ogilvie-Grant also joined them, with responsibility for disinformation. Throughout that year they were kept very busy. After 'A Force' successfully created a fake British division in Cyprus it soon found itself involved in things on a much grander scale in Egypt.

OPERATION *BERTRAM*

Royal Engineer Lieutenant Colonel Geoffrey Barkas served as director of camouflage for Middle Eastern Command. Tony Ayrton, a member of 'A Force', was appointed his deputy. Before the war Barkas had been a movie director, producer and writer, so he was not new to creating make-believe. Steven Sykes, his previous deputy, was taken ill, so Barkas also drafted in Lieutenant Brian Robb – a talented artist – to help.

Before the Battle of El Alamein in 1942 Barkas faced a difficult dual task: he had to hide Montgomery's massive real build-up in the north, while at the same time create a massive fake build-up in the south. Brigadier de Guingand, Montgomery's chief of staff, told Colonel Clarke, who was Barkas's boss, 'You must conceal 150,000 men with a thousand guns and a thousand tanks on a plain as flat and hard as a billiard table […] You can't do it of course, but you've bloody well got to!'

Barkas and his men had just a month to carry out what was known as Operation *Bertram*. First they had to move 6,096 tonnes (6,000 tons) of supplies to the north and somehow conceal them. Barkas and his team came up with a series of inspired plans. About 2,032 tonnes (2,000 tons) of fuel cans were hidden in existing masonry-lined trenches, which had their sides raised to increase capacity. From the air it was difficult to detect the modifications; when the RAF flew reconnaissance flights over them they failed to spot any changes.

Ammunition and food stores were stacked to resemble trucks weighing 3.05 tonnes (3 tons) and covered in camouflage netting. These 'trucks' were scattered across the desert to mimic the dispersal of real vehicles. Similarly, over four hundred 25-pounder field guns were also hidden. Techniques used to conceal them included a device called a 'Cannibal'. This was a canvas-and-pole framework that from the air looked like a lorry. These were used to hide the gun or its Quad gun tractor or the ammunition limber. Hundreds of 'Cannibals' were positioned north and south of Miteiriya Ridge. Likewise, fake pipelines were built.

The next and probably most challenging project was to move forward the British 1st and 10th Armoured Divisions, first to the rear staging areas code-named 'Murrayfield North', 'Murrayfield South' and 'Melting Pot' south of the Borg El Arab railway station and then opposite Rommel's minefields. To mask the forward presence of the tanks 'Sunshields' were built to look like trucks, which were placed over the hull. Built from wood and canvas,

A British 6-pounder anti-tank gun portée cleverly disguised to look like a harmless lorry.

these were designed to fit the Crusader, Grant, Sherman and Valentine tanks equipping Montgomery's 8th Army.

More than 720 'Sunshields' were produced and moved up under the cover of darkness to the 'Martello' holding area south of the El Imayid railway station. Come daylight, the Germans naturally assumed that they were just supply lorries. The tanks then deployed to 'Martello' at night to occupy an allocated pre-positioned 'Sunshield', so as not to arouse German suspicions. On the way, the tanks were fitted with chains that scoured out the telltale marks left by their tracks. Each tank as it deployed from the rear holding areas was replaced by a dummy replica, to convince Rommel that Montgomery's armour had not moved.

The water pipeline running from the El Imayid railway station behind El Alamein was extended south towards Mount Himeimat. An 8 km (5 mile)-long trench was dug and a fake pipe made of 4-gallon fuel cans placed in it during the day. At night the pipe was removed, the trench was filled in and another 8 km (5 mile)-long stretch was built the following day, and so on for 32 km (20 miles). At three points fake pump houses were built, along with can-filling stations. The engineers made sure they did not complete the pipeline until after Montgomery had started his attack, in order to lull Rommel into a false sense of security.

Between the Munassib Depression and Mount Himeimat engineers constructed dummy gun positions and supply dumps. The latter simulated 9,144 tonnes (9,000 tons) of tented supplies controlled by three administrative camps. Hundreds of dummy tanks and other vehicles were deployed out in the desert. The commanding officer of the 2nd Derbyshire Yeomanry, after watching some nearby tanks on exercise, turned to one of his men and observed, 'They make no noise, they've got no tracks, they are lorries with canvas over them made to look like tanks.' Initially, Barkas had proposed creating two dummy armoured brigades, amounting to a division, but Montgomery revised this up to an entire armoured corps consisting to 600 vehicles. In total, over 400 dummy tanks, 100 dummy guns and almost 2,000 dummy soft-skinned vehicles had to be created.

Everything just seemed to fall into place. de Guingand happily reported,'By the end of the third week in October [1942] we began to realise that all these vast preparations were successfully reaching their conclusion.' Rommel was perplexed by the pipeline and the supply dumps. Common sense dictated

Chapter 10

Montgomery would attack north near Kidney and Miteiriya Ridges, yet Montgomery was diverting precious water south and stockpiling supplies there. Would perhaps an attack in the north be a feint while Montgomery's main effort was to the south?

Rommel fully appreciated that some of the British preparations were undoubtedly fake, but the question was, which ones? Fatefully, he was forced to divide his tank forces. He moved his 21st Panzer Division and the Italian 'Ariete' Armoured Division south to cover the sector opposite Munassib, while keeping his 15th Panzer Division and the Italian 'Littorio' Armoured Division in the north. Rommel, who was unwell, convinced by Monty's deception that an attack was not imminent, flew home to Germany.

Monty's attack opened in the north on the night of 23 October 1942, catching the Germans completely by surprise. De Guingand recalled, 'the wireless traffic […] of an armoured division was so employed as to indicate that a large move of armoured forces was taking place in the southern sector.' Montgomery had fooled the Germans into thinking that he had an extra armoured unit simply by employing a 'divisional' headquarters drawn from 8th Armoured Division. Using radio traffic, he created the impression that it was in charge of this new unit. In reality, it commanded no tanks at all.

Montgomery, though, went into battle with a superiority of about 2:1 in troops and 1,100 tanks to Rommel's 500, of which 300 were of an inferior type. On top of this, he had almost 1,000 field guns, eight hundred 6-pounder and five hundred 2-pounder anti-tank guns. Rommel could only marvel at such resources.

Along the Mediterranean coast, a convoy set out from Alexandria as if a landing was to take place behind Rommel's lines. After dark, most of it turned back but some vessels continued and three hours after the ground attack started they proceeded to shell a stretch of shoreline as if an amphibious assault was about to take place. Earlier attempts to capture the ports of Benghazi and Tobruk added to the deception that the British were conducting a naval operation in support of Montgomery.

When Rommel returned to North Africa he found his troops almost beaten. This battle has 'turned the tide of war in Africa against us,' he wrote, 'and, in fact, probably represented the turning point of the whole vast struggle. The conditions under which my gallant troops entered the battle were so disheartening that there was practically no hope of our coming out of it victorious.'

The British 1st Armoured Division had reached Kidney Ridge by 26 October and was threatening to cut the Axis's main north–south line of communication along the Rahman Track. The following day Montgomery reorganized his forces and despite mounting losses maintained his pressure in the northern sector of the battle. Rommel was in an unenviable position: despite all his skills, by the end of October he knew the British had still not committed the bulk of their 800 tanks, against which he could pit just 90 panzers and 140 Italian tanks.

Then on 1 November Montgomery renewed his attack in the north with Operation *Supercharge* and finally overwhelmed the exhausted Axis troops. All Rommel could do was oversee a fighting withdrawal first to Tripoli and then all the way to Tunisia. Following the battle Churchill noted, 'By a marvellous system of camouflage, complete tactical surprise was achieved in the desert. The enemy suspected, indeed knew, that an attack was impending, but where and when and how it was coming was hidden from him.'

After El Alamein 'A Force' was tasked with keeping the pressure up on the Axis by suggesting an Allied threat to occupied Crete and Greece with Operation *Warehouse*. This was designed to distract the Axis from the forthcoming Operation *Torch* and the Allied invasion of French North Africa in November 1942 that would trap Rommel. This was done by leaking fake intelligence through double agents. It was backed by Operation *Cascade*, intended to show that Allied forces in the Mediterranean had increased by 50 per cent.

This was followed in January 1943 by Operation *Withstand*, which suggested that in response to any German move into Turkey the Allies would attack Crete and the Peloponnese. To back this up, amphibious forces were gathered in eastern Mediterranean ports and in Cyprus. British units in Syria also conducted exercises close to the Turkish border. This bluffing had the desired effect, as the Germans cancelled all naval leave in the Aegean for fear of an attack. Thanks to *Cascade*, the German high command erroneously estimated in February 1943 that the Allies had four and a half divisions earmarked for operations against Crete and another four and a half divisions poised in Syria to invade Turkey.

Chapter 11

Dummy Armies

When the Allies decided to invade Sicily in mid-1943 they had to throw the Axis off the scent. Operation *Barclay* was designed to convince them that the Allies were planning attacks throughout the Mediterranean. They also wanted to force the Axis to keep the Italian fleet away from Sicily. To do this they needed to suggest a major threat to the Balkans, which would force the Italians to keep their warships in the Adriatic.

FICTITIOUS FORCES

In Egypt, the Allies created the fictitious 'British 12th Army', consisting of about a dozen fake divisions. These forces were controlled by three British corps and a Polish one, all of which were purely fictional commands, though a few real divisions were added to the army's order of battle to enhance the illusion. Many of the dummy tanks and lorries built to support the fighting at El Alamein were rounded up and sent back to the Cairo area to help flesh out the '12th Army'.

To add to the threat to the Balkans, dummy landing craft and aircraft were positioned along the Egyptian and Libyan coasts for Abwehr agents to spot. It was rumoured that this invasion fleet's task was to take western Crete and the Peloponnese in late May 1943, followed by the Italian islands of Lampedusa and Pantelleria in early June 1943. Once in Greece, the 'British 12th Army' could then link up with the Red Army. Shortly after, an American force was to attack Corsica, Sardinia and southern France. To reinforce the impression that Greece was the target, Operation *Animals* saw guerrilla attacks stepped up on Greek railway bridges and telecommunications.

Hitler took the bait. He assessed the threat from Operation *Barclay* and supporting intelligence from Operation *Mincemeat* to be real. Alarmed by

Chapter 11

intelligence reports of the preparations being conducted by the 'British 12th Army' in early June 1943, he ordered the 1st Panzer Division to be moved from southern France to the Peloponnese. The successful Allied invasion of Sicily commenced on 9 July and by mid-August the island had been secured and the Axis garrison defeated.

A phantom British army was also created in Scotland in 1943 to convince the Germans of an impending threat to Norway. This was known as the 'British 4th Army' under General Sir Andrew Thorne. His headquarters were beneath Edinburgh Castle, from where he commanded two corps, with one located at Dundee and another one at Stirling. Thorne even had a Russian liaison officer, Kliment Budyonny, to make it appear as if Moscow was being kept informed of the preparations.

Thorne was known to the Germans, as he had commanded the British 12th Corps protecting Kent and Sussex from the threat of invasion in the summer of 1940. Initially, in June that year he had just a single division and a motorized brigade under his control, but by August he could muster six divisions. The following year he was appointed the senior commander in Scotland and had been there ever since. In 1944 his '4th Army' became part of *Fortitude North*.

German intelligence was led to believe that Thorne commanded over 250,000 troops supported by aircraft, artillery and tanks. As it was felt any

An inflatable Sherman tank deployed in England as part of Operation Fortitude *in 1944.*

Luftwaffe reconnaissance planes crossing from Norway were likely to be intercepted by the RAF, there was little reliance on physical deception. Instead, the existence of the '4th Army' was a hoax perpetrated by a detachment of radio operators sending out fake orders for German eavesdroppers to pick up. The illusion was backed by Commando raids in Norway in the spring of 1944, which suggested they were preparing the way. The ruse worked because Hitler kept over a dozen divisions in Norway.

DUMMY ARMY GROUP

By the early spring of 1944 Allied preparations in Britain for the opening of the Second Front were hard to hide from prying eyes. The challenge facing Hitler's high command was not so much when an invasion would take place, but rather where. For the Allies, the shortest route would be across the Dover Strait or Pas-de-Calais, where the English Channel is at its narrowest. Once the Allies had selected Normandy as their assault point for Operation *Overlord* they needed to persuade Hitler to keep his forces north of the Seine.

To encourage this, the Allies, under Operation *Fortitude South* and more specifically Operation *Quicksilver*, created the fictitious 'First United States Army Group', or 'FUSAG', under the command of General George Patton. The illusion needed to be created that it was poised in south-eastern England ready to strike the Pas-de-Calais and attack the German 15th Army. 'FUSAG' consisted of the 'US 3rd Army' and the 'Canadian 1st Army', both of which would become real commands once in Normandy.

According to his 'orders' Patton was to launch 12 divisions across the Pas-de-Calais with a follow-up force of 38 divisions. While some of 'FUSAG's divisions were real, others were completely fake. The real ones were actually assigned to take part in *Overlord*. This combination of real and fake helped mask *Overlord*'s build-up in southern England and its destination, while at the same time gave greater credibility to the existence of 'FUSAG'. The presence of Patton as its commander greatly helped with the deception. Patton had led American troops in the invasion of Sicily, so he had the necessary experience.

To support the illusion of a massive build-up of troops and equipment in south-eastern England engineers had to create inflatable rubber landing craft, tanks and trucks. Some were also built from wood. Fake landing craft known as 'Bigbobs' and 'Wetbobs' were moored in the Ramsgate-Hastings area opposite the Pas-de-Calais. Others were placed along the coast from Great Yarmouth

Chapter 11

and the Thames. To convince the Luftwaffe and German spies they were real, tug boats regularly moved some of the craft, while oil spills often appeared and smoke wafted from smoke stacks. In the darkness, floodlights were towed about at sea to mimic moving landing aircraft. Vehicles were moved along the shoreline to simulate resupply operations and at night the illusion of docks was created using lighting.

Inland, daytime decoy airfields known as 'K sites' were built, requiring dummy aircraft, hangars and storage facilities. These were built from wood, fibreboard and canvas. To add to the illusion, some real aircraft and vehicles were added to the sites. At night, patterns dubbed 'Q lights' were used to simulate airfields and runways. 'On the ground in the daytime, the decoys looked pathetic,' recalled an RAF veteran. 'Just a collection of old wooden poles with a tangle of wires and electric bulbs [...] But when you flew over the same spot at night, the effect was amazing.'

To confound and deceive German eavesdroppers, 'FUSAG' set up radio stations in Bury St Edmunds, Dover, Chelmsford, Folkstone, Leatherhead and Wentworth. Occasionally, Calais would be mentioned in the radio traffic. Every now and again it would stop, as if indicating radio silence imposed for security purposes prior to troop movements. 'FUSAG's radio operators were warned by the Allied high command: 'You must realize that the enemy is probably listening to every message you pass on the air and is well aware that there is a possibility that he is being bluffed.'

The illusion of 'FUSAG' was fostered by a number of other deception operations.

General Hans Cramer, who had been captured in North Africa in May 1943 and since held in a Welsh prison camp, was deliberately exposed to 'FUSAG's preparations. Cramer's ill health had made him eligible for a prisoner exchange and repatriation to Germany. While being driven to London his guards accidently mentioned 'FUSAG' and the Pas-de-Calais. They also passed real concentrations of armour, aircraft, soldiers and supplies, which were actually part of *Overlord*. When Cramer got home he naturally repeated everything he had overhead and reported what he had witnessed.

Thanks to 'FUSAG', the German high command decided to prioritize General Hans von Salmuth's 15th Army deployed north of the Seine. This meant that Field Marshal Gerd von Rundstedt's better forces remained in the Pas-de-Calais area due to the Allies' highly successful deception efforts. That

Dummy Armies

General Patton commanded the fictitious 'First United States Army Group' before D-Day.

in turn had a negative impact on General Friedrich Dollmann's 7th Army covering Normandy and Brittany. Most of his divisions were third-rate static fortress units, so he lacked mobile infantry and armour with which to counter-attack. Even when he did receive panzer divisions, the infantry needed to support them remained north of the Seine.

'FUSAG' clearly played a vital part in ensuring that D-Day was a great success on 6 June 1944. A bridgehead was secured. Although the Allies suffered about 10,000 casualties that day, they had anticipated up to ten times this number. The Allied high command feared their troops might be thrown back into the sea either from the beaches or once inland. The deployment of German troops and their poor co-ordination ensured that this never happened.

When the Germans learned that Patton was not among the Allied commanders on D-Day it further convinced them that Normandy was just a diversion. Hitler continued to believe well into July 1944 that Patton's bogus 'FUSAG' was to strike the Pas-de-Calais and attack the 15th Army. The worry remained that if Hitler permitted the immediate redeployment of his infantry divisions from beyond the Seine, this would free up his armoured divisions for a thrust to the coast in Normandy. Instead, Hitler fed his divisions into the battle piecemeal.

THE GAME'S UP

D-Day and the subsequent Battle for Normandy were all about timing. Following the capture of Cherbourg, General Omar Bradley's mission was to swing his forces south and break out of the Normandy bridgehead. The key to a successful outflanking manoeuvre would then be getting over the Sée River at Avranches and the Sélune River at Pontaubault. Rather optimistically, Montgomery wanted to schedule General Bradley's US 1st Army breakout, code-named Operation *Cobra*, for early July. 'We had hoped originally,' said Monty, 'to launch the operation from the line St Lô-Coutances.' This did not happen.

In the meantime, General Dempsey's British 2nd Army had to maintain its pressure on the tough German defences at Caen. Both Montgomery and Bradley appreciated that speed was of the essence because the Germans only had limited armour facing the Americans, while eight panzer divisions were holding the British at bay. Although Patton arrived in Normandy on 6 July 1944, his US 3rd Army did not become operational until 1 August. It first had to be shipped from England amid great secrecy, which caused even more confusion among the German high command.

Hitler, though, would not continue to believe in the Pas-de-Calais bluff indefinitely. This deception would soon crumble once Patton's forces became active. Bradley's breakout from Normandy finally commenced on 25 July and within a week the pulverized German defence had collapsed. On 1 August Patton then swept through Avranches as planned and west into Brittany before turning east at Le Mans. Three weeks later the German army was completely defeated at Falaise, forcing the survivors to retreat across the Seine.

Part 5

Partisans and Guerrillas

Chapter 12

European Resistance

While the military campaigns in North Africa, on the Eastern and Western Fronts and in the Far East are well-known, what is less appreciated is that a secret struggle was waged behind Axis lines. This was fought by unconventional forces that in some cases transitioned from sabotage and guerrilla operations to conventional warfare in order to liberate their countries from Axis occupation. Some succeeded quite dramatically, while others failed spectacularly. To foster mayhem behind the lines the SOE along with MI6 and the American OSS fomented rebellion by arming resistance and partisan forces around the world. In the case of Europe, Winston Churchill's instruction was to set it ablaze.

SOE agents found themselves responsible for the logistical support of a diverse range of resistance and partisan groups. The RAF in support delivered explosives, money, radios and weapons. The SOE provided training and liaison officers. By 1944 the SOE was operating 60 schools producing radio operators, saboteurs and spies. In total, some 7,500 agents were sent into occupied western Europe, not including operations in Italy. Many were captured, tortured and executed. As the war progressed the OSS, with much greater resources at its disposal became the senior partner. The occupied territories not only saw resistanc,e to Axis rule, but in some cases civil war as resisters fought with collaborationist security forces.

In western Europe, apart from France and Italy, the resistance only made a small contribution to the Allied war effort; it never constituted a serious threat to German control. Nor was it strong enough to transition to open warfare. When resistance movements did so in France and Italy the Germans were easily able to defeat them. In contrast, the Balkans and eastern Europe were to see extensive guerrilla warfare. The terrain there was much more favourable: the Balkans were mountainous and western Russia was covered in vast forests and swamps. Such terrain offered safe havens from which to attack exposed supply lines and isolated garrisons.

Furthermore, Germany's occupation policies in eastern Europe were far more repressive than those in the west. These drove many people into the arms of the partisans. In particular, Hitler saw the Slavs as subhumans who should be exploited and exterminated in equal measure. He saw little reason to foster nationalist sentiments among the Soviet republics and failed to recruit them as allies, which fuelled ever greater levels of resistance.

It is notable that the Communist partisans in the Balkans and the Soviet Union were by far the most effective fighters. In the Balkans, many of the democratic and monarchist groups lacked discipline and clear strategic goals. They also hated the Communists as much as they did the Germans, which greatly hampered co-operation against a common enemy. This led to three-way wars with nationalist partisans fighting the occupation forces and the Communists. When Italy collapsed the Germans had to disarm the Italian garrison in the Balkans, where they became ever more reliant on unreliable and ill-disciplined collaborationist forces.

Axis attempts at encouraging rebellion in British colonial possessions and in the Soviet Union had very poor results. In the case of the latter, Hitler refused to encourage nationalists seeking independence from Moscow, a policy that alienated many potential allies. German agents approached nationalists in both British-controlled Egypt and Iraq in the hope of causing trouble. In the case of Egypt, their efforts came to nothing. In Iraq, the Germans encouraged a coup, which sparked a brief conventional war, resulting in the British taking control of Baghdad.

In the Far East, Asia and the Pacific, resistance sprang up against Japanese occupation, but many of the nationalist groups hoped for independence from America, Britain, France and the Netherlands, so sided with Japan. Japanese actions, though, soon affronted the indigenous populations, who saw them as worse than their former colonial masters. This resulted in a number of very confused guerrilla wars. Likewise in China, lines became blurred in the face of collaboration with the Japanese.

EUROPE

BELGIUM Although about a dozen groups emerged in Belgium to oppose the German occupation the resistance was never very strong in military terms.

The government who fled to London collectively dubbed them the 'Secret Army'. The SOE and the exiled Belgian government sent 300 agents into the country. By 1944, with the Allies approaching Brussels, the resistance numbered about 45,000, though only around 7,000 were actually armed. The resistance's biggest contribution to the Allied war effort was preventing the Germans from blowing up Antwerp's docks when they withdrew.

ESTONIA In June 1940 the Soviet Union occupied the three small independent Baltic states of Estonia, Latvia and Lithuania, which prior to the First World War had been part of the Russian Empire. This sparked guerrilla movements in all of them. Initially, they opposed the Red Army and when the Germans invaded they helped hasten it on its way. When it became apparent that Hitler had no intention of restoring their independence the guerrillas began to attack the new occupiers. In Estonia, there were around 50,000 'Brethren of the Forest'. To counter this, thousands of Estonians, Latvians and Lithuanians sided with the Germans, serving in locally raised police battalions. When the Red Army returned in 1944 the guerrillas resumed their hopelessly one-sided struggle.

FRANCE Defeated France was in the unusual position of initially being partitioned into the German-occupied north and the pro-Nazi Vichy south, known as the so-called Free Zone. General de Gaulle fled to Britain to head the Free French, but his authority carried little weight. The Vichy government was not in a position to continue resisting but refrained from declaring war on Britain. This did not stop Churchill from attacking the French fleet and French colonies. Following the Allied landings in French North Africa in late 1942, Hitler invaded the Free Zone to complete France's humiliation.

The Maquis or Resistance was generally dominated by the French Communist Party, which formed a Front National that was open to all. The size of France and its geography greatly aided the Resistance. Initially, the Free Zone provided a relatively safe haven from which to operate. In London, the French section of the SOE also organized its own intelligence-gathering and sabotage operations. However, the SOE's relations with de Gaulle's secret service were never very good.

French security forces were employed against their fellow countrymen throughout occupied France, including Paris. While no organized units of the French armed forces took action against the French Resistance, the

French police and various collaborationist militias did. Vichy, following the occupation of the Free Zone, approved Interior Minister Joseph Darnand to form the Milice Française, whose main force was the Franc Garde consisting of 13,000 personnel. They, along with the French Police's 10,000-strong Groupes Mobiles de Réserve (GMR), regularly supported German security operations against the Resistance.

By 1943 German and Milice convoys were coming under attack and in the spring the Franc Garde first went into action against the Resistance in Haute-Savoie, followed by operations in the old Occupied Zone in December. The Wehrmacht, GMR and the Franc Garde then moved to liquidate a Resistance stronghold on the Glières plateau in early 1944.

Darnand aimed to make the Milice a French version of the Waffen-SS. Initially, it operated in Vichy, but its activities spread north. In his fight against the Resistance he collaborated closely with the feared Higher SS and Police Leader for France, Paris-based Major General Karl Oberg. In January 1944, as a reward for his efforts against his own countrymen, Vichy appointed him to the post of General Secretary for the Maintenance of Order. Darnand became one of the most hated men in France.

As the opening of the Second Front approached, the Resistance stepped up its operations. In the run-up to D-Day the Resistance sabotaged power supplies and railways. Throughout May 1944 the 2nd SS Panzer Division conducted anti-Resistance operations against a force of about 5,000 in the Dordogne and Lot. This culminated in the burning down of Terrou and the arrest of 1,000 people at Gageac. By D-Day enough weapons had been supplied by the SOE, OSS and other organizations to fully arm 20,000 men and partially arm another 50,000.

Once the Allies landed in Normandy the desire to collaborate rapidly crumbled, weakening the Milice. It disappeared completely after Operation *Dragoon*, when the Allies, including Free French forces, landed in southern France.

After D-Day the Resistance were grouped together as the French Forces of the Interior (FFI) by de Gaulle to assist the Allies with the liberation. Notably, they attempted to delay German troops heading for Normandy. On 8 June the 2nd SS conducted anti-partisan operations in the Limoges-Tulle area. When the Resistance captured an SS officer the 2nd SS Division destroyed the village of Oradour-sur-Glane two days later and brutally murdered 643 men, women and children in reprisal. Shortly after, General Blaskowitz, commander of Army Group G, declared the south-west of France a battle zone. It would take the 2nd SS almost three weeks to reach Normandy.

To the south-east, about 4,000 FFI prematurely rose up in the mountains of the Vercors Massif in July 1944. This had long been a sanctuary for the Resistance. The Germans immediately responded by sending 10,000 troops, supported by airborne forces and the Luftwaffe, to swiftly crush them. The FFI were surrounded and overwhelmed, suffering 659 dead. Around 200 civilians were also killed. The region was liberated the following month, after the Allied landings on the French Riviera.

Members of the Maquis or French Resistance in Haute-Loire in southern France.

Chapter 12

When the Resistance rose up in France's main cities de Gaulle moved to ensure that the French Communists did not take power in Paris, Marseilles and Toulon. He also subsumed the FFI into the regular French armed forces to assert further control over them. After the war about 40,000 people were arrested for collaboration and about 10,000 were executed.

LATVIA In Latvia, about 60,000 guerrillas first opposed Soviet occupation, then German occupation and then the Soviets again when they returned. Around 15,000 Latvians sided with the Germans by serving in security battalions.

LITHUANIA Lithuania had by far the largest guerrillas forces in the Baltic states. The Lithuanian Activist Front totalled about 120,000. As a result, when the Red Army returned it took much longer to subdue them. Lithuanian resistance to Soviet rule lasted until the early 1950s. About 13,000 Lithuanians served the Germans.

NETHERLANDS In the Netherlands, in the face of German invasion the Dutch government and royal family fled to Britain. As a result, the country was ruled by Nazi Reichskommissar Arthur Seyss-Inquart. Dutch resistance was regularly compromised by German intelligence and collaboration. The first group was the Orde Dienst, made up of former Dutch army officers planning for the day when the Germans eventually left. In November 1941 the Abwehr caught a number of Dutch SOE agents and gained access to their links with London. Over 450 SOE agents were caught, many of whom were executed. The Germans were able to manipulate their communications and seized equipment sufficient for 10,000 men. Operation *England Game*, as the Germans dubbed it, ended in 1943 when a captured agent escaped and made it back to Britain. Dutch Communists mounted attacks on the Germans and collaborators but were too weak to pose a serious threat. At the end of the war 50,000 Dutch were prosecuted for collaboration, which included serving in the SS in large numbers.

POLAND Hitler partitioned Poland into a series of administrative areas. To maintain order, the Germans kept up to 600,000 police and soldiers in the country. The Poles, though, resisted from the start, coalescing around the

Armia Krajowa (AK) or Home Army in 1942. This recognized the authority of the Polish government in exile in London. It drew on former members of the Polish armed forces and civilians. The AK was by far the largest of the Polish resistance groups. At its height it had about 400,000 under its command. Its constitutionalist and nationalist credentials meant that it was ignored by the left- and right-wing resistance groups such as the People's Guards and the National Armed Forces.

Initially, the resistance refrained from outright guerrilla warfare for fear of the consequences. Its main success early on was sabotaging the railway lines and trains outside Warsaw in late 1941. Crucially, this held up the supply of vital German winter clothing that was desperately needed on the Eastern Front. General Heinz Guderian found his men still in their summer uniforms and suffering terrible frostbite. He had requested warm clothing in September and again in October. His men faced temperatures of -8 °C (17 °F) and the German advance had ground to a halt before Moscow. When he looked into the delay in late November Guderian discovered the supplies had been stranded at Warsaw station for several weeks because of a lack of trains and disruption by Polish partisans.

The AK went into action in the winter of 1942–3 to oppose the German policy of forced evictions. In August 1944, with the approach of the Red Army, it launched the Warsaw Rising. This transition from guerrilla to conventional warfare proved ill-fated. The Russians were unable to reach the city and the Germans brutally crushed the rising and flattened Warsaw. The survivors were marched into captivity and the AK was officially disbanded in January 1945, leaving Poland to the Polish Communists.

SOVIET UNION After Hitler's invasion of the Soviet Union in June 1941 his armed forces soon found the region behind the lines teeming with partisan activity. Stalin had called for the creation of Otryadi or partisan units in all occupied areas. These were each up to 1,000 strong. Byelorussia proved particularly favourable to guerrilla warfare thanks to its forests and swamps. In contrast, Ukrainian nationalism and a historic hatred of rule by Moscow made it an unfavourable area for partisan operations.

German security measures meant that by the end of 1941 only about 30,000 partisans survived. The following year they were bolstered by regular troops, who infiltrated German lines. Partisan attacks became much more effective, forcing Hitler to send increasing numbers of security divisions to the Eastern Front to counter them. The Germans also raised security militias among the nationalists in Byelorussia, Ukraine and in the Baltic states. In fighting for the Germans against their own countrymen, they vainly hoped to gain independence.

Stalin in May 1942 formed the Central Staff of the Partisan Movement at the Red Army's headquarters in Moscow. By the end of the year about 130,000 partisans were controlling large areas in the Germans' rear. They regularly attacked convoys and railways transporting German supplies. Up to 60 per cent of the partisans came from the peasantry, many of them forcibly conscripted, with the rest being mainly army personnel.

These escalating partisan attacks exasperated Hitler, who foolishly hoped to rule and exploit his conquests without opposition. His response was to unleash the SS, supported by the armed forces and military police. By the summer of 1942 Himmler was firmly in charge of pacifying the occupied territories. Hitler instructed: 'The Reichsführer-SS has the sole responsibility for combating banditry in the Reich Commissioner's territories. [...] The Chief of the Army General Staff is solely responsible for action against bandits in operational areas.' Such a demarcation made little difference to the partisans.

Before the Red Army's summer offensive at Kursk in 1943 the partisans stepped up their operations against the German lines of communication. At the end of the first week of March over 1,000 partisans from three different units targeted the Desna railway bridge near Vygonichi. This was a vital link in the supply route to Field Marshal von Kluge's Army Group Centre, taking up to 20 trains a day. One unit made a feint assault from the west to distract the guards. The bridge was then blown up. The same night another team attacked the relief line running from Krichev to Unecha. For a distance of some 97 km (60 miles) they cut the line in 90 different places. The following week they also destroyed the Revna bridge near Sinzoertei.

The destruction of the Desna bridge reduced rail traffic for several crucial weeks. Within five days German engineers built an improvised structure, but it could only safely take one freight wagon at a time, rolled across by hand. After a week the new bridge could take an entire train but not the weight of a locomotive. This meant that the wagons had to be pushed on from one end and pulled off from the other.

Another major choke point for German communications was at Bryansk. The town was the junction for three key railways and a highway. This made it an important staging post on the main line of communications to Orel to the east. Karachev, a third of the way along the line to Orel, was a pinch point. Security for the garrison at Bryansk was a complete headache. The region was heavily forested, which provided sanctuary for three major partisan strongholds to the north and south, as well as to the west of the town. An area of some 6,440 sq km (4,000 sq miles) concealed up to 16,000 partisans. They regularly blew up roads and railways and during 1942 sparked a series of brutal anti-partisan operations by the exasperated Germans.

To the south, Poltava sat astride the main railway to Kharkov and Belgorod and was a key supply point for Army Group South. During the spring and early summer of 1943, across the central sector, attacks on the railways rose from 626 in April to 841 in June. During the latter attacks of the 1,822 trains transiting the area, 296 were derailed.

The Germans conducted Operation *Robber Baron* from 16 May to 6 June 1943 against the southern area, which involved six whole divisions, one of which was armoured. This killed and captured more than 4,000 partisans, and over 200 camps were destroyed. Almost 16,000 civilians were evacuated. Despite this success, as many as 4,000 partisans still remained at large. To make matters worse for the Germans, plans were underway for the partisans to commence in August 1943 a two-month campaign known as the 'Battle of the Rails'.

Zhukov was full of praise for the role played by the partisans in the Battle of Kursk: 'The "railroad war" carried out by the guerrillas of Byelorussia, Smolensk, and Orel oblasts and the Dnieper valley was especially effective in cutting enemy supply lines. The guerrillas blew up trains, stations and yards and provided the Soviet command with intelligence data that enabled it to assess the strategic situation and enemy intentions.'

Although these partisan attacks showed that great swathes of territory behind German lines were bandit country, the build-up for Hitler's Operation *Citadel* at Kursk went according to plan and the offensive was not delayed due to logistical problems. After the Desna attack German security forces ensured that the partisans did not achieve such a success again. There were German ammunition shortages but the partisans never came close to strangling Army Group Centre or preventing the withdrawal of 2nd Panzer Army and 9th

Army from the Orel salient. Likewise, in the south, while they were troubling to Army Group South, they did little to disrupt German operations in the Belgorod salient. Their greatest role was undoubtedly intelligence-gathering, which was probably far more harmful to the German war effort than their military activities.

Soviet partisan forces had grown to about 200,000 by early 1944. As a prelude to Operation *Bagration* that summer Soviet partisan forces set about Army Group Centre's rear areas and lines of communication. On the night of 19–20 June 1944 they blew up 40,000 tracks in occupied Byelorussia. The supply lines of 3rd Panzer Army were the main targets, as it was to bear the brunt of the first assault. In just one night 15,000 demolitions were conducted, 10,500 of which were successful.

Army Group Centre found all double-track lines blocked for about 24 hours and the single-track ones out of action for 48 hours. Colonel G. Teske, Chief of Transportation of Army Group Centre, later recorded: 'The lightning operation conducted during the night by partisan detachments halted all railway traffic on individual sections of all the principal communications leading to the breakthrough areas… This operation was carried out brilliantly.' Army Group Centre was methodically cut off from the outside world.

After this the existence of the partisans as a separate entity from the Red Army was soon brought to an end. The Central Staff was abolished and as the partisan-held areas were liberated, their units were absorbed into the army.

To confuse matters on the Eastern Front, some Ukrainian guerrillas hoping for independence fought both the Germans and the Soviets. They wanted the restoration of the short-lived Ukrainian National Republic, which had come into being after the First World War. Soviet Russia had annexed it in 1921. Key among the nationalist Ukrainian guerrilla organizations was the Ukrainian People's Army, which by 1944 numbered up to 30,000. Often their priority was fighting Soviet partisans and the Red Army. This sometimes led to co-operation with German and Hungarian occupation forces and with collaborationist Ukrainian units.

After the German retreat the UPA's numbers swelled with Ukrainians who had fought for the Germans. When the war ended they desperately continued to hold out against the Red Army from Ukraine's forests. In 1947 some of them fought their way into the American Zone in Austria seeking sanctuary. The following year those still in Ukraine were largely destroyed by joint Czech,

Polish and Soviet military operations. Nonetheless, sporadic resistance to Soviet rule continued in Ukraine well into the early 1950s.

The Germans only recognized Ukrainian independence in March 1945, by which time it was too late. The Ukrainian National Army created by the Germans consisted of two divisions, one of which was a former Ukrainian SS division. These units soon found themselves disowned by the Germans and on their own. They ended the war in Austria and Czechoslovakia and were swiftly rounded up by the Red Army.

Chapter 13

Resisting on the Flanks

Resistance not only took place in Europe: it spread across Scandinavia, the Balkans, the Mediterranean and even down into the mountains of the Caucasus. This widespread resistance on the Axis's flanks caused them unending security problems.

SCANDINAVIA

DENMARK At first occupied Denmark was treated leniently and none of its institutions, including the armed forces and the police, were disbanded. Lacking a government in exile, easy communication with Britain or suitable geography, Danish resistance was slow in starting. The most effective were the Danish Communists, who were banned after Hitler's invasion of the Soviet Union. They formed the Borgerlige Partisaner and were followed by other non-Communist groups.

In 1943, following a series of strikes and demonstrations, the Germans fearing a coup disbanded the Danish armed forces. The resistance groups then formed the Denmark Liberation Committee that included a Danish SOE representative. This formed a secret army that was about 45,000 strong by the time of the German surrender. After the war some 16,000 Danes were arrested for collaboration.

NORWAY The Norwegian resistance benefitted from its relative closeness to Britain. Communication between the two was maintained by what was quaintly called the 'Shetland bus', which was a regular fishing boat run across the North Sea.

Despite the ever-present danger of being intercepted by the German navy or the Luftwaffe, it helped ferry to Norway enough weapons for 35,000 men.

The Norwegian government in exile also arranged for the training of 15,000 'police' in neutral Sweden.

Unfortunately, differences of opinion between the various resistance organizations over strategy and tactics meant they were not very active. Their greatest success was the destruction of the Norsk Hydro 'heavy water' plant in 1943, a vital part of Hitler's atomic bomb research. By the end of the war the Milorg group, founded by former Norwegian army officers, had 40,000 men ready to assist disarming the German garrison.

BALKANS

ALBANIA Albania was invaded by Italy in early April 1939 and its 10,000-strong army disintegrated. King Zog fled to London and the Italian King Vittorio Emmanuel III seized his throne. The country was garrisoned by four Italian divisions. After Hitler's invasion of the Balkans in 1941, Yugoslav Kosovo, Western Macedonia and Greek southern Epirus, which had majority Albanian populations, were ceded to Albania.

In southern Albania the Communist Party, under Enver Hoxha, started ambushing Italian patrols during the summer of 1941. A British Military Mission to assist the Albanian resistance was set up in April 1943. Soon the National Liberation Army under General Hoxha numbered 10,000. Anti-Communists established the Balli Kombëtar in the south, but Hoxha's forces proved significantly more effective. In northern Albania, the resistance was far less organized.

After the Italian armistice in September 1943 the occupying garrison either fled into Yugoslavia or defected to the partisans. When the Germans sent two divisions the Albanian National Committee declared the country neutral and severed all ties with Italy. In Kosovo, the Germans recruited 6,500 Albanians into an SS division to fight the partisans. This ill-disciplined rabble was swiftly disbanded after a series of atrocities. In late 1943 the Germans attacked Hoxha's army, now some 35,000 strong. It withdrew into the mountains.

The following year Hoxha reoccupied the south and marched north. The Germans and the Balli Kombëtar responded by driving the partisans into central Albania. By the summer of 1944 Hoxha's forces had doubled and in October he took the capital, Tirana. The Germans withdrew from Albania leaving Hoxha and the Communists in power.

GREECE Resistance to the Axis occupation of Greece ended up a complete mess, with the Greeks more intent on fighting each other than their occupiers. During the 1930s Greece was a military dictatorship under General Metaxas. He had banned the Communist Party. The Italian invasion of 1940 temporarily united the country behind Metaxas. However, German intervention the following year sealed Greece's fate. King George II left to form a government in exile, but the Greek free forces were split between the royalists and the republicans. German resources were such that they could only hold Salonika, Athens and Crete. Wider security operations were left to the Italians and the Bulgarians.

Resistance from two main organizations sprang up in Greece's mountains. The Communist ELAS (National Popular Liberation Army) constituted the largest guerrilla force and operated throughout the country. It numbered about 50,000 armed fighters. Its rival was the EDES (National Republican Greek League), which was mainly confined to Epirus, and totalled about 10,000. These two groups spent more time fighting each other than the Germans. British attempts to get them to co-operate consistently failed. This civil war greatly aided the occupation.

Following Italy's defection the Germans managed to disarm the Italian divisions in the Balkans and take some of the Aegean islands. Their lack of forces on the mainland forced them to extend the Bulgarian security area and raise an anti-Communist Greek militia. The growing threat of an Allied landing in the Balkans and the approaching Red Army encouraged the Germans to withdraw from Greece in late 1944. They deliberately left behind weapons caches, hoping the guerrillas would use them to fight each other rather than harass their retreat.

Britain rushed troops and Greek royalist forces to Athens and the country fell into a second bout of civil war. EDES was defeated in the mountains but with British help was able to force ELAS into Communist Albania and Yugoslavia. There they prepared for a third round of civil war, which would end with its defeat in 1949.

YUGOSLAVIA Yugoslavia had only come into existence after the First World War and was a hodge-podge of races and religions who had little in common other than deep-rooted historical animosity. During the Axis occupation, like Greece, it was the scene of highly confused infighting. King Petar II, after

Chapter 13

the brief and highly successful German-led invasion in April 1941, fled to British-controlled Egypt. There he tried in vain to raise a liberation army. The Communist-led resistance would have far greater appeal than the pro-monarchy groups.

Hitler dismembered Yugoslavia just as he did Czechoslovakia and Poland. Pro-Nazi Croatia became independent and annexed neighbouring Bosnia and Herzegovina. Pro-Nazi Serbia also became independent and Central Slovenia was taken by Germany and Western Slovenia and Dalmatia by Italy. The Italians set up a puppet state in Montenegro and annexed Kosovo as part of Albania. The Bulgarians occupied Eastern Macedonia. The relatively small German garrison in Croatia and Serbia was there to guard communications with Greece.

Yugoslav partisans successfully tied down large numbers of Axis troops.

In July 1941 there was a rising in Montenegro against the Italians. This spread to Slovenia, Bosnia and then Serbia. In the latter, Communist leader Josip Broz, better known as Tito, orchestrated a general rising. His partisans rapidly controlled a large area south of Belgrade in short-lived co-operation with the nationalist Serb Chetniks. In September the Germans counter-attacked and by the end of the year the revolt had been crushed. Tito withdrew into Italian-occupied eastern Bosnia to regroup.

German and Croatian forces attacked Tito's headquarters in January 1942 but he escaped. The Germans tried again the following month and again he escaped, this time to Montenegro. By the summer he had liberated a great swathe of Bosnia. At the end of the year his forces numbered about 150,000, which were designated the Yugoslav National Liberation Army.

In January 1943 German, Italian and Croatian forces attacked his stronghold at Bihać, known as 'Titoland'. Tito withdrew and then counter-attacked the Italians, driving them back. German forces, though, pushed him over the Neretva River. There he mauled the Chetniks and then moved into Montenegro. Once more the Chetniks withdrew to their heartland in Serbia. The Allies, who had previously been supporting the Chetniks, now started supplying Tito's partisans. King Petar also now recognized the partisans, as the Chetniks had been compromised by their collaboration with the Axis.

Once more the Germans surrounded Tito, this time at Mount Durmitor in Montenegro. Tito escaped to Bosnia. When Italy defected, 18,000 interned Yugoslav troops returned home to join Tito and some Italian units defected to him. He also received a massive windfall of Italian weapons. By 1944 the partisans numbered about 250,000 but still the Germans fought to hold down Yugoslavia. In May they launched one last desperate attempt to crush the partisans at Dvar.

Tito's luck held and yet again he got away. His troops, now really a conventional army, numbered 390,000. In October 1944 the Red Army arrived to help liberate Belgrade as the Germans withdrew. The partisans, organized into four armies totalling 800,000, proceeded to liberate the rest of Yugoslavia and install a Communist government.

MEDITERRANEAN

CRETE After the Allies were driven from Crete in May 1941 many locals took to the caves in the White Mountains ready to resist the occupiers. The island was divided between German and Italian forces. The latter were disarmed after the Italian armistice. Cretan resistance, starting with acts of revenge and small skirmishes, gradually escalated from late 1941. Germans reprisals were brutal, with whole villages being massacred. As in Greece, the resistance was dominated by the Communist-led ELAS. On the island it never exceeded 5,000 men, including reserves. Non-Communist Cretans were grouped under the National Organization of Crete (EOK). Both were supported and encouraged by the SOE and MI6.

The Cretans launched a revolt in eastern Crete in September 1943 following the Italian surrender but were forced to retreat westwards. In response, the Germans proceeded to burn down a number of villages and carry out bloody reprisals. One of the resistance's greatest successes, along with British officers, was the kidnapping of General Heinrich Kreipe, the German garrison commander on 26 April 1944. He was grabbed on the open road, then whisked off to Egypt by boat. Despite the ongoing resistance, Crete would have to wait until May 1945 and Germany's surrender to be liberated.

EGYPT Generally, the people of North Africa attempted to keep out of the conflict between the European colonial powers. When the fighting spread there nationalists did not try to capitalize on the situation. The Egyptian government, although keen to see the British military presence gone, refrained from causing trouble when Mussolini attacked. Instead, nationalist ringleaders were rounded up and arrested. Despite the known anti-British sentiments of the Egyptian armed forces and the Muslim Brotherhood, neither took up arms, hoping the Axis would grant them full independence if Cairo was taken. Egyptian guerrilla attacks could have threatened the vital Suez Canal.

Suspecting the Egyptian army's loyalty, the British ensured it was only deployed for internal security and was not involved in the fighting in the Western Desert. The British and Egyptian governments agreed it would protect communications, vital installations and the Suez Canal, and man anti-aircraft guns in Cairo and Alexandria. This kept young nationalists such as Lieutenants Gamal Abdel Nasser and Anwar Sadat out of the way. The Germans did contact General Aziz el Masri, who had served as the inspector general of the Egyptian army until he was dismissed for his anti-British sentiments.

Sadat recalled: 'Now seemed to be the golden opportunity for General Aziz el Masri. No one could do more than he to hold the Egyptian forces together and to win vital German support for the Arab cause.' Instead he tried to flee to Iraq and was arrested. It was rumoured when Rommel was approaching El Alamein that if he broke through, Egyptian nationalists would rise up in support of him in Cairo. He was defeated and this never happened.

LIBYA During the Second World War the Libyans offered little if any opposition to the Italian occupation. Italy had seized control of Libya from the Ottoman Empire just before the First World War. After that conflict the Italians had to contend with a major rebellion, which they ruthlessly crushed. Resistance leader Omar al-Mukhtar was executed in 1931. Any surviving rebels were pushed into Libya's vast interior and they did not have the strength to challenge Italian rule again. As a result of this the Italians did not altogether trust the Libyans. At the outbreak of the Second World War Mussolini only had two Libyan divisions and when these were lost in the fighting with the British in 1940 the survivors were relegated to security duties.

The Libyans, who had been brutalized by the Italians for three decades, had no real reason to welcome the arrival of Rommel's Afrika Korps in early 1941, which would temporarily save Mussolini's colonial regime. However, the Libyans made no attempt to obstruct Italian and German lines of communication during the war: they did not cut the long coastal road, known as the 'Via Balbia', running all the way from Tunisia to Egypt. Instead, they largely kept out of the way, no doubt for fear of retribution, and hoped that if the Axis lost then they would get independence.

THE CAUCASUS

CHECHNYA Chechen nationalists in the Caucasus, like some of their Ukrainian counterparts, ended up fighting both the Germans and the Soviets in a little-known guerrilla war. When Hitler attacked the Soviet Union the Caucasus had little love for Soviet rule. The North Caucasus and the lower and middle Volga were some of the most important food-producing regions in the country. Together they were designated the Soviet Union's main grain-producing area. The administrative capital was Rostov on the Don. The Krasnodar area, with a number of other areas that later became autonomous republics (North Ossetia, Chechen-Ingush Republic and the Kabardino-Balkar Republic), also formed part of the larger administrative territory run by the North Caucasian Communist Party committee in Rostov.

Muslim Chechen leader Khasan Israilov and his brother Hussein launched a Chechen insurgency against Moscow in 1939. They were greatly encouraged by the Red Army's failures in the Winter War against Finland. They set up a guerrilla organization in the mountains of south-eastern Chechnya. 'The valiant Finns are now proving that the Great Enslaver Empire is powerless against a small but freedom-loving people,' declared Israilov. 'In the Caucasus you will find your second Finland and after us will follow other oppressed peoples.'

Although Lavrenti Beria's feared NKVD internal security troops were sent to deal with the Chechen rebels, they were rapidly defeated in the mountains. Hitler would have done well to heed the nationalist aspirations of the Chechens. His invasion of the Soviet Union inflamed the Chechen rebellion further. The Israilovs set up the 'Provisional Popular Revolutionary Government of Chechen-Ingushetia'. By the end of the summer of 1941 they had rallied over 5,000 fighters and some 250,000 sympathizers operating in five military districts, including Grozny, Gudermes and Malgobek.

In January 1942 the brothers expanded the rising to encompass a dozen other ethnic groups, creating the Special Party of Caucasus Brothers. The following month Mairbek Sheripov led a rebellion in Shatoi and his men united with the Israilovs. Insurrection also broke out in neighbouring Dagestan. Desertions from the Red Army began to mount, with reports of over 60,000 men fleeing into the mountains to join the guerrillas. Soviet diplomat Konstantin Oumansky doubted the loyalty of the entire region: 'I must say I am a little worried about the Caucasus. [...] Like the Crimean Tartars, they are Muslims and they still remember the Russian conquest of the Caucasus which ended not so very long ago – in 1863.'

It was not until the summer of 1942 that the Abwehr attempted to capitalize on the Chechens' hatred of Stalin and his cronies. German commandos landed at the village of Berzhki in the Galashki area on 25 August. Their mission was to recruit locals. By September some 40 Germans had been dropped at various locations where the inhabitants were deemed to be anti-Soviet. Their task, along with the Chechen rebels, was to secure the Grozny refinery before the 1st Panzer Army arrived and to stop the withdrawing Red Army from destroying it.

Attempts at a German–Chechen alliance soon floundered. In keeping with Hitler's policy in the rest of the occupied territories, he showed no inclination to cut a deal with the Chechen rebels. If he had promised them independence then they may have aided his war effort; indeed, he could have incited rebellion across the Caucasus. Perhaps Grozny might have been within his grasp.

The Abwehr, though, was unable to recruit Khasan Israilov and his men because of Hitler's refusal to recognize Chechen independence. In turn, Israilov refused to place his guerrillas under German control, as he saw them as little more than imperialists in the same mould as the Soviets. To further aggravate the volatile Chechens, the Germans courted the Kuban and Terek Cossacks, who were their traditional enemies. Mairbek Sheripov warned the Germans that: 'If the liberation of the Caucasus meant only the exchange of one coloniser for another, the Caucasians would consider this only a new stage in the national liberation war.' In other words, they would resist the Germans as well as the Soviets.

The German defeat in the Caucasus in early 1943 and their retreat from the region sealed the fate of the Chechen rising. In December Soviet counterintelligence arrested the last of the Abwehr's operatives in Chechnya. This ended German involvement in the region and indeed the Caucasus as a whole. Stalin's retribution was swift: deportations at gunpoint continued into 1944. Some 47,000 Meskhi – Turkish-speaking Georgians living near the Turkish border – were sent to Central Asia. Also, 1,400 Hemshins (Muslim Armenians), 9,000 remaining Kurds in Armenia and 30,000 other people were deported.

In the meantime Khasan Israilov's Chechen guerrillas were mercilessly hunted down and shot. Many of those who surrendered were massacred. Israilov lasted until December 1944, when he was killed by two of his own men. His successor, Qureish Belhorev, was captured in 1947, but the Chechen insurgency operating from the Caucasus mountains lasted until the mid-1950s. Upwards of 200,000 Chechens are estimated to have been killed between 1944 and 1948.

Stalin had no intention of leaving those who survived in their homes. Nearly 500,000 people from Checheno-Ingushetia were deported to Central Asia and Siberia. Around another 200,000 people from the region's various other ethnic groups were also sent into exile.

Chapter 14

Guerrillas in the Far East and Pacific

Guerrilla and resistance movements in the Far East and Pacific were often very conflicted in their political aims. While many indigenous people were glad to see the back of the colonial powers, the arrival of the Japanese proved little cause for celebration.

FAR EAST

BORNEO In early 1942 the Japanese seized the island of Borneo, which was under British and Dutch colonial control. The indigenous, Chinese and Malay population soon suffered at the hands of the occupation. The Sino-Japanese War showed that the Japanese had little regard for Chinese life. Albert Kwok organized a resistance movement known as the Kinabalu Guerrillas Defence Force in North Borneo. This carried out the Jesselton revolt in early October 1943.

Kwok's forces took control of Jesselton, Kota Belud and Tuaran. In the process they killed 90 Japanese troops. The Japanese responded by bombing local villages and executing up to 4,000 civilians. To stop the killing, Kwok and other leaders surrendered and they were executed on 21 January 1944. Borneo's Dayak tribesmen also conducted guerrilla warfare against the Japanese, killing 1,500, and assisted Allied special forces' operations until liberation.

BURMA Although a Burmese division fought with the British in the face of the Japanese invasion in 1942, many of Burma's different races sided with the Japanese, hoping for independence from Britain. Nationalist leader Aung San formed the Burma National Army, some 15,000 strong, to fight alongside the Japanese. He had received military training with other nationalists in Japan.

The Japanese hoped to use Burma as a base from which to invade British-controlled India. They proclaimed Burmese independence in August 1943, with Aung San appointed minister of defence. Japanese arrogance and brutality, though, soon alienated the Burmese, who realized their new occupiers were a lot worse than the old ones.

When the Japanese attack on India failed at Imphal and Kohima in 1944 Aung San formed the Anti-Fascist People's Freedom League and sided with the British. In November 1944 a British agent and former member of the BNA was dropped to liaise with the nationalists. General Slim recalled, 'My opinion was that the B.N.A, prowling on their lines of communication, could not fail to be a nuisance to the Japanese and give them an uncomfortable feeling on dark nights.' He hoped they would conduct guerilla operations and provided them with supplies. Aung San's troops attacked the Japanese rear in the Rangoon area in late March 1945, which greatly helped the British advance. 'They proved definitely useful in gaining information,' said Slim, 'and in dealing drastically with small parties of Japanese.'

Two years after the war ended Aung San and seven of his ministers were assassinated by a rival. Burma's Red Flag and White Flag Communists waited in the wings to seize power when independence came in 1948. They and other factions plunged the country into decades of civil war.

EAST INDIES After Germany invaded the Netherlands in 1940 the Dutch East Indies were left on their own. These consisted of 1,700 islands with a population of over 60 million. Following Pearl Harbor they declared war on Japan. Resistance to the Japanese invasion of the Dutch East Indies in 1942 mainly came from Dutch nationals and Moluccans serving in the Dutch armed forces. One such group was the Java Legion in Bandung led by Dutch captain De Lange. Jan Kaihatu led a group of Moluccans in Batavia while his brother Job Kaihatu led another in Bandung.

After the Japanese invasion some Dutch troops escaped to Australia; ten small units then returned to the East Indies to gather intelligence. Another group known as the Insulinde Corps sailed from Ceylon by submarine to Sumatra. They established contact with the local population.

Many Indonesians, however, regarded the Japanese as liberators. This attitude changed when thousands were forced into slave labour. There were three major revolts by Indonesians in Java, which were brutally supressed. At the end of the war there were some 300,000 Japanese troops and civilians in the East Indies. The Indonesians did not welcome the return of Dutch authority, assisted by British troops. Although the Indonesians declared independence and revolted, the Dutch did not relinquish control until 1949.

INDIA In the summer of 1942 the Quit India revolt inspired by Gandhi sought to end the Raj just as the British were being driven from Burma by the Japanese. After the loss of Malaya and Singapore, British prestige was at rock bottom. The civil unrest was supported by the nationalist Hindu Indian National Congress but not the Muslim League, which backed the British authorities. In response, Lord Linlithgow, the Viceroy of India, declared the Congress illegal and its leaders were arrested.

There were demonstrations, sit-ins, riots, murders and acts of sabotage across India. The riots in Delhi were swiftly contained but spread in Calcutta and other major cities. Railway tracks were torn up, telegraph wires cut and police stations set on fire. This posed a threat to the supply lines of British forces in north-eastern India and northern Burma. The British 26th Division was deployed in Bengal and the 70th Division in Bihar to help quell the unrest. In Bombay, the British 2nd Division was also sent to deal with demonstrators.

'I am engaged here in meeting by far the most serious rebellion since that of 1857,' Lord Linlithgow signalled to Churchill, 'the gravity and extent of which we have so far concealed from the world for reasons of military security.' Fortunately, the Indian Army and the Indian police remained loyal, otherwise law and order would have completely collapsed. About 100,000 British and Indian troops were tied up putting down the insurrection. This greatly hampered British preparations for operations against the Japanese.

Order was eventually restored in the cities but regaining control in the rural areas proved much harder for the police. By the end of August 1942 around 2,500 people had been killed and 66,000 arrested. The trouble had died down and rail communications were restored by the middle of the following month. India, though, would have to wait until 1947 for independence.

Chapter 14

INDOCHINA In December 1941 Japanese troops passed through French Indochina to attack Thailand, Burma, Malaya and Singapore. The isolated Vichy authorities there were in no position to stop them. The Japanese also insisted on extensive basing rights. In March 1945 they completely occupied Indochina and disarmed the small French garrison, although part of it managed to escape to China. The Japanese permitted Vietnam, Cambodia and Laos to declare independence, though they were really puppet states.

The local Communists, known as the Viet Minh, under Ho Chi Minh were encouraged by the OSS to resist. In return for intelligence on the Japanese, the Viet Minh were supplied with American weapons. This would prove fatal to French authority. Ho Chi Minh, in co-operation with the non-Communist United Party, seized territory in the north, especially around Hanoi. Minh also had supporters in central and southern Vietnam.

The Viet Minh not only resisted the Japanese, but they also moved to eliminate those collaborating with the French colonial administration. They then waited for the end of the war with the intention of declaring independence. Following the Japanese surrender in August 1945 the Viet Minh filled the vacuum and declared the Democratic Republic of Vietnam, sparking the Indochina War with France.

MALAYA In Malaya, the SOE sought to encourage the population to resist the Japanese occupation. They did this by supplying weapons to the Malayan Communist Party and its guerrilla organization, the Malayan People's Anti-Japanese Army (MPAJA). This was largely composed of Chinese who had gone to Malaya looking for work in the tin mines and rubber plantations. Among its ranks was Chin Peng, future leader of the Malayan Communist Party. He worked as a liaison officer with the British. While the Japanese treated the Malays relatively leniently, they considered the Chinese outright enemies after their long war with China. Thousands of Chinese settlers were executed and thousands more fled into the jungle.

The MPAJA was never really tested in combat and at the end of the war, with the return of British rule, it was disbanded and handed over most of its weapons. In the late 1940s its members were recruited into the Malayan People's Anti-British Army, which became the Communist-dominated Malayan Races Liberation Army. This opposed the creation of the Federation of Malaya and sparked a long guerrilla war.

ASIA

CHINA While the Allies' preoccupation was fighting the Japanese in Burma and the Pacific, as well as supporting the Chinese Nationalists against the Japanese, countless forgotten guerrilla campaigns were fought across China. These resisted the Japanese and their Chinese proxies. In the 1920s and 1930s China was blighted by a Communist insurgency that waged a guerrilla war against the Nationalist government. Both sides temporarily buried their differences in the face of Japanese invasion in the late 1930s.

Resistance to Japanese occupation was swift. Chinese guerrillas in Shandong forced the Japanese to evacuate the road between Yantai and Weifang in early 1938. This opened up a large area of the province to guerrilla activity and they were able to retake Jinan and Yantai. By the spring, guerrilla operations had spread in southern Shandong, eastern Anhui and northern Jiangsu. Chinese partisans also penetrated Hangzhou, forcing the Japanese to conduct a five-pronged operation in the Jiangsu-Zhejiang-Anhui border area. Zhao Tong's guerrilla group even raided Beijing prison and released 570 prisoners under the very noses of the Japanese guards.

Chinese guerrillas in Guangzhou opposed to the Japanese occupation, February 1941.

Chapter 14

One of the most daring acts of resistance in the occupied parts of China occurred in the autumn of 1940. The valet of Fu Xiao'en, the mayor of Shanghai, was recruited to hack his master to death with a meat cleaver. This was the traditional punishment for a traitor. Although Fu Xiao'en was well-guarded by Japanese soldiers, the valet, with his weapon concealed up his sleeve, easily passed them. After the deed was done he escaped the city to join the guerrillas. Nationalist Juntong agents operating in concert with the Green Gang triad during 1937–41 murdered 150 Chinese collaborators and 40 Japanese officers in Shanghai. There was, however, no shortage of Chinese who were prepared to collaborate with the Japanese. One Chinese partisan recalled, 'Our work among the people is too inadequate [...] there are so many traitors [...] But they are driven by hunger and they are so ignorant.'

During the Sino-Japanese War the Japanese created a series of puppet states in their occupied zones of China. These included Peking (Beijing) in northern China, Nanking (Nanjing) in eastern central China, Shanghai in the east and Manchuria in the north-east. They were allowed to raise armies to help maintain law and order. Many of the recruits were deserters from the Nationalist Army. These forces fought alongside the Japanese against Communist and Nationalist guerrillas during the Second World War.

In 1940 the Japanese set up a puppet government in Nanking, under Wang Ching-wei, that was nominally in charge of all of China. Nanking troops conducted anti-guerrilla operations on their own behalf of the Japanese, but these were stopped following mass desertions. The Communists saw such forces as a welcome source of weapons, which were often handed over without a fight. The Nanking government collapsed in 1944 and many of its soldiers sided with the guerrillas. The Japanese consistently treated the Chinese with such appalling brutality that it constantly undermined their rule and fuelled resistance until the end of the Second World War.

FORMOSA (TAIWAN) The island of Formosa was annexed from China by Japan in 1895, becoming its first colony. Armed resistance by the Chinese had been overcome by 1902, though sporadic rebellions continued. However, the indigenous people in the mountains, who the Japanese tried to displace, resisted into the early 1930s. During the war, to head off further resistance, the Japanese recruited over 200,000 Formosans into their armed forces in non-combatant roles. Formosa was used as a naval base and airbase for the attacks on the Chinese island of Hainan and then the Philippines. Both would present major resistance to Japanese occupation.

HAINAN The Japanese invaded Hainan in 1939. The regular Chinese Nationalist forces under Wang Yi withdrew to the central mountains. There, the ethnic Li rebelled against them but were swiftly crushed with the loss of 7,000 people. Chinese Communists led by Feng Baiju and supported by the Li fought a guerrilla war against the Japanese in western Hainan. The Japanese responded by massacring 30,000 people in Danzhou. Feng and his men as well as Nationalist fighters continued to hold out until the end of the war. However, the partial occupation of the island enabled the Japanese to use it as a base for operations against Guangdong province and French Indochina.

KOREA Korea was annexed by Japan in 1910 following the Russo-Japanese War. Japan then proceeded to colonize the country. It also recruited Koreans into the Japanese armed forces and used them as slave labour throughout the Empire of Japan. All this led to the rise of the Korean independence movement. The Japanese suppressed all opposition in the Korean peninsula and thousands fled to China. From neighbouring Manchuria, numerous groups waged guerrilla warfare against the occupation, until the Japanese invaded Manchuria, forcing them back deeper into China and the Soviet Union.

Kim Il Sung, the future leader of North Korea, conducted armed resistance in the Sino-Korean border region after the Japanese created the puppet state of Manchukuo in Manchuria. Pursued by Japanese troops, he was forced into the Soviet Union in 1940, where he joined the Red Army. He was assigned to the 88th Separate Rifle Brigade, which was made up of Chinese, Koreans and Soviet Central Asians. It sent small groups into Manchuria and Korea to conduct intelligence-gathering and sabotage operations. By 1945 most of Kim Il Sung's comrades had been killed in the guerrilla war. His return home would eventually spark the Korean War in 1950.

MANCHURIA In the early 1930s the Japanese took over Manchuria's three provinces in north-eastern China, creating a puppet state known as Manchukuo. They appointed the last and deposed Chinese emperor, Pu Yi, to rule it. This process was overseen by Major General Togo, who was head of the Kempeitai, Japan's military police at the time. Large numbers of Japanese and Korean settlers moved into the region. The vastness of Manchuria made it impossible to completely control; large areas were infested by bandits and guerrillas.

In the north and east, Communist guerrillas resisted the Japanese and the Manchukuo Imperial Army throughout the 1930s and 1940s. The Japanese considered the latter unreliable and were reluctant to supply it with heavy equipment, such as artillery or tanks. They sent some of its units to Burma and Sumatra on garrison duties. Many of the Manchurian troops had no option but to serve the Japanese: their families were registered with the authorities and if they refused to fight or deserted, their loved ones faced execution. In August 1945 the Soviet Red Army stormed into Manchuria, which it then handed over to China's Communists. This provided them with a base from which to resume the Chinese Civil War and ultimately take power.

PACIFIC

NEW GUINEA The Japanese invaded the island of New Guinea, north-east of Australia, which was under the control of Australia and the Netherlands in 1942. The eastern half comprised Australian Papua and New Guinea and to the west, Dutch New Guinea. The Japanese occupied the northern half of the island along with the Bismarck Archipelago and the Solomon Islands to the east, which were under British rule.

In New Guinea, guerrilla skirmishes commenced in the Markham Valley and in the Owen Stanley Range. Attacks were carried out by the New Guinea Volunteer Rifles, supported by Papuan porters. As both sides poured in more troops, the fighting turned into full-scale jungle warfare. The Allies' main concern was to prevent the Japanese from taking Port Moresby.

In the occupied Dutch area, a guerrilla group, comprising four combat units, was led by Mauritz Christiaan Kokkelink and Willemsz Geeroms. They gathered intelligence and with the assistance of the native Papuans attacked Japanese patrols. Geeroms was eventually captured and beheaded by the Japanese. Pieter de Kock, with one of the units, fought on until October 1944, when they made contact with the Allies. Captain Jean Victor de Bruijn held out with a group of 40 Papuan and Indonesian supporters in the highland region of western New Guinea for two years. In July 1944 they were evacuated to avoid becoming trapped.

PHILIPPINES In late 1941 the Japanese invaded the US-controlled Philippines. They defeated the American and Filipino forces in Bataan and on Corregidor the following year. Some Filipino politicians were prepared to support the Japanese in order to protect their positions and in the hope of independence from the USA. Their administration, though, struggled to recruit security forces to assist the occupation.

Japanese brutality ensured most Filipinos remained loyal to the Allied war effort and many fled to the jungles to take up the fight against their occupiers. Numerous groups conducted guerrilla warfare against the Japanese, which resulted in them controlling some 60 per cent of the islands. During the war, half a million Filipinos would die.

In Central Luzon, the Communist-inspired People's Anti-Japanese Army numbered about 30,000. They not only fought the Japanese garrison, but also American-led guerrilla units. On Mindanao, there were almost 40,000 guerrillas under American Colonel Wendell Fertig. The Muslim Moro population on Mindanao also fought against the Japanese, as well as the Filipinos and Americans. Radio communication was lost with the resistance until late 1942, when the reformed Philippine 61st Division on Panay established contact with US headquarters in Australia. Supplies and radios were delivered to the resistance by US submarines.

The Japanese did not declare the Philippines an independent republic until October 1943. American troops under General MacArthur returned to the Philippines the following year on 20 October with an assault on the island of Leyte. At the end of the war the Japanese only controlled 12 of the 48 Filipino provinces. By this stage the resistance had around 260,000 men under arms, who continued to harass the Japanese until they surrendered. The USA granted the Philippines independence in 1946.

SOLOMON ISLANDS The British Solomon Islands, east of New Guinea, became the scene of fierce fighting between the Americans and the Japanese in 1943, most notably on Guadalcanal. They also hosted a major intelligence-gathering operation conducted by the Coastwatchers. This organization was created by Australia before the war and code-named 'Ferdinand'. Its members were initially recruited from civilians working as plantation managers and serving as district officers with the Colonial Service, but they were joined by Australian and New Zealand servicemen and islanders. The Coastwatchers monitored Japanese activity across the thousand islands making up the Solomons. Submarines were used to ferry them and reconnaissance teams between the islands. They were constantly at risk of ambush or capture by the Japanese.

The Coastwatchers were greatly assisted by the Solomon Islander Scouts and members of the British Solomon Islands Protectorate Defence Force. They also operated guerrilla groups, which conducted sabotage and generally harassed the Japanese. The success of Solomon islanders' ambushes against Japanese patrols became such that in late 1942 Japanese units would not go into the bush unless in strength. The Japanese took revenge for these attacks by destroying the islanders' canoes, churches and vital vegetable gardens. This did nothing but alienate the islanders further and made them more determined than ever to exact revenge on the invaders.

Coastwatcher Sergeant Major Jacob Vouza of the Defence Force was awarded the George Medal and Silver Star for courage and devotion to duty after being captured and tortured by the Japanese. Despite being terribly wounded, he escaped and warned the Allies about a surprise Japanese attack on Guadalcanal. In 1943 the Scouts helped rescue future US president John F. Kennedy after his torpedo boat was rammed by a Japanese destroyer west of Kolombangara Island.

TIMOR The island of Timor, north-west of Australia, was divided in two with West Timor ruled by the Dutch and East Timor by the Portuguese. In 1941 the Allies occupied Dili but were thrown out when the Japanese invaded both halves of the island the following year. The mountainous interior became the scene of a vicious guerrilla war. This was waged by survivors from Sparrow Force, which consisted of Australian, Dutch and British troops.

Notably, in the south and east of Timor, Australian guerrillas successfully tied down a Japanese division and killed about 1,500 men. Although Portugal was neutral, many Portuguese civilians as well as Dutch and Timorese fought with the Allies. After the Australians withdrew in early 1943 some Timorese continued to resist. Japanese reprisals resulted in the death of up to 70,000 civilians. Timor remained under brutal Japanese control until the end of the war.

Part 6

Opposition Within the Axis

Chapter 15

Defying Militarism

GERMANY

Nazi Germany was a highly effective police state that stamped out dissidents with unwavering brutality. This made resistance to Hitler's government extremely tough. Over the years, though, there were numerous plots to kill him. During the war the only coherent opposition emerged from within the German military, most notably among officers serving with Army Group Centre. Some veterans increasingly felt that Hitler's conduct of the war was leading their country to ruin and were prepared to take matters into their own hands. Colonel Henning von Tresckow, one of the leading plotters, served as Field Marshal Günther von Kluge's chief of staff at Army Group Centre. This command played a key role in a series of failed assassination attempts on Hitler.

Colonel Rudolf Christoph Freiherr von Gersdorff, Army Group Centre's intelligence officer, later admitted: 'One of the most active cells in the conspiracy was to be found in the staff of Army Group Centre on the Eastern Front, in which I was G2 [intelligence] from 1941 to 1943. It is here that we meet von Tresckow, at that time a colonel in the General Staff and G3 [operations] of the Army Group.' Gersdorff was impressed by him and sympathetic to the anti-Hitler cause, adding, 'A man of dominating personality, he handled with great energy both discussion and action. […] he turned to me in early 1942, as I remember, with his first request to prepare the explosive and fuse for the actual attempt.'

Nonetheless, killing Hitler was not something to be undertaken lightly. Gersdorff was rightly worried about the impact removing Hitler would have on the German war effort. 'The conspirators fully realised that the existence and unity of the German Army must not be jeopardised by the planned coup

Chapter 15

d'état,' he noted. 'A Russian breakthrough on the Eastern Front would bring chaos to the heart of Europe; Germany would be overrun by millions of Slavs and Asiatics.'

Regardless of these concerns an attempt was made on Hitler's life on 13 March 1943 when he flew from his Werwolf (Werewolf) forward headquarters near Vinnitsa in central Ukraine to the Wolfsschanze (Wolf's Lair) outside Rastenburg in East Prussia. He broke his journey by stopping at Army Group Centre's headquarters at Smolensk. 'The first assassination attempt was carried out by Tresckow,' recalled Gersdorff. Tresckow personally escorted Hitler from the airfield with the intention of placing a bomb in the side pocket of the staff car, next to where Hitler was to sit. He failed in this and the bomb was instead put on Hitler's plane. It was timed to explode near Minsk so that it would appear Hitler had been shot down by the Red Air Force. The bomb failed to detonate and Hitler was not shot down.

Gersdorff made a second attempt a week later when Hitler was visiting Berlin's old armoury, called the Zeughaus, on Unter den Linden. According to Gersdorff's account, 'Army Group Centre had prepared in the armoury in Berlin an exhibition of captured Russian arms and equipment, war pictures, models etc, and a few days prior to 15 March 1943 General Schmundt gave out information that Hitler would personally open the exhibition on the occasion of Heroes Memorial Day.'

As an expert on Russian equipment, Gersdorff was an ideal guide. Unfortunately, on 21 March Hitler hurried through the exhibits with such speed that Gersdorff was obliged to defuse his bomb. This second failure temporarily discouraged the plotters at Army Group Centre. Gersdorff's role was not discovered and he returned to the Eastern Front. In 1944 he transferred to Army Group B in France, where he served with valour during the Battle for Normandy, leading the escape of several thousand men from the Falaise pocket.

The plotters had not given up. Hitler was thoroughly distracted from the conduct of the war by an almost successful attempt on his life at the Wolf's Lair in the summer of 1944. This was carried out by veteran Colonel Claus von Stauffenberg, who had gone to a meeting with Hitler carrying a briefcase containing a bomb. This he left under a table in the conference room. Although four people were killed and 20 injured, Hitler, screened by a table leg, survived the blast with only minor injuries. As a result, a planned coup in Berlin, which was to announce a new government, quickly collapsed.

'On the evening of 22 July,' recalled Lieutenant Armin Scheiderbauer of the 252nd Infantry Division, 'it was announced that an assassination attempt had been made on the Führer on 20 July. Among us there was more surprise than fury.' After hearing of the failure of the bomb plot, Tresckow, who was on the Eastern Front, wandered out into some woods and killed himself using a grenade.

Hitler's sense of betrayal knew no limits and resulted in a bloody purge. He spent the following weeks devoting his time and that of the Gestapo to tracking down the plotters. This was at a critical period for both the Eastern and Western Fronts, where the Allies were making considerable progress against his forces. In total, some 7,000 people were arrested and almost 5,000 executed, including Stauffenberg. Many of the latter had nothing to do with the plot whatsoever but fell foul of the Gestapo for their political views.

Hitler's trust in the German army plummeted further when Field Marshals von Kluge and Rommel took their own lives to avoid public disgrace over their complicity. Although neither had been active supporters of the plotters, von Kluge knew about Tresckow's plan to shoot Hitler during a visit to Army

The shattered conference room where Hitler was almost killed on 20 July 1944.

Group Centre. He had been informed by his former subordinate, Georg von Boeselager, who served under Tresckow. Boeselager was dispatched by Tresckow in mid-1944 to urge his old commander to change his strategy and to join the conspiracy against Hitler. Kluge, though, had waivered.

Trying to claim credit for the army and the upper classes, Gersdorff concludes, 'In closing, it must be said that the conspiracy of 20 July was the only active effort to overthrow the National Socialist government and to remove the chief criminals. It should be emphasised that this only attempt was planned and executed by members of the officer corps and that the dominant role was played by the General Staff, the nobility, and the large landowners.' The resistance had failed.

AUSTRIA

Austria, following Anschluss with Germany in 1938, was fully integrated within the Nazi security apparatus, so any resistance was inevitably penetrated by Nazi spies and sympathizers. In April 1945 the approaching Red Army called on the Viennese to revolt against German rule. 'People of Vienna help the Red Army liberate your city,' Marshal Tolbukhin declared, 'and make your contribution to the liberation of Austria from Nazi tyranny.'

A delegation from the clandestine Austrian Resistance Movement informed Tolbukhin that the citizens of Vienna were ready to rise up. They said two reserve infantry battalions and an artillery battery under Major Karl Sololl were poised to take up arms against their one-time allies. Another 1,200 soldiers from various other units were also reportedly prepared to support a rebellion. In addition, up to 20,000 inhabitants were ready to help kick out the German administration. Tolbukhin instructed them to take and guard the city's vital Danube bridges and key communication centres and to attack German military facilities and police headquarters. The Soviet press reported: 'The Viennese are helping the Red Army, and they fully understand that the Soviet Union is not fighting against Austrians.'

The Viennese uprising was timed for 12:30 hours on 6 April 1945, to provide a diversion for the Red Army. Tolbukhin published an appeal to the city, 'People of Vienna […] The hour of the liberation […] has come, but the retreating German troops are out to turn the city into a battlefield just as they did in Budapest. This threatens […] the same destruction and horrors that were inflicted by the Germans on Budapest and its inhabitants.' He went on to urge the population to remain in the city to help protect Vienna's historic artworks, buildings and monuments from damage.

Although the Soviets hoped that the Austrian Resistance Movement would hand over the city intact, they were partly thwarted in this by the presence of the SS and the German 6th Panzer Division. Furthermore, the Germans were tipped off and the very morning of the uprising many of the resistance leaders were swiftly arrested and shot. Nonetheless, the Soviet official history claimed that Tolbukhin's appeal had the desired effect: 'The response was immediate, and many Viennese took part in the fighting against the invaders.' In reality, most feeling trapped in the middle stayed at home and prayed for it all to be over. Nonetheless, by 7 April the Red Army was in Vienna's southern suburbs and the following day entered the western suburbs, followed by the eastern and northern ones. The German defence quickly disintegrated.

BULGARIA During the Second World War a little-known guerrilla war was fought in Bulgaria. Although the Bulgarians joined the Axis alliance in March 1941, it was an uneasy relationship. They took part in the invasions of Greece and Yugoslavia but then tried to keep out of the war. Despite Bulgaria successfully resisting calls to join the war in Russia, it did provide reinforcements to alleviate pressure on German security forces in the Balkans. Bulgaria's biggest concern was the potential of war with Turkey should it side with the Allies. Resistance to Hitler's wishes by King Boris III of Bulgaria proved fatal. Following a meeting with Hitler in the summer of 1943 he was allegedly poisoned for refusing to declare war on the Soviet Union and to deport Bulgarian Jews. Many Bulgarians then took to the hills to oppose the country's role in the Axis.

By the summer of 1944 Hitler's relationship with Bulgaria was rapidly deteriorating. The Bulgarian army, in addition to its commitments in Greece and Yugoslavia, at home found itself countering some 18,000 Bulgarian partisans, known as the People's Liberation Army. Other factions numbered about 12,000. They were fighting to bring down the government and extricate the country from the war. These groups suffered heavy casualties in engagements with the Bulgarian army and police.

When Romania swapped sides in August 1944, Bulgaria began secretly negotiating with the Allies. On 5 September 1944 the Soviet Union declared war on Bulgaria and three days later commenced hostilities. The Bulgarians sought to save themselves by declaring war on Germany. The factory workers downed tools in Sofia on 6 September and three days later an armed uprising took place in the city. Bulgarian troops, though, offered no resistance and in many cases they joined the insurgents. The Red Army rolled into Sofia on 15 September 1944. After that the Bulgarians fought alongside the Russians in the Balkans against the Germans.

CZECHOSLOVAKIA

Czechoslovakia languished under German control from the late 1930s until the arrival of the Red Army in 1945. The country had been divided up into the Protectorate of Bohemia and Moravia and the Slovak Republic, both of which were Nazi satellite states.

SLOVAKIA

In the spring of 1944 Soviet troops reached Slovakia's frontier. Slovak partisans were transported from the Soviet Union to join other resistance groups. That summer they began operations against the Germans and the Slovak government. They were joined by part of the Slovak army, which had fought on the Eastern Front supporting the Axis. By the end of August they had taken control of much of central and north-eastern Slovakia. German troops, while holding off the Red Army, proceeded to crush the rising by the end of October. The remaining partisans were forced back into the mountains to await the liberation of Bratislava by the Russians.

BOHEMIA AND MORAVIA

The Czechs likewise had to wait until the end of the war to throw off Nazi control. Limited fighting broke out in Prague on 1 May 1945 with a general uprising four days later. The tension was ramped up on the afternoon of 4 May when a German prison train tried to leave, carrying political prisoners. Angry inhabitants surrounded it and demanded the release of the captives. When a German guard lifted his rifle and aimed at the crowd he was shot by a Czech policeman. Around the city, German-language signs were torn down and Czech and Allied flags began to appear. German soldiers caught on their own on the streets were accosted by hostile locals and disarmed.

General Kutlvašr launched his uprising on 5 May 1945 in the Old Town Square. While the Germans were distracted by demonstrators in

Wenceslas Square a convoy of armed insurgents made their way towards the Old Town Hall and the Radio Building. Crucially for the rebels, they were joined by the police and the protectorate guard. This meant that Kutlvašr was able to talk to the insurgents throughout the city via the police communications network.

Several hundred Czechs barricaded themselves in the Old Town Hall, though they were critically short of weapons. At the Radio Building the staff blocked the entrances and issued a plea for help. Broadcasting in Czech they said, 'We appeal to all members of the police, army and government to join the patriots who are already defending our radio station.'

German troops tried to secure the Radio Building by infiltrating across the rooftops. From there they managed to gain entry to the upper storeys. Kutlvašr sent a battalion of Czech police to drive them out. The fighting was at close quarter as the Czechs fought their way along the corridors, forcing the Germans into the basement. Explosives were hurled down the stairwells to finish them off. The Czech National Council announced at 14:00 hours that the Nazi puppet Protectorate of Bohemia and Moravia was at an end.

By the evening of 5 May around 30,000 Czech insurgents had seized the city's central telephone exchange, post office, power station, the radio station, most of the railway stations and the bridges over the Vltava. Some 1,600 barricades appeared overnight to impede German military movement. The workers rose up in Kladno to the north-west of Prague, one of the largest industrial centres, followed by those in Pilsen.

The following day the Germans launched a series of counter-attacks, pushing the insurgents back into the city centre. The Czechs had few anti-tank weapons and were unable to prevent the panzers from smashing their barricades. However, in the face of the advancing Red Army it became increasingly obvious that the Germans would have to withdraw or become trapped. This they did and the Russians entered the city from multiple directions on 9 May 1945, to be greeted by joyous citizens.

ITALY

Italy, rather like France after its defeat, ended up partitioned following Mussolini's fall from power in the summer of 1943. Hitler, in response to Allied landings in Sicily and then the Italian mainland, occupied northern Italy as well as Rome. Mussolini was rescued and installed as the head of a fascist puppet government in the north. Italy, once a staunch German ally, became a battlefield on multiple fronts.

In the south, the new government sided with the Allies while in the north, Italian Communist partisans resisted the Germans and Mussolini's fascist military. The partisans also fought each other. This plunged the country into a terrible civil war. The conflict in Italy proved more bitter than in any other western European country.

Resistance in the north escalated during the first half of 1944. The fall of Cassino and the subsequent Allied liberation of Rome in June 1944 sped up the Allies' advance. The partisans used terror tactics, which sparked bloody reprisals by the Germans. However, by the winter the Allies were tied down by the Germans on the Gothic Line, which forced the partisans to scale down their activities. It has also been argued the Allies deliberately reduced their logistical support to prevent the Communists from seizing power in the north.

The guerrilla forces comprising Communist, Socialist and Christian Democratic brigades numbered about 250,000. During April 1945 there were major partisan risings in Genova, Milan and Torino. The partisans caught Mussolini and executed him on 28 April. Following the Allied victory the partisans embarked on an orgy of retribution.

JAPAN

There was surprisingly some resistance to Japanese militarism within the country and outside. This was usually passive in nature, although there were strikes and sabotage in Japan's weapons factories. A report in July 1944 estimated that 10 per cent of aircraft produced were defective. Absenteeism among factory workers was also a problem. Pacifists and other anti-war campaigners were targeted by the Tokkō and imprisoned, where they were maltreated.

There was a low level of resistance to war within the Japanese armed forces, especially from Communist sympathizers and other left-wing supporters. The Japanese Communist Party had been banned in Japan since the mid-1920s. In China, some Japanese deserters and prisoners joined the Chinese resistance. Founded in China in 1939, the League to Raise the Political Consciousness of Japanese Troops sought to recruit prisoners of war to the Chinese Communist cause. Similarly, the Japanese People's Anti-War Alliance formed in China in 1942 appealed to Japanese soldiers to surrender or refuse to fight and to take part in the anti-war movement. The Chinese Nationalists disbanded it, fearing it was a Communist organization similar to the Japanese People's Emancipation League/Japanese People's Liberation Alliance. The latter operated in Chinese-liberated areas. Japanese resistance on the whole never seriously affected Japan's war effort.

Chapter 16

The Jews Fight Back

Hitler conducted a secret war of extermination against Europe's Jews. Although word leaked out about his Final Solution, no one wanted to believe the enormity of what was happening. Not all Jews went passively to their deaths. Some took up arms and fought back, determined to die on their own terms. Warsaw, after the conquest and dismemberment of Poland, became a police state. By 1943 the German garrison included some 6,000 military police. German was made the official language and the Germans controlled the media. Many buildings and streets were given German names. Apartheid became a way of life with 'Germans Only' signs springing up throughout Warsaw. Any resistance was punishable by firing squad or hanging. Hans Frank, the German governor, authorized the Gestapo to shoot on suspicion in the autumn of 1943

WARSAW GHETTO

That year Warsaw became the scene of a horrific tragedy. It occurred because of Hitler's abhorrent anti-Semitic policies and his determination to wipe out the Jews. The previous year the Communist underground become active and the Germans escalated their arrests, especially in the Polish capital. Mass shootings also escalated outside Warsaw. The Germans then decided to liquidate the Jewish Warsaw ghetto. This had not existed before the war but the Germans had started segregating the population on the basis of Jewish and non-Jewish in November 1939.

All non-Jews in the designated ghetto area were expelled and the city's Jews were herded in and surrounded by a wall. The latter was 6 m (20 ft) high and topped with barbed wire. It was patrolled by armed guards, who shot any Jews caught outside the ghetto without permission. There were two areas west of the Vistula joined by a footbridge known as the 'Large' and 'Small' ghettos. The former was some three times the size of its southern neighbour. The 'Small Ghetto' was filled with affluent residents and was considered the better place to live. In October 1940 Hitler's henchmen decided that Warsaw would be a good place to gather all European Jews.

The Gestapo controlled the Jewish population with the assistance of the Ghetto Police and the Jewish Council. The two prisons operated by the Gestapo, the 'Pawiak' and the 'Serbia', were inside the ghetto perimeter. This meant that all those non-Jews who were arrested in Warsaw were sent there for interrogation, torture, execution or shipment to the concentration camps.

At first those in the ghetto were free to pass through the gates during the daytime as long as they were wearing a yellow Star of David. Then from 15 October 1941 the gates were sealed and the ghetto effectively became a concentration camp. The following year the forced deportations to the death camps started. By then children living on the streets had begun to die of starvation despite the presence of some well-stocked food shops.

THE FINAL SOLUTION

Around 380,000 Jews from Poland and across Europe were crammed in the ghetto under the administration of the SS-appointed Council of Jewish Elders. Inside, communication was a problem, as the Poles spoke Polish or Yiddish so could not easily understand the German, French and Greek Jews. Every day 5,000 were sent to the gas chambers at the Treblinka concentration camp.

A Jewish policeman called Szmerling, known as 'the Jewish Torturer', oversaw this process at the Umschlagplatz (Collection Point) rail siding. This was located at the northern edge of the 'Large Ghetto' and was concealed from the rest of the area. The entrance was near the junction of Zamenhoff and Low Streets and led via a maze of pathways to an open square. From there the people were herded into an old hospital forecourt, where they spent the night before being put into cattle trucks in the morning. Around 150,000 Jews had been murdered in this way by early August 1942.

In October 1942 the Germans set up a little-known concentration camp within the city limits known as KZ Warschau. It consisted of five sub-camps linked by railway lines. Two were located in the area of the ghetto and two were near Warsaw's Western Station. The fifth had served as a transit camp for prisoners of war. The KZ Warschau complex had space for over 41,000 inmates. It included gas chambers. The camps operated until August 1944, by which time up to 200,000 people had died there.

Although conditions in the ghetto were increasingly appalling, the Jews remained compliant for fear of repercussions. By 10 September 1942 there were just 30,000 left with another 40,000 in hiding across the city. In desperation, the underground Polish Home Army offered to conduct diversionary attacks if there was a Jewish revolt. However, the ghetto's leaders felt it best if they continued co-operating with the Nazis. The younger Jews, though, decided to fight back and created the Jewish Fighting Organization. The Home Army did what it could to assist smuggling in small quantities of arms and ammunition.

WARSAW RISING

Reichsführer-SS Himmler made a surprise visit to Warsaw in January 1943 to see how the liquidation of the Jews was progressing. By now the remaining Jews were confined to an area of just over 2.6 sq km (1 sq mile). It was evident that at this rate the Jewish presence in the city could not last much longer.

Himmler, convinced his work was almost done, ordered the complete destruction of the Warsaw ghetto by 16 February 1943. In light of commitments elsewhere, especially at Stalingrad, there were not the resources to carry this out. SS-Oberführer von Sammern-Frankenegg was initially in charge but was relieved by SS-Brigadeführer Jürgen Stroop. He commenced the operation on 19 April. The units involved were largely newly formed and consisted of two reserve SS training battalions, plus some army cavalry and Panzergrenadiers. In all they numbered just over 2,000 men. The SS was reinforced by Lithuanian militia and some Polish police and firemen.

Himmler did not oversee things personally and hurried back to Berlin. It was anticipated that this 'special action' would last just three days – in the event it took four weeks. Earlier in the month a Jewish revolt had brought the deportations to a halt. The resistance killed some of the Jewish collaborators and built barricades. These fighters belonged to either the Jewish Fighting Organization or the Jewish Military Union. They then waited for the inevitable German assault. About 600 armed Jews stopped the initial attack but the Germans quickly brought up artillery with which to bombard their positions.

'Hardly had [the] operation begun,' reported Stroop, 'than we ran into strong concerted fire by the Jews and bandits.' A panzer and two armoured cars leading the advance were attacked using Molotov cocktails and forced to retreat. 'About 1730 hours we encountered very strong resistance from one block of buildings, including machine gun fire,' adds Stroop. A German assault party stormed the buildings but the Jews slipped away. Stroop's first attack cost him 12 men. On the second night the Red Air Force bombed the city but it did little to help the uprising.

BATTLE FOR SURVIVAL

Slowly but surely the defenders were driven back by Stroop's artillery, flame-throwers and tanks. Stroop was baffled by why the Jews did not simply give up. During the first phase of his operation it was possible to round up large numbers of Jews; by the second phase it had become much more difficult. As soon as resistance was overcome his forces would encounter another Jewish battle group of 20–30 men supported by a similar number of women. The latter fought using pistols and hand grenades.

By day five Himmler was getting increasingly impatient for results. 'I therefore decided,' said Stroop, 'to destroy the entire Jewish area by setting every block on fire.' He hoped this would drive the Jews out but many preferred to perish. His flame-throwers rapidly helped set the ghetto ablaze. The flames were soon threatening the factories that made spare parts and uniforms for the Germans. However, when the Polish fire brigade turned up to try and prevent the fire from spreading they were stopped by the SS. The Jewish fighters trapped in the burning buildings were forced to jump from the upper storeys. Those who survived tried to reach the neighbouring blocks, but most were too badly injured or were shot.

Himmler was informed on 25 April that 27,464 Jews had been captured. Many were sent to Treblinka. The following day Stroop signalled to Himmler to report that his forces had killed 362 Jews in 'battle' and shot another 1,330. Just 30 prisoners were taken. In early May the Germans rounded up members of the Jewish Council and executed them. Community Chairman Chernyakov took his own life. In London, Shmuel Zigelbaum, a member of the National Council of the Polish Government in Exile, also committed suicide to draw attention to the terrible plight of the ghetto. The fighting continued. Stroop even resorted to flooding the sewers in an effort to flush out the remaining Jews. His men then dropped smoke bombs down the manholes.

Jewish resistance was finally overcome on 16 May 1943. 'One hundred and eight Jews, bandits and subhumans were destroyed,' reported Stroop triumphantly. 'The former Jewish quarter of Warsaw is no longer in existence.' At 20:15 hours his men blew up the Warsaw Synagogue.

According to Stroop's figures, 56,065 Jews were killed or captured. This included 7,000 killed in the ghetto and 6,929 sent to Treblinka. A further 6,000 perished in the flames of the burning ghetto. This left around 36,000 unaccounted for but it was assumed they had gone to the gas chambers. Stroop claimed he had lost 16 dead and 90 wounded, but this seemed suspiciously low.

Stroop treated the destruction of the ghetto as if it were a military campaign rather than a police operation. His 75-page report and photographs were bound as an album called *The Warsaw Ghetto is No More!* and presented to Himmler. The latter used this to convince Hitler that the Jews had built strongpoints in the ghetto and that the SS had fought a real battle.

REVENGE

The Warsaw ghetto was not the only one, as the Germans established similar ghettos elsewhere – most notably at Lodz, where up to 250,000 Jews were herded together. There was no rebellion. In September 1942 17,000 people were removed and killed. In December of that year another 25,000 suffered the same fate. There were just 74,000 left by the beginning of January 1944. Himmler gave the order to liquidate the Lodz ghetto on 10 June 1944. By the time the Red Army arrived there were just 850 people remaining.

In the wake of the destruction of the Warsaw ghetto the Polish Home Army stepped up its attacks on the occupiers. A casino frequented by German officers was blown up. The Gestapo and German police were attacked on the streets. Five insurgents gunned down SS-Oberscharführer Franz Bürkl, the deputy commander of Pawiak prison on 7 September 1943. In the western Praga district, fuel supplies for the German armed forces were set alight. Then on 8 October the Home Army blew up all the railway lines leading out of the city. This paralyzed supplies being sent to the Eastern Front. The Polish Home Army would not follow the Jews' example of rising up until August 1944, with similarly tragic results.

Part 7

Scientific War

Chapter 17

Radar Wars

While the spying, eavesdropping, deception and resistance behind the lines was going on, so too was a top-secret hi-tech scientific struggle. The Allies and the Axis each turned to technology to give them a decisive advantage. Scientific developments made during the 1930s were turned to military use on land, air and sea. This then spawned ever more sophisticated counter-measures. The scientific war became like a giant game of chess with each side trying to predict the other's next move with their technological advances.

POWER OF RADAR

After the Fall of France in June 1940, in the air battle that was to follow, Britain had one key technological advantage: early warning radar known as Radio Direction Finding or RDF for short. This was RAF Fighter Command's eye in the sky. By 1940 Britain had 18 large Chain Home radar stations covering the southern and eastern coast stretching from the Isle of Wight to Scotland. These could detect aircraft out to 290 km (180 miles) and up to 5,490 m (18,000 ft). Below 915 m (3,000 ft) was covered by the Chain Home Low stations.

While British radar at the time was good at tracking targets over the sea, it was not so efficient over land. This gap was filled by the eyeballs of the Observer Corps. Its volunteers were tasked with the visual detection, identification and tracking of aircraft over Britain. Once the Phoney War came to an end the Observer Corps had their hands full monitoring the Luftwaffe and passing intelligence to RAF Fighter Command. Thanks to the vital part it played in Britain's early warning system, King George VI in the spring of 1941 made it the Royal Observer Corps.

Edward Fennessy, a radar expert at the Air Ministry, knew in the run-up to the Battle of Britain that the RAF's radar network was at risk: 'General

Chapter 17

Martini, the Luftwaffe Chief Signals Officer, had by this time a pretty shrewd idea that we had an RDF system operational and he had to argue very forcibly with Göring to allow the Luftwaffe to attack the RDF stations.' These attacks started on 12 August 1940. However, it proved difficult to damage the RDF sites. Unless struck by a direct hit, the British radar masts proved blast-proof. German bombers could not see the masts from the air and even dive-bomber attacks were not very effective.

'The lattice masts can't be seen from the air,' noted Ernest Clark, a wireless operator at one of the stations, 'and they were so designed that they could stand up on any two of their gimbals. And the blast used to go through them.' That day, the Luftwaffe tried to destroy the radar stations at Folkstone, Pevensey, Rye and Ventnor. Only the latter on the Isle of Wight remained off air for three weeks; the others were back up and operating within hours. The following day the Luftwaffe's massed assault went horribly wrong.

On 18 August 1940 the Poling Chain Home and Chain Home Low radar stations were attacked by 31 German Stuka dive-bombers. They dropped a total of 80 bombs and hit only one Chain Home receiving mast, taking off the top. The Germans completely missed the Low installation. Nor were any of the radar staff injured. The radar was fixed within three days. The failure to silence Britain's radars convinced Göring that he was wasting his time and fortuitously for Fighter Command, he ordered that there be no further attacks.

During the Battle of Britain the RAF had the advantage of early warning radar.

In contrast, in the Pacific, the newly installed radar on Oahu did nothing to prevent the surprise Japanese air attack on the US naval base at Pearl Harbor in December 1941. A radar warning system had been set up that summer but it functioned on a part-time basis. The radar was only operated from 04:00 to 07:00 hours. The situation was further aggravated by a turf war between the US Signals Corps and the Army Air Corps. As a result, the Americans were caught completely by surprise.

BATTLE OF THE BEAMS

Dr Reginald Victor Jones had started the war as a scientific officer serving on the staff of the Air Ministry looking at air defence. He was soon facing numerous challenges. Another scientific struggle took place during the Battle of Britain, especially after the German bombers turned their attentions from the RAF's airfields to Britain's cities. The ferocity of the resistance by RAF Fighter Command eventually forced the Luftwaffe to stop daylight raids after October 1940. Celestial navigation was notoriously ineffective, so the Luftwaffe employed radio navigation for night bombing during the Blitz.

At Bletchley, a new Enigma system, which the code breakers in Hut 6 called 'Brown', started to be used on a communication link between a Luftwaffe base in France and a German experimental research establishment that was developing navigational beams. Professor Frederick 'Bimbo' Norman in Hut 3 called Dr Jones, who knew this information would be vital in him devising counter-measures to the beams.

Beam radio navigation had originally been developed in the 1930s as a blind landing aid. This technology was essentially reversed. The Germans had two systems, known as Knickebein (Crooked Leg) and X-Gerät (X-Apparatus). These greatly helped bombers find their targets in the opening stages of the Blitz, which lasted until May 1941. Dr Jones was in the forefront of British efforts trying to counter this.

Jones, thanks to the prior intelligence, on 21 June 1940 had the RAF put up aircraft to locate the two Knickebein radio signals, which crossed over at the intended target. Once they had verified the correct frequency Jones built jammers that 'bent' the signal by sending a counter-signal diverting the German bombers off-course, resulting in them dropping their bombs over open countryside. 'The knowledge that Knickebein was jammed spread through the Luftwaffe and there was a story […] that although the pilots were well aware of it,' explains Jones, 'no one wanted to take responsibility [...] with the result that Knickebein was persisted in for the next two months although it was substantially useless.'

It did not take Jones and his team long to find the ground stations. 'On 8th September Enigma gave us the pinpoint to the nearest mile of the Cherbourg Knickebein,' he wrote. This was then confirmed through reconnaissance photographs. The RAF now knew exactly what they were looking for.

When the Luftwaffe realized what was happening it sparked the Battle of the Beams, with the Germans developing new systems, which the British then had to counter.

The more sophisticated X-Gerät employed a series of beams named after German rivers. Weser, the first, was the main navigational beam, which was crossed by three single beams: Rhine, Oder and Elbe. These guided the navigator on how far the aircraft was from the target. This added complexity made it much more difficult to counter. X-Gerät was employed for a series of raids code-named by the Germans 'Moonlight Sonata', against Coventry, Birmingham and Wolverhampton. Fortunately for the British, they successfully salvaged X-Gerät equipment from a ditched bomber on 6 November 1941. This enabled Jones and his team to modify the jammers.

Jones was also prepared for the introduction of Y-Gerät thanks to Enigma decrypts and the Oslo Report written by Hans Ferdinand Mayer. The Germans had code-named it 'Wotan', who was a one-eyed god. This tipped off Jones that it used a single beam. The bombers did not track this; instead, they were directed by a ground station. The BBC transmitter at Alexandra Palace was used to intercept the return signal, and this was retransmitted, causing feedback.

Eventually this forced the Luftwaffe to give up using electronic navigation aids against Britain. 'By February 1941 the Battle of the Beams was as good as won,' said Dr Jones. 'We had another three months of bombing to endure, but all three major German systems, Knickebein, and X and Y, were defeated.' By the spring the Luftwaffe's bombers were not only missing their targets, but they were also suffering heavy losses.

BLINDING THE GERMANS

By 1944 Dr Jones and his colleagues were grappling with numerous intelligence problems. He recalled, 'At the same time as we were watching the flying bomb trials, dealing with the Baby Blitz, and wrestling with the

German night defences, another problem was approaching its climax: this was the coming operation to land in force in Normandy. Ever since 1940 I had known what my part must be, whether or not it was formally assigned to me: to see that everything possible was done to knock out by jamming, deception, or direct action, the chain of coastal radar stations that the Germans would inevitably build up.'

Jones, his fellow scientists and the intelligence gatherers had catalogued 600 German radar installations serving 200 stations. These extended from Bayonne in western France to Skagen in northern Denmark. Such a vast sweep seemed wholly unnecessary, but Jones pointed out, 'Even though we knew that the attack was to be made in Normandy, we covered a very much wider coastline, so that if any leakage of information were to occur, the Germans would have no clue regarding the selected area.'

Prior to D-Day Jones had co-opted RAF Rhubarb missions, whereby although they had no specific tasking, they collected intelligence on German radars even when not specifically targeting them. When Jones approached Air Marshal Arthur Tedder to ask what the Allies intended to do about Hitler's coastal radars, Tedder admitted that little thought had been given to this issue. A team was immediately set up ready to target Hitler's radars in the run-up to D-Day.

Jones set about coming up with the best way to destroy the enemy's radars. He appreciated that there were three options in dealing with them: they could be deceived, jammed or destroyed. A very low-tech solution had been found in 1942. Dr Robert Cockburn devised 'Window', essentially foil strips designed to fool enemy radar during bombing raids. Jones reasoned that if they destroyed some of the stations the remaining ones would not fully appreciate the significance of jamming and 'Window' when the time came.

The Allies then deliberately blinded the Germans along the English Channel by knocking out the radars. This had to be done in such a manner as not to alert the Germans as to the true location of the amphibious assault. Rocket-armed RAF Typhoon fighter-bombers played a key role in these operations, striking sites from Ostend to Cherbourg and the Channel Islands. To help foster the illusion that the Pas-de-Calais was the most likely crossing point some radars in this area were left alone. Along the coast, out of 92 radar sites only 18 were operational by the time of D-Day, and they were to be further misled by dummy invasion fleets.

Cockburn reasoned that 'Window' could be used to create the impression of vast armadas. The first was to cover an area 26 km (16 miles) long and 22.5 km (14 miles) wide. Motor launches would also be deployed under the 'Window' to boost and extend the radar echoes. It was therefore important that the Fécamp radar station be left functioning. Squadron Leader John Shannon, 617 Squadron, who was to be involved recalled, 'The operation was called Operation *Taxable* and it was one of the biggest spoofs ever played on the Germans.'

German air defence radars were to be jammed by a large-scale operation. According to RAF radar and jamming expert, Sergeant Jack Nissen, 'Two hundred ships were each equipped with two to three kilowatts of Mandrel jammers, which were used on that "one-night-only" basis. When Eisenhower said "Go", everybody on board their ships, wherever they were, threw this big master switch.' The jammers would create 'hash' on German radar screens, which was consistent with a faulty valve. The hope was that the operators would wait till morning before calling the engineer, by which time it would be too late.

GERMAN COUNTER-MEASURES

The Germans were fully aware of the Allies' radar-jamming capabilities. Reichsmarschall Hermann Göring, commander of the Luftwaffe, grumbled, 'Whatever the equipment we have, the enemy can jam it without so much as a by-your-leave.' Amazingly, the Germans had been incredibly slow, if not downright resistant, to waging electronic warfare. Ironically, General Wolfgang Martini, the Luftwaffe's Chief of Air Signals, opposed a jamming campaign against the British on the grounds that: 'There is a simple means whereby the enemy can jam our entire radar system, against which we have no antidote.' As a result, no research was carried out for six months.

Their hand was forced once RAF Bomber Command started employing 'Window'. In light of his lack of counter-measures against British radar, Göring had raged at Martini, 'What am I supposed to tell the Führer! He would think me a complete nincompoop if I repeated to him what you tell me.' Infuriated by Martini's intransigence, and what he saw as incompetence, Göring took responsibility for electronic research and development from him.

The Germans eventually developed jamming transmitters to interfere with radar carried by Allied bombers. British intelligence erroneously concluded that

Sonar helped locate, track and destroy Hitler's U-boats.

the Germans had 23 jamming stations, but only five of these were confirmed and only four were in the D-Day invasion area. These could interfere with the assault fleet's navigational aids.

LISTENING AT SEA

Just before the Second World War broke out Germany had 17 U-boats deployed in the Atlantic and 14 in the North Sea. The Battle of the Atlantic commenced the very day that Britain declared war on Germany. The first victim of the U-boat war was the passenger liner SS *Athenia*, which was sunk on 3 September 1939 on the way from Glasgow to Montreal by *U-30*. The vessel went down with 128 passengers and crew. The aircraft carrier HMS *Courageous* was torpedoed west of the British Isles a fortnight later.

From that point on it was open season on British warships and merchantmen. By the end of the year the U-boats had claimed 114 ships. After the Fall of France the assault on shipping escalated as the Luftwaffe joined the fray from French airbases. The U-boats also began to operate in what were dubbed Wolfpacks and in October 1940 they sank 63 ships. The Royal Navy quickly had to perfect the use of such measures as sonar and anti-submarine warfare.

During the First World War the British had sought to design a submarine detection system through the use of sound. By the end of the conflict prototypes had been built called ASDIC (better known by its American name, sonar). Production did not commence until the early 1920s. It would become a vital tool in the deadly Battle of the Atlantic as Hitler's U-boats sought to strangle Allied transatlantic shipping. Initially the U-boats reigned supreme, causing great losses, then slowly but surely the Allies began to turn the tide through a combination of technology and improved tactics.

The Royal Navy found the use of anti-submarine depth charges caused a loss of ASDIC contact. This was because a warship had to pass over the target before attacking. Contact was lost just before the depth charges were dropped. This gave the submarine commander a chance to take evasive action. As a result, tactics using one or more ships to first hunt submarines were developed. The detector would guide in a vessel that had its ASDIC turned off. The directing ship would then make a follow-up attack.

This type of warfare also led to the production of new weapons such as the forward-throwing anti-submarine weapon known as the Hedgehog in 1942. This fired 24 spigot mortars ahead of the ship. These used contact fuses rather than timed or depth fuses. This made them more deadly because they only exploded when the mortar touched the hull of the submarine. The Hedgehog was followed by the similar Squid in 1943.

ASDIC technology was transferred to the USA in 1940. However, the Americans had already produced their own underwater sound detection technology in the 1930s. This was known as sonar. There were two types: active sonar, which emits pulses of sound to detect echoes from passing vessels; and passive sonar, which listens for sound made by vessels. Both types were used by surface craft during the Second World War, but submarines avoided using active sonar, as it could reveal their presence. Being able to listen for vessels both on the surface and underwater ultimately gave the Allies a war-winning advantage at sea.

In the air, the RAF's Coastal Command deployed the Airborne Surface Vessel Mk II Radar. This, though, could not help pilots spot surfaced submarines at night. In March 1941 Coastal Command began experimenting by fitting its submarine hunters with a searchlight known as the Leigh Light after its inventor. This meant that even in the darkness submarines had nowhere to hide; it proved a great success.

By September 1941 Germany had lost 43 U-boats. However, German production meant that by August 1942 Hitler had 300 U-boats. In response, the Allies' tactics became ever more aggressive, supported by sonar and radar. By May 1943 the tide had begun to turn and the U-boats were temporarily forced out of the Atlantic. When they returned, they lost the war of attrition and by 1944 they were no longer a menace.

Chapter 18

Wonder Weapons

Hitler, having failed to bomb Britain into submission, sought a way to replicate the Blitz by employing unmanned aerial weapons in 1944. In great secrecy, his scientists worked to develop two terror weapons that would rain death and destruction down on British cities.

FLYING BOMBS AND ROCKETS

Dr Jones was closely involved in countering Hitler's V-1 flying bomb and V-2 rocket programmes. The Polish Home Army helped gather vital intelligence about their development at Peenemünde on the island of Usedom from 1941. It set up the Lombard group to spy on German V-weapon activities in the occupied territories. They were assisted in their work by Polish engineer Antoni Kocjan and Austrian anti-Nazi Roman Traeger, who was stationed on Usedom. The RAF bombed Peenemünde on 18 August 1943, which delayed the V-2 by up to two months.

The Poles proved particularly successful in gathering intelligence on the V-2 tests, including smuggling parts of a rocket out of Poland in July 1944. By this stage the Germans had conducted major building works in Belgium and France to both store and launch the V-weapons. It was anticipated that these would be ready to commence attacks on London from around mid-1944. This intelligence added impetus to the requirement for D-Day to be conducted as soon as possible. The V-1 was first launched against London on 13 June 1944, just a week after D-Day. It would also be used against Antwerp and Brussels.

In France, Nazi armaments minister Albert Speer and his deputy Xaver Dorsch were shadowed by the French Resistance, who seemed to dog their every step with the construction of the Atlantic Wall. The Organization Todt, responsible for the work, had its headquarters at Audinghen in the Pas-de-

Chapter 18

Calais bombed twice by Americans on 11 November 1943. That same day the bombers also struck one of the network of new V-weapon launch sites being built in the Cotentin Peninsula at Couville, south-west of Cherbourg. The bombs wrecked the 5 m (16.4 ft)-thick concrete bunker roofs and damaged much of the nearby village. At Audinghen, the first attack flattened the village, while the second hit the Todt building, scattering frightened staff.

What Speer did not know was that in between the raids at Audinghen, Michel Blot, a French agent, had slipped in and photographed plans for over a hundred V-1 flying-bomb sites and stolen secret documents dealing with coastal defences. Controlled from Caen, a network of some 1,500 agents systematically plotted German defences. They included a painter and decorator who managed to steal blueprints from the Organization Todt.

Colonel Wachtel, commander of Regiment 155, had been given the task of setting up the fixed launch sites along the north coast of France and Belgium in the summer of 1943. Thanks to the French Resistance, the Allies knew all about Wachtel. His preparations were constantly attacked by Allied bombers in the run-up to D-Day. Wachtel, concerned by the breach in his security, abandoned his headquarters at Doullens and established a new one at Creil, north of Paris, in early 1944.

He was so alarmed at the prospect of British commandos trying to kill him that he grew a beard, dyed his hair and assumed the name 'Max Wolf'. His men changed their uniforms and transport in an effort to throw spies off their trail. Wachtel also instructed that over the telephone his unit was to be referred to as 'Flak Group Creil'. All this subterfuge did him no good. 'Colonel Wachtel himself will not be in continual residence at his HQ', reported a French agent after the move, 'for he goes on inspection missions in Belgium and also makes frequent journeys.'

In the three months of April, May and June 1944 the US 8th Air Force dropped 109,101 tons (110,834 tonnes) of bombs in direct tactical support of the Allied armies and the assault on Hitler's V-weapon sites. On the ground, the French Resistance also co-ordinated their efforts with the SOE and OSS to hinder the German movement of reinforcements by road and rail towards Normandy once the Allies' invasion was underway.

Owing to the bomber attacks, Wachtel and his boss Lieutenant General Walther von Axthelm opted for using more temporary sites. By the end of August 1944 they had launched 8,554 V-1s, most of which were aimed at

London. Although about a third proved faulty and a third were shot from the skies, a large enough number were still hitting the British capital to please Hitler.

After the German collapse in Normandy, Colonel Wachtel's men withdrew from France and Belgium into the Netherlands and Germany. When the Allies overran Creil, they captured all his launch data. They learned that the Luftwaffe had conducted no photographic missions over London from 10 January 1941 to 10 September 1944. This indicated they had little idea of how their V-weapons were actually performing.

Hitler hoped the V-1 flying bomb would batter Britain into submission.

Chapter 18

Continual RAF raids on the V-2 base at Peenemünde persuaded Hitler to relocate the programme to Nordhausen, Germany. Likewise, the launch sites built in France in early 1944 were attacked before they could be completed. The largest V-2 rocket base in northern France was at Méry-sur-Oise. On 24 August the Germans abandoned it in the face of the Allied advance. To oversee mobile launches, two units were formed: Battery 444 and Group North. These had been deployed to create the launch sites around The Hague. Battery 444 conducted its first V-2 combat launch on 8 September 1944, when a rocket was fired at newly liberated Paris. Shortly afterwards Group North targeted London and Antwerp.

In terms of countering Hitler's terror weapons it proved possible to shoot down the V-1 using anti-aircraft artillery or tilt it off-course and into a terminal dive using fighters. Aircraft such as the British Hawker Tempest and de Havilland Mosquito and North American Mustang were employed as interceptors. British Meteor jets, which had the speed to catch it, were also used to shoot them down from early August 1944. In contrast, the V-2 proved impossible to counter other than by destroying its launch sites. The last V-1 and V-2 rockets were fired defiantly at Britain at the end of March 1945.

Allied intelligence on the V-2 rocket was very good.

HITLER'S JETS

Hitler's other wonder weapons were his state-of-the-art jet aircraft, which were also developed under great secrecy. Behind the scenes, he hoped his scientists could give him victory in the air. Ironically, he proved to be his own worst enemy when it came to his jet programmes. Field Marshal Erhard Milch, Inspector General of the Luftwaffe, was responsible for the world's very first turbojet fighter, known as the Messerschmitt (Me) 262. General Adolf Galland, in charge of the Luftwaffe's fighter forces, was in need of such an aircraft by 1944. Initially, Hitler and Galland anticipated that it would drive the Allies from the skies.

When Hitler authorized production of the Me 262 in November 1943 it could have proved a game-changer. Powered by two wing-mounted jet engines giving a top speed of 869 km/h (540 mph), it was considerably faster than any other Allied aircraft. It also had considerable firepower with four 30 mm (1.2 in) cannons and air-to-air rockets. Furthermore, the Me 262 was fuelled with low-grade petrol, of which there was a plentiful supply, so it was not greatly affected by the mounting oil crisis in Germany.

Hitler foolishly decided it should serve solely as a fighter-bomber to counter the anticipated Allied invasion of France, which meant major structural changes. Luftwaffe chief Hermann Göring and his commanders were horrified when Hitler announced, 'In this aircraft, which you tell me is a fighter, I see the Blitzbomber with which I will repulse the invasion.' He then instructed, 'The aircraft does not interest me in the least as a fighter.'

However, carrying two 250 kg (550 lb) bombs beneath the nose greatly hampered the aircraft's combat performance. Eventually a compromise was reached and both types were produced, but it was much too late and the Luftwaffe was deprived of a jet fighter that could have been invaluable in opposing D-Day. The bomber variant only entered service in July 1944 and the fighter did not see action until October 1944. Both were only available in limited numbers

Hitler sought to support his troops with a 'People's Fighter' or *Volksjäger*, which would be a single-engine jet fighter. After all the problems with the Me 262 he needed a jet as quick as possible and at the lowest cost. Messerschmitt introduced small numbers of the Me 163 Komet into service in May 1944. This diminutive interceptor was powered by a rocket motor using very volatile fuel. The Komet's 959 km/h (596 mph) top speed meant it rapidly overshot

Chapter 18

its intended target. Also, heavy landings often caused the engine to explode, instantly killing the pilot.

The other candidate for the *Volksjäger* was the Heinkel He 162 Salamander. This turbojet fighter was far from ready for mass production, as the requirement was only issued in mid-September 1944. The first prototype, featuring the engine mounted above the fuselage, crashed on 10 December 1944, killing the test pilot. He had conducted a high-speed, low-level pass during which the leading edge of the starboard wing failed. Subsequent prototypes were likewise found to be structurally unsound and suffered aerodynamic problems. As a result, a limited production run did not start until the New Year and by then it was too late to introduce it into active service.

Hitler had one more single-seat jet-powered aircraft. This was the Arado Ar 234 Blitz, which was the very first turbojet-powered bomber and the only one to be operational during the Second World War. It suffered a chequered history and although work had commenced in 1940 it was three years before the first prototypes were flown. Although the two-engine turbojet bomber/reconnaissance variant flew in December 1943, and a four-engine version in early 1944, it was not ready to oppose D-Day. Just four reconnaissance variants were issued to an experimental unit in Rheine in the summer of 1944.

Jet fighters such as the Me 262 arrived too late to save the Luftwaffe.

The bomber version became operational in October 1944 with a bomber group based at Achmer and Rheine. By early December 1944 it had been issued with 51 Ar 234s. These were hampered by fuel shortages and an engine life of just 25 hours. The engine proved prone to cracking. Another hazard was discovered when cold weather caused condensation problems on the inside of the canopy. While the Ar 234 could release its bombs in a shallow dive it was not suitable for dive-bombing. A multi-role version capable of ground attack was under development but was not ready for deployment.

The net result of all this was that Hitler's jet programmes never posed a real threat to Allied air superiority. His appliance of science and the use of flying bombs, rockets and jet engines was simply too little too late.

Conclusion

It is impossible to quantify the results of the secret war, though it undoubtedly had a seriously detrimental effect on the Axis war effort. The spies and their handlers, the eavesdroppers, the deception operations and the resistance all played their part – but was it a decisive contribution? The fighting, in what essentially became a war of attrition, is what really settled the outcome of the Second World War. The Axis proved incapable of standing against the grand alliance of Britain, the USA and Russia and their industrial muscle. Nonetheless, in the case of the Allies, the secret war certainly helped them gain victory.

Most notably the penetration of Enigma by the code breakers of Bletchley Park was hailed as one of the greatest British achievements of the Second World War. It has been estimated that thanks to Bletchley cracking both the Enigma and Lorenz cyphers the conflict was shortened by as much as two years. Just imagine if the Second World War had dragged on until 1947. Therefore, the significance of Bletchley and Ultra cannot really be overstated.

Ultra was not perfect, nor was it infallible as a source of intelligence, but it gave the Allies a much-needed edge that they would otherwise not have had. It helped them, as Sun Tzu put it, to 'know the enemy'. Time and time again Allied victories were facilitated by a timely tip-off, though as in the case of the Atlantic, Matapan and Midway, the sailors and aviators still had to win the actual battles. Churchill rightly feared that strangulation of the shipping lanes by the U-boats could have spelled ultimate defeat for Britain. Luckily for him and the country, Ultra had a far greater impact on the war at sea than on land. It repeatedly turned the tide at crucial moments in the battle.

Generally, though, signals intelligence did not guarantee victory; that was up to the skill of admirals and generals. What Ultra meant was that when commanders looked to be taking a gamble, behind the scenes they were often backed by sound intelligence. General Patton's daring breakout from Normandy proved to be a fine example of this. Common sense suggested that the Germans could easily pinch off his breakthrough and trap his men

Conclusion

in Brittany. Patton already knew, thanks to Ultra, that the German army was overstretched and did not have the manpower to do it. When they attempted to counter-attack him their operation quickly turned into a farce. In the meantime, Patton was busting open the Western Front and rapidly heading for Paris.

The Allies also became masters at tactical and strategic deception. Prior to D-Day Patton's phantom 'FUSAG' exemplified this. It completely convinced Hitler that the Allies had an entire army group poised to assault the Pas-de-Calais. Even when Hitler rightly deduced that the Allies would first land in Normandy, he continued to believe that this was a feint and that their main thrust would come north of the Seine. Likewise, the perceived threat to Norway from a fake army in Scotland kept a huge German garrison needlessly tied up there. All this was enhanced by the remarkable success of the Double-Cross System. The steady drip of information from the double agents helped create a completely false picture of Allied intentions.

On the Eastern Front, just how much value did Stalin gain from his spies in Britain and Switzerland? The answer is probably very little. By the time decrypted intelligence reached Moscow it was often days if not weeks out of date. John Cairncross, Leo Long and Anthony Blunt liked to think they were instrumental in changing the course of the war. This was a deluded view. Sándor Radó and Rudolf Roessler were fed intelligence direct from the German high command, but whether this was better than the intelligence gained from the Lorenz decrypts is unknown. Stalin had numerous sources of information, and his spy networks were just one small part of his vast information-gathering operation.

Did Churchill facilitate the Red Army's victory at Kursk in the summer of 1943? His understandable reluctance to reveal the source of Ultra inevitably did little to enhance its credibility with Stalin. Furthermore, after intercepts had been decrypted units were often long gone, having been redeployed elsewhere. Stalin got much better intelligence from his partisans and spies behind enemy lines monitoring German-controlled airfields, railways and roads. Likewise, the Red Army ran its own radio intercept operations, and the Red Air Force conducted regular photographic reconnaissance flights.

Nonetheless, the value of Enigma and Lorenz intelligence passed to Stalin officially or unofficially should not be dismissed. If Stalin was never ready to acknowledge the part played by Lend-Lease, then he was certainly never going to accept that he won the war thanks to British and American intelligence.

Conclusion

Code breaker Captain Jerry Reynolds was in little doubt that information supplied by Bletchley Park was crucial in shortening the war and hastening Hitler's final defeat. He pointed out that Churchill 'gave the Russians full details of the plans three months before the battle took place and allowed them to deploy the maximum number of tanks and win the Battle of Kursk'.

Until his dying day Reynolds championed the unsung heroes of Bletchley: 'Most people in Britain are unaware of the Kursk story and its enormous significance, and of the major contribution made by the Lorenz decrypts to its successful outcome. I wonder whether the Russian authorities ever realized the importance of the help that Britain had given.' If they did, they were never prepared to admit it. In the same way, Ultra and the deception operations' contribution to the Allied victory in the West still remains relatively unsung. What they did was help ensure that D-Day did not become a bloodbath and that the invasion was not thrown back into the sea. Meticulous planning of course also ensured that it was a complete success.

Behind the lines, the brave resistance and partisans played a major role by being a massive drain on Axis resources. Sabotage and guerrilla activity required regular security operations, which did nothing but alienate the local population. In the Balkans and the Soviet Union they tied up a huge number of divisions that were badly needed elsewhere. The Allies' deception operations had a similar effect. In the case of Britain's Double-Cross System, it proved remarkably successful at turning Nazi agents against their masters. Ultimately, the Axis lost the secret war because they could not compete at any level, despite their best efforts.

Glossary of Deception and Intelligence Code Names

Airborne Cigar Allied jammer used against German night-fighter radio frequencies, to help RAF Bomber Command.

'Aspidistra' Secret radio station set up in Britain to send clandestine messages to occupied Europe.

Aztec, **Operation** Airborne operations conducted by the OSS to assist Italian partisans in the Venice area in October and December 1944.

Barclay, **Operation** An Allied plan prior to Operation *Overlord* to encourage the Germans to reinforce the Balkans and southern France rather than the Low Countries and northern France. This was done by giving the impression that a major operation would take place in the eastern Mediterranean.

Bernhard, **Operation** A German plan to drop forged £5 notes in Britain to destabilize the British wartime economy.

Bertram, **Operation** This operation conducted in September–October 1942 was designed to fool Rommel into believing that Montgomery was planning to attack in the south at El Alamein and not in the north. It consisted of seven subsidiary operations.

'Black Radio' These were radio stations masquerading as those of another country. The British Political Warfare Executive ran over 40 such radio stations pretending to be broadcasting from inside Germany. The Germans only had four radio stations operating against Britain.

Blue, **Operation** The French Resistance sabotage of electrical power supplies in support of Operation *Overlord*.

Bodyguard, **Operation** An overall Allied strategic deception plan for the invasion of France, designed to shield Operation *Overlord* from German intelligence. This encompassed Operations *Copperhead*, *Fortitude*, *Graffham*, *Ironside*, *Quicksilver*, *Royal Flush*, *Vendetta* and *Zeppelin*.

'Boozer' A British radar-detection device designed to test the ability of the German Würzburg fire-control radar to detect small aircraft.

Glossary of Deception and Intelligence Code Names

Braddock, **Operation** Air supply of munitions to resistance fighters in Europe.

'Carpet' The name for the American and British radar jammer designed for use against the German Würzburg fire-control radar.

Cascade, **Operation** A deception plan designed to mislead the Axis as to the true strength of Allied forces in the Mediterranean. It was followed by Operation *Zeppelin*.

Cloak, **Operation** The British deception scheme to cover the presence of 4th Corps in the Myittha valley in late 1943 and early 1944.

Cockade The designation of multiple Allied diversionary schemes in 1943 to prevent German forces in western Europe from being deployed to the Eastern Front. These included Operations *Harlequin*, *Starkey*, *Tindall* and *Wadham*.

Conclave A deception scheme to shield the left flank of General Slim's 14th Army in Burma during its march down the Irrawaddy and Sittang rivers towards Rangoon in April 1945.

Copperhead, **Operation** This involved Montgomery's body double travelling around the Mediterranean to deceive the Germans about Monty's location in the run-up to Operation *Overlord*.

Corona, **Operation** This operation involved broadcasting of false information to German night-fighter crews by German-speaking Allied speakers to divert them from Allied bomber raids.

Crossbow, **Operation** British intelligence and photo-reconnaissance operations to gather information on the development of German secret V-weapons at Peenemünde in the Baltic.

Diamond, **Operation** An operation to create a fake water pipeline at El Alamein to distract the Germans from the real one.

Diver, **Operation** Allied air attacks on German V-1 launch sites in northern France and along the Belgian coast in the spring and summer of 1944.

Double-Cross Created by the British XX Committee, this system was designed to feed disinformation to enemy spies and double agents. About 120 Abwehr agents ended up working for Double Cross and none were unmasked.

Glossary of Deception and Intelligence Code Names

***Error*, Operation** This was designed to convince the Japanese that General Wavell, the British commander in India, had been killed in a car crash in Burma and that fake information at the scene indicated British forces were stronger than they really were.

***Ferdinand*, Operation** By threatening an invasion of Genoa, it was hoped to draw more German forces to Italy.

***Fortitude (North and South)*, Operations** Allied deception plans designed to convince the Germans that their main invasion of the continent would occur in Norway or the Pas-de-Calais area.

***Game Against England*, Operation** This was the Abwehr's counter-espionage operation against SOE agents in the Netherlands.

***Graffham*, Operation** A fictitious plan for the Allies to invade Sweden, which was expanded to include Spain and Turkey to became Operation *Royal Flush*.

***Green*, Operation** The plan by SOE for operations by the French Resistance against German rail communications in northern France in support of Operation *Overlord*.

***Harlequin*, Operation** Part of Operation *Cockade* in 1943, this envisaged an amphibious training exercise in the English Channel with a feint towards the Pas-de-Calais. It did not take place.

***Ironside*, Operation** An effort to dupe the Germans into believing the Second Front would be opened in the Bordeaux area.

***Kremlin*, Operation** A German deception plan in early 1942 designed to convince Stalin that Hitler's summer offensive would be towards Moscow, whereas it was actually towards the Caucasus and Stalingrad.

***Martello*, Operation** This was designed to mask the movement of Montgomery's tanks at El Alamein.

***Mincemeat*, Operation** This Allied deception plan was intended to fool the Axis into believing that the Allies did not intend to invade Sicily in 1943.

***Quicksilver*, Operation** Part of Operation *Fortitude,* which covered the fictitious 'US 1st Army Group' under General Patton in south-east England, poised to strike across the Pas-de-Calais. *Quicksilver* was divided into six elements, all working to the same goal. These continued well after D-Day had taken place.

***Royal Flush*, Operation** This was part of Operation *Bodyguard* in support of D-Day, intended to make the Germans think the Allies were recruiting neutral Spain, Sweden and Turkey to their cause or intended to invade them.

Glossary of Deception and Intelligence Code Names

'Ski Site' The Allied designation of the V-1 ramp launch sites in northern France and the Low Countries in June 1944. These had first been detected in October 1943 and were subsequently subjected to regular air attack.

***Solo I*, Operation** This was a deception scheme intended to convince the Germans that the Allies were planning to invade Norway in the winter of 1942. In reality, their intended target was Algeria and Morocco with Operation *Torch*.

***Starkey*, Operation** A combined RAF and US Army Air Force offensive in the Boulogne area followed by a fictitious British and Canadian amphibious assault on Boulogne.

***Taxable*, Operation** A British radar decoy operation to deceive the Germans into thinking Operation *Overlord* was taking place in the Pas-de-Calais and not Normandy. This involved the RAF dropping 'Window' over a small invasion fleet to convince German radar operators that it was bigger than it was.

***Tindall*, Operation** This was a fictitious operation against Norway with Stavanger as the objective.

***Tortue*, Operation** An operation by the French Resistance to hamper the movement of German reinforcements towards Normandy in support of *Overlord*.

***Trojan Horse*, Operation** The original code name for Operation *Mincemeat*.

***Wadham*, Operation** This suggested that the Allies intended to land in Brittany with the aim of capturing Brest.

***Warehouse*, Operation** This operation posed a fictional threat to Crete.

***Withstand*, Operation** This also posed a fictional threat to Crete and followed on from Operation *Warehouse*.

***Vendetta*, Operation** An operation designed to convince the Germans that D-Day would take place in southern France.

***Violet*, Operation** A plan by the French Resistance, with support from the SOE and the OSS, to cripple France's phone and telegram network once Operation *Overlord* commenced.

***Zeppelin*, Operation** A deception plan designed to convince the Germans that the Allies would attack Crete or western Greece from the Mediterranean, or Romania via the Black Sea.

Endnotes

Introduction

'If you know the enemy and know yourself': Tucker-Jones, *Sun Tzu's The Art of War: Illustrated Edition*, p.47

'O divine art of subtlety and secrecy!': Ibid., p.71

'I must say, quite frankly, that I hold it perfectly justifiable': *Hansard, Vol 385*, 11 November 1942

Chapter 2: Spymasters

'Admiral Canaris came to my headquarters': Gehlen, *The Gehlen Memoirs*, pp.86–7

'By 9 November 1942, ten days before the beginning of the Soviet counter-attack': Ibid. p.70

'Only a meagre reserve is available over and above the armed forces': Ibid. p.65

'inexperienced and naïve': Montefiore, *Stalin: The Court of the Red Tsar*, p.298

'A spy should be like the devil': Ibid.

'Find out who the author is and punish him': Ibid., p.315

'The story of Richard Sorge, Soviet master spy': Willoughby, *Sorge: Soviet Master Spy*, p.v

'Unlike Japan, Shanghai at that time was comparatively safe': Ibid., p.146

'The espionage group which I operated in Japan': Ibid., p.125

'I stood firm on the view that Japan had no intention': Ibid., p.184

Chapter 3: Agents and Double Agents

Jarrot had 'seriously harmed German industries on French soil': *Washington Post*, 21 April 2000

'Wing Commander Yeo-Thomas thus turned his final mission into a success': *London Gazette*, 15 February 1945

Endnotes

'She fought for the cause of the Indian people struggling against British oppression': Willoughby, *Sorge: Soviet Master Spy*, p.206

Chapter 5: The Impact of Bletchley Park

'Enigma gave a general warning of the approach of the Battle of Britain': McKay, *The Secret Life of Bletchley Park*, p.98

'Ultra never mention Coventry': Ibid., p.107

'it was important to maintain an appearance of normality [...] lest the enemy should "smell a rat"': Grehan & Mace, *The War at Sea in the Mediterranean 1940-1944*, p.53

'Tell Dilly that we have won a great victory': Kerrigan, *How Bletchley Park Won World War II*, p.78

'By the summer of 1942 [...] there can have been little Enigma traffic': McKay, *The Secret Life of Bletchley Park*, p.188

'We told Monty over and over again how few tanks Rommel had got': Ibid.

'earning the comment from Churchill, "I had not been content with this form of collective wisdom"': Jones, *Most Secret War*, p.205

'I remember saying that the attack would take place on 22 or 29 June': Cradock, *Know Your Enemy*, p.21

'the prospect of a German defeat of Russia has receded to vanishing point': Ibid.

'The Russians, both on land and in the air, had now the upper hand': Churchill, *The Second World War, Vol V*, p.229

'We were able to warn them what army groups were going to be used': McKay, *The Secret Life of Bletchley Park*, p.237

'Hitler and his commanders expected an Allied invasion along the French coast at Calais': Roberts, *Lorenz*, p.53

'Patton studied every Ultra signal': Kerrigan, *How Bletchley Park Won World War II*, p.212

'I remember a particular night when I was working on a message': Smith, *Station X*, pp.181–2

'Then there came through this detailed order that four or five German armoured divisions were to go hell for leather': Ibid.

'The message was to say how the Germans were planning to get out of this impasse': Ibid, p.183

Chapter 7: Allied Deception Operations

'special section of Intelligence for Deception': Darman, *Deceptions of World War II*, p.40

'The enemy certainly got badly "bogged down" in this area': De Guingand, *Operation Victory*, p.148

'Sicily lay within striking distance': Kesselring, *The Memoirs of Field Marshal Kesselring*, p.159

'we shall have to get the body back and give it another swim': Smyth, *Deathly Deception*, p.88

'At the time of the capitulation of Tunis [...] the outlook in Sicily, as everywhere, was very black': Kesselring, *The Memoirs of Field Marshal Kesselring*, p.161

'Mincemeat swallowed rod, line and sinker by right people and they look like acting on it.' Pack, *Operation Husky*, p.26

'The deception bolstered the German High Command's assumption that the Balkans would be the objective for the next attack': Ibid.

'Soon afterwards ULTRA decrypts revealed that the Germans had been comprehensively deceived': Andrew, *The Defence of the Realm*, p.287

'Everything will be all right. Don't worry about it': Rankin, *Churchill's Wizards*, p.554

'From all I could gather, the plan worked to perfection': Butcher, *Three Years with Eisenhower*, p.501

'In fact there was nothing in Ultra messages or in German documents': Haswell, *The Intelligence and Deception of the D-Day Landings*, p.140

'thus playing himself being himself as well as playing the man he had been playing at being': Pearson, *Achtung Schweinehund!*, p.34

'It is a one-horse show,' noted Fleming, 'and I am the horse': Rankin, *Churchill's Wizards*, p.488

'With a resounding thump it was blown at 2359 hours on 30th April': Slim, *Defeat into Victory*, p.88

'The stage was set for the most dramatic of all military operations': Ibid., p.406

'The gradients and the dust were at times such that the tanks had to tow their own transporters': Ibid., p.404

'Their eyes, we hoped, were still fixed on Mandalay, not Meiktila': Ibid., p.406

'The enemy had no suspicion that a major crossing was about to be attempted here': Ibid., pp.423–4 'the strongest fortress in the world': Tucker-Jones, *The Changing Face of Aerial Warfare 1940–Present Day*, p.38

'It is our considered opinion that Japan envisages early hostilities against Great Britain and the United States': Ibid.

Chapter 8: Deception on the Eastern Front

'The troops stationed on our western borders were not moved up to their defence line': Tucker-Jones, *Slaughter on the Eastern Front*, p.71

'A railroad stretched beneath us almost the whole time': Ibid., p.68

'We'll be lucky if it doesn't begin in the next fifteen to twenty days': Ibid., p.69

'Everything is normal with us.' Werth, *Russia at War 1941-1945*, p.143

'My thoughts were depressing': Tucker-Jones, *Slaughter on the Eastern Front*, p.70

'stamping around in various tactical battalion and regimental exercises': Ibid.

'MAX must be regarded as a success': Hastings, *The Secret War*, p.235

'All there is left to take is a couple of little scraps of land. […] Time is of no importance': Bastable, *Voices from Stalingrad*, p.144

'Despite persistent attacks Army Group Centre had retained a considerable part of White Russia': Mellenthin, *Panzer Battles*, p.335

Chapter 9: Japan's Great Con

'Japanese troops have made a surprise attack and crossed into friendly Mongolia': Zhukov, *Reminiscences and Reflections, Vol I*, p.177

'pull no punches': Ibid., p.178

'I had to keep a constant watch on Japan's troop strength in China': Willoughby, *Sorge: Soviet Master Spy*, p.163

'It is not a good idea […] to undertake large-scale action': Chang & Halliday, *Mao: The Unknown Story*, p.246

'I remember in particular Ozaki's report on his meeting with Prince Konoye in 1941': Willoughby, *Sorge: Soviet Master Spy*, p.169

'To everyone's surprise, the Japanese armed forces had carried through a very large reinforcement programme': Ibid., p.163

'A correct knowledge of the scope of the mobilization and its direction': Ibid., p.168

'I maintained that the great mobilization of August 1941 was not directed primarily against the Soviet Union': Ibid., p.184

'preparations for Southward Move': Jeffrey, *MI6: The History of the Secret Intelligence Service 1909-1949*, p.574

'The Russians were so prone to suspect that the Japanese and German foreign policies': Willoughby, *Sorge: Soviet Master Spy*, p.163

Chapter 10: Hiding in Plain Sight

'Every vehicle was covered with tree branches and moved along hedges': Tucker-Jones, *Falaise: The Flawed Victory*, p.48

'By the end of the day I had lost forty tank trucks carrying fuel': Ibid.

'You must conceal 150,000 men with a thousand guns and a thousand tanks': Darman, *Deceptions of World War II*, p.52

'They make no noise, they've got no tracks, they are lorries with canvas over them made to look like tanks': Dimbleby, *Destiny in the Desert*, p.380

'by the end of the third week in October we began to realise': De Guingand, *Operation Victory*, p.160

'the wireless traffic […] of an armoured division was so employed': Ibid., p.156

'turned the tide of war in Africa against us': Liddell Hart (ed), *The Rommel Papers*, p.302

'By a marvellous system of camouflage, complete tactical surprise was achieved in the desert': Reit, *Masquerade: The Amazing Camouflage Deceptions of World War II*, p.159

Chapter 11: Dummy Armies

'On the ground in the daytime, the decoys looked pathetic': Ibid., p.53

'You must realize that the enemy is probably listening to every message': Ibid., p.40

'We had hoped originally to launch the operation from the line St Lô-Coutances': Montgomery, *The Memoirs*, p.258

Chapter 12: European Resistance

'the Reichsführer-SS has the sole responsibility for combating banditry in the Reich Commissioner's territories': Trevor-Roper (ed), *Hitler's War Directives*, p.199

'The "railroad war" carried out by the guerrillas of Byelorussia, Smolensk, and Orel oblasts and the Dnieper valley': Salisbury (ed), *Marshal Zhukov's Greatest Battles*, p.257

Endnotes

'The lightning operation conducted during the night by partisan detachments halted all railway traffic': Tucker-Jones, *Stalin's Revenge*, p.32

Chapter 13: Resisting on the Flanks

'Now seemed to be the golden opportunity for General Aziz el Masri': Cooper, *Cairo in the War 1939-1945*, p.105

'In the Caucasus you will find your second Finland and after us will follow other oppressed peoples': Tucker-Jones, *The Battle for the Caucasus 1942-1943*, p.2

'I must say I am a little worried about the Caucasus': Ibid., p.33

'if the liberation of the Caucasus meant only the exchange of one coloniser for another': Ibid., pp.53–4

Chapter 14: Guerrillas in the Far East and Pacific

'My opinion was that the B.N.A, prowling on their lines of communication': Slim, *Defeat into Victory*, pp.484–5

'They proved definitely useful in gaining information': Ibid., p.520

'I am engaged here in meeting by far the most serious rebellion since that of 1857': French, *Liberty or Death*, p. 161

'Our work among the people is too inadequate […] there are so many traitors': Wilson, *When Tigers Fight*, p.146

Chapter 15: Defying Militarism

'One of the most active cells in the conspiracy was to be found in the staff of Army Group Centre on the Eastern Front': Tucker-Jones, *Stalin's Revenge*, pp.44–5

'On the evening of 22 July […] it was announced that an assassination attempt had been made on the Führer': Ibid., p.95

'People of Vienna help the Red Army liberate your city': Tucker-Jones, *Battle of the Cities*, p.189

'The Viennese are helping the Red Army, and they fully understand that the Soviet Union is not fighting against Austrians': Ibid., p.190

'People of Vienna […] The hour of the liberation […] has come': Ibid.

'The response was immediate, and many Viennese took part in the fighting against the invaders.' Ibid.

'We appeal to all members of the police, army and government to join the patriots': Ibid., p.205

Endnotes

Chapter 16: The Jews Fight Back

'Hardly had [the] operation begun, than we ran into strong concerted fire by the Jews and bandits': Tucker-Jones, *The Battle for Warsaw 1939-1945*, p.44

'About 1730 hours we encountered very strong resistance from one block of buildings, including machine gun fire': Ibid.

'I therefore decided to destroy the entire Jewish area by setting every block on fire.' Ibid.

'One hundred and eight Jews, bandits and subhumans were destroyed': Ibid., p.45

Chapter 17: Radar Wars

'General Martini […] had by this time a pretty shrewd idea that we had an RDF system operational': Levine, *Forgotten Voices of the Blitz and the Battle for Britain*, pp.256–7

'The lattice masts can't be seen from the air': Ibid., p.257

'The knowledge that Knickebein was jammed spread through the Luftwaffe': Jones, *Most Secret War*, p.129

'On 8th September Enigma gave us the pinpoint to the nearest mile of the Cherbourg Knickebein': Ibid., p.132

'By February 1941 the Battle of the Beams was as good as won': Ibid., p.179

'At the same time as we were watching the flying bomb trials, dealing with the Baby Blitz': Ibid., p.400

'Even though we knew that the attack was to be made in Normandy, we covered a very much wider coastline': Ibid., p.401

'The operation was called Operation *Taxable* and it was one of the biggest spoofs ever played on the Germans': Tucker-Jones, *D-Day 1944: The Making of Victory*, p.91

'Two hundred ships were each equipped with two to three kilowatts of Mandrel jammers': Ibid.

'Whatever the equipment we have, the enemy can jam it without so much as a by-your-leave.' Ibid., p.90

'There is a simple means whereby the enemy can jam our entire radar system, against which we have no antidote': Ibid.

'What am I supposed to tell the Führer!': Ibid.

Endnotes

'Colonel Wachtel himself will not be in continual residence at his HQ': Jones, *Most Secret War*, p.374

'In this aircraft, which you tell me is a fighter, I see the Blitzbomber with which I will repulse the invasion': Fitzgerald, *Hitler's Secret Weapons of Mass Destruction*, pp.54–5

'The aircraft does not interest me in the least as a fighter': Irving, *The Rise and Fall of the Luftwaffe*, p.425

as Sun Tzu put it, to 'know the enemy': Tucker-Jones, *Sun Tzu's The Art of War: Illustrated Edition*, p.46 & p.127

'gave the Russians full details of the plans three months before the battle took place': Roberts, *Lorenz*, p.135

'Most people in Britain are unaware of the Kursk story and its enormous significance': Ibid., p.131

Bibliography

Andrew, Christopher, *The Defence of the Realm: The Authorized History of MI5*, London: Allen Lane, 2009

Bastable, Jonathan, *Voices from Stalingrad*, Newton Abbot: David & Charles, 2006

Butcher, Captain Harry C., *Three Years with Eisenhower*, London: William Heinemann, 1946

Caballero-Jurado, Carlos, *Resistance Warfare: Resistance and Collaboration in Western Europe 1940-45*, London: Osprey, 1985

Chang, Jung & Halliday, Jon, *Mao: The Unknown Story*, London: Jonathan Cape, 2005

Churchill, Winston S., *The Second World War, Volume V, Closing the Ring*, London: Cassell, 1965

Clark, Lloyd, *Kursk: The Greatest Battle Eastern Front 1943*, London: Headline Review, 2012

Clifton James, M.E., *I Was Monty's Double*, London: Rider, 1954

Collier, Richard, *Ten Thousand Eyes*, New York: The Lyons Press, 2001

Cooper, Artemis, *Cairo in the War 1939-1945*, London: Hamish Hamilton, 1992

Cooper, Matthew, *The Phantom War: The German struggle against Soviet partisans 1941-1944*, London: Macdonald & Jane's, 1979

Cradock, Percy, *Know Your Enemy: How the Joint Intelligence Committee Saw the World*, London: John Murray, 2002

Dargie, Richard, *The Plots to Kill Hitler: The Men and Women Who Tried to Change History*, London: Arcturus, 2020

Darman, Peter, *Deceptions of World War II: From Camouflage Techniques to Deception Tactics*, Bicester: Aura, 2023

De Guingand, Major General Sir Francis, *Operation Victory*, London: Hodder & Stoughton, 1947

Dimbleby, Jonathan, *Destiny in the Desert: The Road to El Alamein – The Battle that Turned the Tide*, London: Profile, 2013

Dumbach, Annette & Newborn, Jud, *Sophie Scholl and the White Rose*, Oxford: Oneworld, 2006

Bibliography

Fitzgerald, Michael, *Hitler's Secret Weapons of Mass Destruction: The Nazi Plan for Final Victory*, London: Arcturus, 2018

Fitzgerald, Michael, *Hitler's War Beneath the Waves*, London: Arcturus, 2020

Ford, Ken, *El Alamein 1942: The Turning of the Tide*, Oxford: Osprey, 2001

French, Patrick, *Liberty or Death: India's Journey to Independence and Division*, London: Harper Collins, 1997

Galante, Pierre & Silianoff, Eugene, *Hitler Lives – and the generals die*, London: Sidgwick & Jackson, 1982

Gehlen, Reinhard, *The Gehlen Memoirs: The first full edition of the Memoirs of General Reinhard Gehlen 1942-1971*, London: Collins, 1972

Grehan, John & Mace, Martin, *Despatches from the Front: The War at Sea in the Mediterranean 1940-1944*, Barnsley: Pen & Sword, 2014

Hastings, Max, *The Secret War: Spies, Codes and Guerrillas 1939-45*, London: William Collins, 2015

Haswell, Jock, *The Intelligence and Deception of the D-Day Landings*, London: B.T. Batsford, 1979

Hinsley, F.H. & Stripp, Alan (ed), *Codebreakers: The Inside Story of Bletchley Park*, Oxford: Oxford University Press, 2011

Holzman, Michael, *Spies and Traitors: Kim Philby, James Angleton and the Betrayal that Would Shape the Cold War*, London: Weidenfeld & Nicolson, 2023

Irving, David, *The Rise and Fall of the Luftwaffe*, London: Weidenfeld & Nicolson, 1973

Jeffery, Keith, *MI6: The History of the Secret Intelligence Service 1909-1949*, London: Bloomsbury, 2011

Jones, R.V., *Most Secret War: British Scientific Intelligence 1939-1945*, London: Hamish Hamilton, 1978

Jowett, Philip, *Japan's Asian Allies 1941-45*, Oxford: Osprey, 2020

Kennedy, Paul, *Engineers of Victory, The Problem Solvers who Turned the Tide in the Second World War*, London: Penguin, 2014

Kerr, Walter, *The Secret of Stalingrad*, London: Macdonald and Jane's, 1979

Kerrigan, Michael, *How Bletchley Park Won World War II*, London: Amber, 2018

Kesselring, Albert, *The Memoirs of Field Marshal Kesselring*, London: William Kimber, 1974

Levine, Joshua, *Forgotten Voices of the Blitz and the Battle for Britain*, London: Ebury, 2007

Lewis, Damien, *The Flame of Resistance: The Untold Story of Josephine Baker's Secret War*, London: Quercus, 2023

Liddell Hart, B.H. (ed), *The Rommel Papers*, London: Collins, 1953

Macintyre, Ben, *Agent Zigzag: The True Wartime Story of Eddie Chapman – The Most Notorious Double Agent of World War II*, London: Bloomsbury, 2016

Marshall, Bruce, *The White Rabbit*, London: Cassell, 2000

Mayer, S.L., (ed), *The Japanese War Machine*, London: Bison, 1976

Mazower, Mark, *Hitler's Empire: Naz Rule in Occupied Europe*, London: Penguin, 2009

McDonough, Frank, *The Hitler Years: Disaster 1940-1945*, London: Head of Zeus, 2020

McKay, Sinclair, *The Lost World of Bletchley Park: An Illustrated History of the Wartime Codebreaking Centre*, London: Aurum Press, 2013

McKay, Sinclair, *The Secret Life of Bletchley Park: The WWII Codebreaking Centre and the Men and Women Who Worked There*, London: Aurum Press, 2011

Mellenthin, Major General F.W. von, *Panzer Battles*, London: Futura, 1984

Melton, H. Keith, *Ultimate Spy*, London: Dorling Kindersley, 2002

Montefiore, Simon Sebag, *Stalin: The Court of the Red Tsar*, London: Weidenfeld & Nicolson, 2003

Montgomery, Bernard, *The Memoirs of Field Marshal Montgomery*, London: Collins, 1958

Mortimer, Gavin, *World War II in Secret: The Hidden Conflict 1939-1945*, Bicester: Aura, 2023

Muñoz, Antonio J., (ed.), *Wehrmacht Rear Guard Security in the USSR 1941-1945*, Bayside, NY: Europa Books/Washington DC: Department of the Army Pamphlet 20-240, 1951

Pack, S.W.C., *Operation Husky: The Allied Invasion of Sicily*, New York: Hippocrene, 1977

Paterson, Michael, *Voices of the Code Breakers: Personal Accounts of the Secret Heroes of World War II*, Barnsley: Greenhill, 2018

Bibliography

Pearson, Harry, *Achtung Schweinehund!: A Boy's Own Story of Imaginary Combat*, London: Little, Brown, 2007

Rankin, Nicholas, *Churchill's Wizards: The British Genius for Deception 1914-1945*, London: Faber and Faber, 2009

Reit, Seymour, *Masquerade: The Amazing Deceptions of World War II*, London: Robert Hale, 1979

Roberts, Captain Jerry, *Lorenz: Breaking Hitler's Top Secret Code at Bletchley Park*, Stroud: The History Press, 2017

Roland, Paul, *Life in the Third Reich: Daily Life in Nazi Germany 1933-1945*, London: Arcturus, 2019

Roland, Paul, *The Secret Lives of the Nazis: The Hidden History of the Third Reich*, London: Arcturus, 2017

Salisbury, Harrison E. (ed), *Marshal Zhukov's Greatest Battles*, London: Macdonald, 1969

Sebag-Montefiore, Hugh, *Enigma: The Battle for the Code*, London: Weidenfeld & Nicolson, 2001

Slepyan, Kenneth, *Stalin's Guerrillas: Soviet Partisans in World War II*, Kansas: University of Kansas, 2006

Slim, Field Marshal Sir William, *Defeat into Victory*, London: Cassell, 1956

Smith, Michael, *Bletchley Park: The Code-Breakers of Station X*, Oxford: Shire, 2013

Smith, Michael, *Station X: The Codebreakers of Bletchley Park*, London: Pan, 2004

Smyth, Denis, *Deathly Deception: The Real Story of Operation Mincemeat*, Oxford: Oxford University Press, 2011

Spector, Ronald H., *Eagle Against the Sun: The American War with Japan*, London: Cassell & Co, 2000

Terraine, John, *Business on Great Waters: The U-Boat Wars 1916-1945*, London: Leo Cooper, 1989

Thomas, Nigel & Abbot, Peter, *Partisan Warfare 1941-45*, London: Osprey, 1983

Toland, John, *Infamy: Pearl Harbor and Its Aftermath*, London: Penguin, 2001

Trevor-Roper, H.R. (ed), *Hitler's War Directives 1939-1945*, London: Pan, 1983

Bibliography

Tucker-Jones, Anthony, *Battle of the Cities: Urban Warfare on the Eastern Front*, Barnsley: Pen & Sword, 2023

Tucker-Jones, Anthony, *D-Day 1944: The Making of Victory*, Stroud: The History Press, 2019

Tucker-Jones, Anthony, *Falaise the Flawed Victory: The Destruction of Panzergruppe West – August 1944*, Barnsley: Pen & Sword, 2008

Tucker-Jones, Anthony, *Kursk 1943: Hitler's Bitter Harvest*, Stroud: The History Press, 2018

Tucker-Jones, Anthony, *Slaughter on the Eastern Front: Hitler and Stalin's War 1941-1945*, Stroud: The History Press, 2017

Tucker-Jones, Anthony, *Stalin's Revenge: Operation Bagration and the Annihilation of Army Group Centre*, Barnsley: Pen & Sword, 2009

Tucker-Jones, Anthony, *Sun Tzu's The Art of War: Illustrated Edition*, London: Bloomsbury, 2019

Tucker-Jones, Anthony, *The Battle for the Caucasus 1942-1943*, Barnsley: Pen & Sword, 2018

Tucker-Jones, Anthony, *The Battle for Warsaw 1939-1945*, Barnsley: Pen & Sword, 2020

Tucker-Jones, Anthony, *The Changing Face of Aerial Warfare 1940-Present Day*, Cheltenham: The History Press, 2023

Turner, Des, *The Secrets of Station 14: Briggens House, SOE's Forgery and Polish Elite Agent Training Station*, Cheltenham: The History Press, 2022

Werth, Alexander, *Russia at War 1941-1945*, New York: Skyhorse Publishing, 2017

Williamson, Gordon, *German Military Police Units 1939-45*, Oxford: Osprey, 1989

Willoughby, Major General Charles, *Sorge: Soviet Master Spy*, London: William Kimber, 1952

Wilson, Dick, *When Tigers Fight: The Story of the Sino-Japanese War 1937-1945*, London: Hutchinson, 1982

Winterbotham, Group Captain Frederick William, *The Ultra Secret*, London: Weidenfeld & Nicolson, 1974

Winterbotham, Group Captain Frederick William, *The Ultra Spy: An Autobiography*, London: Macmillan, 1989

Zhukov, G., *Reminiscences and Reflections, Vol I*, Moscow: Progress Publishers, 1985

Index

Abewehr 20, 33–4, 35, 36, 37, 46, 47, 48, 49, 50, 51, 52, 59, 95, 98, 101, 110, 146, 161
Air Intelligence Department 88
Akin, Spencer 72
al-Mukhtar, Omar 159
Albanian resistance groups 154
Alexander, Hugh 79
Allen, Maurice 68
Allied Forces Information and Censorship Section 43
Allied powers
 deception operations 95–105
 signals intelligence 63–74
 spies 45–56
Amè, Cesare 36
Anti-Fascist People's Freedom League 164
Armia Krajowa (AK) (Home Army) 146–7
Army and Luftwaffe Signals School 87
Art of War, The (Sun Tzu) 9
Astor, Hugh 29, 31
Atlantic, Battle of the 78–9, 89
Aung San 163–4

Austrian resistance groups 178–9
Austrian Resistance Movement 178–9
Axis powers
 resistance groups 175–83
 signals intelligence 87–92
 spies 56–7
Axthelm, Walther von 204
Ayrton, Tony 125

Balli Kombëtar 154
Banza, Elyesa 56
Barkas, Geoffrey 125, 127
Battle of Britain 10, 77–8, 193–6
Bayerlein, Fritz 124
beam radio navigation 195–6
Beaverbrook, Lord 31
Belgian resistance groups 142–3
Bennet, Ralph 81
Bentivegni, Franz Egbert von 33
Bentley, Elizabeth 37, 39
Beria, Lavrentiy 37
Bismarck 79
Blaskowitz, General 145
Bletchley Park 10, 15, 16, 18, 30, 31, 32, 49, 51, 57, 63–71, 77–86, 96, 195, 211–12
Blitz, The 78
Blot, Michel 204
Blunt, Anthony 38, 57, 58, 212
Boeselager, Georg von 178
'Boniface' spy network 70
Borgerlige Partisaner 153
Bormann, Martin 34
Borneo resistance groups 163
Bradley, Omar 86, 136
Brailly, Gaston 51–2
Bridges, Sir Edward 89
Britain
 intelligence services 15–18
 spymasters 29–33
British Security Coordination 15
Bruijn, Jean Victor de 170
Budyonny, Kliment 132
Bulgarian resistance groups 179–80
Burgess, Guy 38, 57
Bürkl, Franz 189
Burma
 deception operations 102–4
 resistance groups 163–4

233

Index

Burma National Army 163–4
Busch, Ernst 112, 113, 144
Butcher, Harry C. 101

Cairncross, John 57, 84, 212
Calvert, Mike 102
Cambridge Five 9, 10, 39, 57–8
Canaris, Wilhelm 33–4, 35, 37, 52
Carboni, Giacomo 36–7
Caracristi, Ann Z. 71
Cavendish-Bentinck, William 29, 82
Central Bureau 72
Central Intelligence Agency (CIA) 42, 45
Central Social Affairs Department 18–19, 33
Central Staff of the Partisan Movement 148
Chapman, Edward 'Eddie' 45
Chen Yi 117
Chiang Kai-shek 19
Chin Peng 166
China
  intelligence services 18–19
  resistance groups 167–70
  spymasters 33
Churchill, Peter 51
Churchill, Winston 9, 15, 16, 29, 30, 31, 32–3, 42, 43, 77, 78, 82, 83, 84, 89, 129, 165, 212
Clark, Ernest 194
Clarke, Carter W. 72
Clarke, Dudley 95, 125
Clayton, Aileen 81
Clegg, Arthur 60
Coastwatchers 171–2
Cockburn, Robert 197, 198
Colby, William Egan 45–6
Cotton, Sidney 46
Cramer, Hans 134
Crossman, Richard 29
Cunningham, Admiral 80
Cypher Department of the High Command of the Wehrmacht 87–8
Czechoslovakian resistance groups 180–1

D-Day landings 11, 17, 20, 46, 52, 54, 70, 85–6, 99–100, 133–7, 144
Dai Li 19
Dalton, Hugh 17
Danish resistance groups 153
Darnand, Joseph 144
Dawson, Harry 32
de Gaulle, General 19, 20, 33, 47, 143
Delhi Intelligence Bureau 15
Delius, Wagner 110
Delmer, Sefton 29–30
Demyanov, Alexander 37–8, 110
Denniston, Alastair 30, 63–4
Detachment 101 42–3
Deutsch, Arnold 38
Dewavrin, André 33
Diepenbroek, Pieter 46
Donovan, William J. 42
Dorsch, Xaver 203
Double-Cross System 10, 16, 18, 29, 32, 51, 110, 212, 213
Dowding, Sir Hugh 77
Dulles, Allen 33, 42, 49

East Indies resistance groups 164–5
Eastwood, Sir Ralph 'Rusty' 101
Eifler, Carl 42–3
Eisenhower, Dwight 43, 86
Eitel, Karl 46
Ershakov, F.A. 108
Estonian resistance groups 143

Fabia, Rudolph 73
Far East Combined Bureau 15
Far East
  deception operations 102–4
  resistance groups 163–70
Faye, Leon 49
Federal Bureau of Investigation (FBI) 26–7, 37, 43
Fellers, Bonner 22
Fellgiebel, Erich 34

234

Index

Fennessy, Edward 193–4
Fertig, Wendell 171
Fiocca, Henri Edmond 53
Fleet Radio Unit, Melbourne (FRUMEL) 73–4
Fleet Radio Unit Pacific (FRUPAC) 74
Fleming, Peter 102
Foote, Allan 58, 59
France
  intelligence services 19–20
  resistance groups 143–6
  spymasters 33
Free French Intelligence Service 19–20, 33
French Forces of the Interior (FFI) 20
Friedman, William F. 71
Frutos, Juan 46
Fu Xiao'en 168

Gabas, Alfred 56
Gamba, Vittorio 36
García, Juan Pujol 46–7
Garrow, Ian 53
Geeroms, Willemsz 170
Geheime Staatspolizei *see* Gestapo
Gehlen, Reinhard 34–5, 110
George VI, King 42
  intelligence services 20–2

resistance groups 175–8
signals intelligence 87–90
spymasters 33–6
Gersdorff, Christoph Freiherr von 175–6, 178
Gestapo 20, 22, 35, 36, 46, 52, 53, 55, 186
Gisevius, Hans Bernd 35, 53
Glad, Tor 47
Godfrey, John 80
Goebbels, Joseph 42
Golikov, Filipp 38–9
Golos, Jacob 37
Göring, Hermann 89, 194–5, 198, 207
Gorsky, Anatoli 39, 84
Görtz, Hermann 56
Government Code and Cypher School 15–16, 30, 31, 32, 63, 69
Government Communications Headquarters (GCHQ) 32
Greece
  invasion 81, 91
  resistance groups 155, 157–8
GRU 25, 38, 39, 110
Guderian, Heinz 147
Guingand, Major General de 97, 125, 127
Gunn, Bill 18

Haswell, Jock 101
Hayabuchi Detachment 22

He Yizhi 55–6
Himmler, Heinrich 20, 21, 33, 187, 188, 189
Hinsley, Harry 77, 78–9, 85
Hitler, Adolf 11, 29, 34, 35, 38–9, 42, 70, 77, 81, 91, 107, 109, 110–11, 112, 120, 131–2, 136, 137, 148, 160–1, 175–8, 207
Ho Chi Minh 166
Hoover, J. Edgar 51
Hoxha, Enver 154

I Was Monty's Double (James) 102
Ilyichev, Ivan 39
Indian Political Intelligence Office 16
Indian resistance groups 165
Indochinese resistance groups 166
Insulinde Corps 164
Israilov brothers 160, 161
Italy
  intelligence services 22
  resistance groups 181–2
  signals intelligence 90–1
  spymasters 36–7

James, Meyrick Edward Clifton 101–2

Index

Japan
  deception operations 115–20
  intelligence services 22–5
  resistance groups 182–3
  signals intelligence 91–2
  spymasters 37
Japanese Army Intelligence 91
Japanese Cypher Bureau 91–2
Japanese Naval Intelligence Division 92
Japanese People's Anti-War Alliance 182–3
Jarrot, André 47
Java Legion 164
Jeannin, Paul 47
Jebsen, Johann 47–8
jet aircraft 207–9
Jewish resistance groups 185–9
Joint Intelligence Committee (JIC) 16, 83
Jones, Reginald Victor 30, 49–50, 82, 195–7, 203
Jordan, Hans 113

Kang Sheng 33
Katamura, Lieutenant General 103–4
Kazakov, M.I. 108, 109
Kempeitai 22–3, 25, 92
Kendrick, Tony 69
Kennedy, John F. 172
Kenyan Directorate of Intelligence and Security 16
Kesselring, Albert 97, 98, 99
KGB 26
Khan, Noor Inayat 48, 49
Khrushchev, Nikita 85
Kielmannsegg, Colonel Count 114
Kim Il Sung 169
Kimmel, Husband 74
Kinabalu Guerrillas Defence Force 163
King, Admiral 73
Kinzel, Eberhard 35
Kita, Nagao 73
Kluge, Günther von 86, 176, 177–8
Klugmann, James 57
Knox, Dilly 67, 69, 70, 80
Kocjan, Antoni 203
Kock, Peiter de 170
Koda-Ha 24
Koenig, General 20
Kokkelink, Mauritz Christiaan 170
Kokuryūkai (Black Dragon Society) 24
Kolbe, Fritz 49
Korean resistance groups 169
Kreipe, Heinrich 158
Kühlenthal, Karl-Erich 36, 98
Kullback, Solomon 71
Kurochkin, P.A. 108
Kursk offensive 11, 25, 35, 83–5, 148, 149, 212, 212

Kutlvašr, General 180–1
Kuznetsov, Admiral 39
Kwok, Albert 163

Lais, Alberto 53
Latvian resistance groups 146
Lauwers, Hubert 49
League to Raise the Political Consciousness of Japanese Troops 182
Lena network 20
Lever, Mavis 67
Li Zongren 55
Liddell, Guy 30, 32
Linlithgow, Lord 165
Lithuanian resistance groups 146
Lockart, Robert Bruce 30–1
Long, Leo 58, 84, 212
'Lucy' spy ring 34, 59, 84
Lukin, M.F. 108

MacArthur, Douglas 32, 40, 72, 73
Maclean, Donald 57–8
Main Intelligence Directorate see GRU
Malayan People's Anti-Japanese Army (MPAJA) 166
Malayan Races Liberation Army 166
Malayan resistance groups 166
Mao Zedong 33, 117, 118

Index

Marshall, George C. 105
Martini, Wolfgang 198
Masterman, John 31
Matapan, Battle of 79–80
Mayer, Hans Ferdinand 49–50, 196
McClure, Robert 29, 43
Mediterranean deception operations 95–9
  dummy armies 131–2
  resistance groups 157–9
Mellenthin, General von 112
Melville, John 98
Menzies, Sir Stewart 30, 31, 32
MI5 16, 18, 19, 29, 31–2, 45, 50–1, 57
MI6 16, 17, 18, 31, 32, 46, 50, 53, 57, 63, 119–20, 141, 158
Michael, Glyndwr 98
Midway, Battle of 74–5
Milch, Erhard 207
Military Information Service (MIS) 22, 36–7, 90–1
Milorg group 154
Miyagi, Yotoku 58
Moe, John 47, 50
'Monastery' spy network 37–8

Montgomery, General 81, 95–6, 97, 101–2, 128, 129
Morgan, Frederick 99
Morton, Desmond 31
Müller, Heinrich 36
Mussolini, Benito 36, 81, 181–2

National Bureau of Investigations and Statistics 19
National Organization of Crete (EOK) 158
National Popular Liberation Army (ELAS) 155, 158
National Republican Greek League (EDES) 155
National Revolutionary Army Intelligence Service 19
National Security Agency 71
Nearne, Jacqueline 50
Netherlands resistance groups 146
New Guinea resistance groups 170
Nimitz, Admiral 73
Nissen, Jack 198
NKVD 25–6, 37, 110
Norland, Selmer 86
Norman, Frederick 'Bimbo' 195
North Africa campaign 81
  deception operations 95–7
  decoys 123–9

resistance groups 158–9
Norwegian resistance groups 153–4
Noyce, Wilfrid 68
Nye, Sir Archibald 98

Observation Service 88–9
Office of Chief of Naval Operation (OP-20-G) 72–3
Office of Naval Intelligence (ONI) 27, 59, 73
Office of Strategic Services (OSS) 17, 19, 27, 37, 42, 43, 45, 46, 141, 144, 166, 204
Office of War Information 43
Onoda, Hiroo 23
Operation *Bagration* 11, 111–14, 150
Operation *Barbarossa* 10–11, 107–9
Operation *Bertram* 125–9
Operation *Bodyguard* 11, 51, 70, 111
Operation *Cascade* 129
Operation *Citadel* 34, 85, 149–50
Operation *Cloak* 103
Operation *Cockade* 99, 100
Operation *Conclave* 14
Operation *Copperhead* 101
Operation *Dragoon* 144

Index

Operation *Error* 102–4
Operation *Fortitude* 48, 51, 101, 109–10, 133
Operation *Harlequin* 99
Operation *Lena* 20
Operation *Lüttich* 86
Operation *Mincemeat* 36, 97–8, 131–2
Operation *Monastery* 109–10
Operation *Oatmeal* 50
Operation *Overlord* 70, 99
Operation *Quicksilver* 46, 101, 133
Operation *Robber Baron* 149
Operation *Second Period of the Nomonhan Incident* 116
Operation *Solo* I 50
Operation *Starkey* 99–100
Operation *Stencil* 103
Operation *Supercharge* 129
Operation *Taxable* 198
Operation *Tindall* 100
Operation *Torch* 129
Operation *Typhoon* 35
Operation *Uranus* 109–11
Operation *Wadham* 100
Operation *Warehouse* 129
Operation *Withstand* 129
Orde Dienst 146
Organisation F 24

Ōshima, Hiroshi 37
Ott, Eugene 40
Oumansky, Konstantin 160
Owens, Arthur George 36, 50–1
Ozaki, Hotsumi 40, 58, 59

Pack, Stanley 99
Pacific resistance groups 170–2
Panfilov, Alexei 39
Patton, General 85–6, 133, 135, 136, 137, 211–12
Pearl Harbor 27, 51, 72–4, 82–3, 104–5, 195
Pearson, Harry 102
People's Commissariat for Internal Affairs *see* NKVD
Pers Z S 89
Petar II, King 155–6, 157
Petrie, Sir David 31
Philby, Kim 37, 38, 57
Philippines resistance groups 171
Phillips, William 43
Polish resistance groups 146–7, 185–9
Political Intelligence Department 16
Political Warfare Executive (PWE) 17, 29, 30, 31, 43
Popov, Dušan 48, 51
Prestwich, John 86
Pridham-Wippell, Sir Henry 80

Proskurov, Ivan 38
Psychological Warfare Division 17, 29, 43
Pu Yi, Emperor 57, 92, 169

radar 193–5, 196–8, 199
Radó, Alexander 26, 58–9, 212
'Red Orchestra' spy network 26, 36, 42, 58
Reichspost 89
Reinhardt, General 113
Rejewski, Marian 69
Research Office of the Reich Air Ministry 89–90
Reynolds, Jerry 213
Richter, Karel 56–7
Ritter, Nikolaus 36
Robb, Brian 125
Roberts, Jerry 83–4, 85
Robertson, Thomas 'Tar' 31–2
Rochefort, Joseph 73
Roessler, Rudolf 59, 84, 212
Rommel, General 81, 95–6, 97, 128–9, 159, 177
Roosevelt, President 42, 83, 89
Rosen, Leo 71
Rowlett, Frank 71
Rundstedt, Gerd von 70
Sadat, Anwar 158–9

Index

Safford, Laurance F. 72
Sansom, Odette 51–2
Sansom, Roy 51–2
Scheiderbauer, Armin 177
Schmidt, Hans-Thilo 51
Schmidt, Wulf 51
Schneider, Christian 59
Scott, Sandy Reid 102
SD 22
Second Bureau of the General Staff 19
Secret Intelligence Service (SIS) *see* MI6
Section 5 90–1
Sergeyev, Lily 52
Seyss-Inquart, Arthur 146
Sheripov, Mairbek 160
Sicherheitsdienst *see* SD
Sicherheitspolizei (SiPo) 22
Sicily 97–9, 131–2
Signal Intelligence Service (SIS) 71–2, 74
'Silvermaster' group 26, 37, 39
Silvermaster, Nathan Gregory 39
Sinclair, Hugh 63
Sinkov, Abraham 71, 72
Skorzeny, Otto 55
Slim, General 102–3, 104
Smedley, Agnes 59–60
SMERSH 26
Solomon Islands resistance groups 171–2
sonar 200–1
Sorge, Richard 23, 25, 39–42, 58, 59, 60, 117, 118, 120
Soviet Union
 deception operations 107–14
 intelligence services 25–6
 invasion of 81–2
 resistance groups 147–51, 159–61
 spymasters 37–42
 spies 57–60
Special Branch 17
Special Operations Executive (SOE) 17, 19, 27, 29, 31, 42, 46, 49, 50, 52, 53, 54–5, 141, 143, 144, 146, 153, 158, 166, 204
Speer, Albert 203, 204
Stalin, Joseph 10, 11, 25, 38, 39, 42, 72, 81–2, 83, 84, 107, 108, 109, 110, 111, 116, 120, 147, 212–13
Starr, John Renshaw 49
Stephenson, Sir William 32
Stevens, Robin 'Tin Eye' 32
Strachey, Oliver 65
Stroop, Jürgen 187–8, 189
Suma, Yakichiro 37
Sun Tzu 9–10, 11, 211
Suñer, Ramón Serrano 37
Sutherland, General 71
Szabo, Violette 52
Szymańska, Halina 52–3

Target Intelligence Committee (TICOM) 90
Tegart, Charles 53
Teske, G. 150
Thiele, Fritz 34
Thorne, Sir Andrew 132
Thorpe, Amy Elizabeth 53
Tiltman, John 70, 82
Timorese resistance groups 172
Timoshenko, Semyon 107, 109
Tito 157
TO network 25, 37
Togo, Major General 169
Tojo, Hideki 23
Tokkō 24–5, 92
Tokubetsu Keisatsutai (Tokkeitai) 25
Tokumu Kikan 25, 92
Tolbukhin, Marshal 178–9
Tosei-ha 24
Traeger, Roman 203
Travis, Edward 30, 32

239

Index

Trepper, Leopold 26, 42
Tresckow, Henning von 175, 176, 178
Trevor-Roper, Hugh 110
Turing, Alan 65, 69, 79
Tutte, Bill 70
Twinn, Peter 69, 70

Ubbink, Johan 46
Ultra Secret, The (Winterbotham) 63
United States
  intelligence services 26–7
  spymasters 42–3

V Force 17–18
V-1 flying bombs 203–5, 206
V-2 rockets 205–6
Vasilevsky, Aleksandr 109
Viet Minh 166
Voronov, General 107
Voroshilov, Kliment 116
Vouza, Jacob 172
Vukelić, Branko 60

Wachi Takaji 55–6
Wachtel, Colonel 204
Wake, Nancy 53–4
Wang Yi 169
Wavell, General 102

Wedemeyer, Albert 43
Wenham, Susan 86
Western Front
  deception operations 99–102
  decoys 124
  dummy armies 133–7, 212
White, Dick 32
Wilkinson, Gerald 32–3, 105
Willoughby, Charles A. 32, 73
Wilson, Sir Henry Maitland 101
Winterbotham, Frederick 63, 69, 86
Wolmer, Lord 17

XX Committee 16, 18, 29, 31, 52

Y Service 18, 68–9, 81
Yamamoto, Admiral 75
Yeo-Thomas, Forest Frederick Edward 54–5
Yomas Intelligence Service 18
Yoshikawa, Takeo 74
Yoshioka Yasunori 57
Yugoslavia
  invasion 81, 91
  resistance groups 155–7

Zhao Tong 167
Zhou Enlai 33, 117
Zhukov, Georgy 38, 85, 107, 108, 109, 110, 116, 149
Zigelbaum, Shmuel 188

All images © Getty Images except for p.23 and p.79 Public Domain and p.66 Shutterstock.